The Collapse of the Self
And Its Therapeutic Restoration

The Collapse of the Self

And Its Therapeutic Restoration

Rochelle G. K. Kainer

THE ANALYTIC PRESS

1999 Hillsdale, NJ   London

Published by The Analytic Press, Inc.
101 West Street, Hillsdale, NJ 07642

Typeset in Caslon by EvS Communication Networx, Pt. Pleasant, NJ

Library of Congress Cataloging-in-Publication Data

Kainer, Rochelle G. K.
    The collapse of the self and its therapeutic restoration /
Rochelle G. K. Kainer.
        p.   cm.
    Includes bibliographical references and index.
    ISBN 0-88163-317-8
    1. Self.   2. Psychoanalysis.   I. Title.
RC489.S43K35   1999
616.89´17—dc21   99-28906
                                                         CIP

Printed in the United States of America
10 9 8 7 6 5 4 3 2 1

For Selig,
and in memory of my family of the past and
love for those who carry its future.

For my students and especially for my
patients who made these efforts worthwhile.

Contents

What all students should have as prerequisites, are courses in the part of 20th century psychology which deals with the human capacity for imagining, dreaming, making up stories, defending the self against brutal realities by building up fictions, that at the same time reflect these realities.
                                                                —LEON EDEL

Foreword

James S. Grotstein

As the smoke and din of distant ecclesiastic cum psychoanalytic wars have cleared away and the now mythical giants of that bellicose age have fought their *Iliad* to a standstill, another generation of psychoanalysts, distant from the heat and embers, is free to view the psychoanalytic episteme from broader perspectives and to see overlaps, integrations, complementarities, and congruencies in what in yesteryear were considered heretical and demonic. Dr. Kainer presents us with a body of work that is well in keeping with this new integrating period. Her work is wonderfully integrative and constitutes a scholarly and cogent "therapeutic restoration" of old wounds.

Dr. Kainer's task in this contribution is an ambitious one. She seeks to bridge many current as well as all but abandoned streams of psychoanalytic thought in order to put forward a cohesive prospectus that includes a theory of thinking, of creativity, of identification, and of the formation of psychic structure. I believe that she adds a new and unusual perspective to our understanding. Her broad theoretical focus pans from Rank to Kohut, from Klein and Fairbairn to Hartman and Mahler, and takes in a number of others in her sweep.

A RECONSIDERATION OF IDENTIFICATION

One of the great schisms of the previous psychoanalytic generation was between the largely internal object relations theories of Klein and the largely external object relations theories of Fairbairn, Winnicott, and Bowlby. Much of the wisdom of Fairbairn and Winnicott crossed the ocean and became the template of self psychology, intersubjectivity, and relationism. Dr. Kainer ably unites some of these once disparate themes using the instrument of *identification*, a mechanism and phenomenon that has previously lent itself to considerable misunderstanding. The concept of identification has been taken very much for granted by most analysts and psychotherapists and has generally been considered to be a normal and healthy developmental process. I think this conclusion is unwise.

To Dr. Kainer's credit, she goes to great lengths to distinguish between pathological and normal identifications. She believes that we normally make "selective" (Jacobson) or "partial" identifications with ideal objects in order to achieve personality growth, whereas we form pathological identifications by default with nonnurturing but greatly needed objects. The distinction she makes between partial and total (often adhesive) identifications is a very important one, in my opinion, and is seldom grappled with in the literature.

DEFINING PSYCHOANALYSIS

One of the themes that Dr. Kainer ably discusses is the alleged demise of the orthodox/classical, one-person model for psychoanalysis in favor of the two-person model, one that is today called the intersubjective, or relational, model. This model has found consummate expression in Ogden's (1994, 1997) concept of the "intersubjective third subject of analysis," which is created in the analytic relationship itself. This whole issue of "one-person" versus "two-person" (and Ogden has added the relationship itself as a virtual "third person") raises another question: What actually is psychoanalysis?

I believe that we must be very careful to distinguish between *psychic realty* and *actual reality*. If we are considering the creation of the former, then the one-person model is requisite. What actually happened to the analysand is one thing (external reality, secondary process, bivalent logic, classical Aristotelian logic). How the analysand unconsciously *believes* (autochthonously) that he *created* that reality is another matter, a psychoanalytic matter of prime importance (Grotstein, 1997). Analysis of this omnipotent belief must first take place in order for the analysand to realize that the analyst operates from a separate scheme of causality. Dr. Kainer's emphasis on the creative aspects of the mutually constructed psychoanalytic narrative takes both models into account.

A NOTE ON SOME OBJECT FUNCTIONS

In her careful delineation of the functions of objects and selfobjects, Dr. Kainer refers to the concept of transformational objects, a notion that owes its origins to the works of Bion (1965, 1970) and Bollas (1979). She goes so far as to state that, in the psychoanalytic situation, the trial iden-

tifications must go both ways; that is, the analysand must be able to identify with some aspect of the analyst, and the same for the latter in regard
to the former. With this I agree. I would like to suggest that the transformational object function may be thought of both as "scaffolding" function and as an "exhortative" function, much like an "existential coach."

Bollas (1987) proffers another object category, however, that of the
"aleatory" (i.e., winged) object. As its name suggests, it is a chance object
that unpredictably appears in one's life and evokes or accesses aspects of
oneself that were hitherto inaccessible. In some ways, psychoanalysis
itself, not just the analyst per se, functions as an aleatory object. Dr. Kainer
speaks to the "found" nature of one's object both in life and in the creative
potential of the analytic encounter itself.

CONSIDERATIONS OF THE DEATH INSTINCT

In her laudable and successful attempt to integrate Kleinian thinking with
that of other current schools, such as intersubjectivity and self psychology, Dr. Kainer discusses the controversial death instinct. Like her, I also
believe that the death instinct is not necessarily the origin of aggression
or of hate. It is the foundation of destructiveness itself. This destructiveness can be silent and unconscious. Infants, children, and adults will all
become aggressive or assertive in support of their life instincts to survive
and thrive. It is only when life itself or the quality of life seems to be
endangered that the death instinct comes into play.

We may see aspects of the death instinct in the neonate in the phenomenon of *apoptosis*, the principle of synaptic death that occurs in the
first 15 months of life. We may see it in operation when certain death is
known to be approaching, in which case the death instinct may operate
so as to "endeaden" us—protectively. We saw it in operation in Spitz's
(1945) hospitalism cases, most of whom died by age four of advanced
deteriorative somatic states, such as senile brain disease, arteriosclero-
sis, or the like. Spitz believed that the self-destructive process had been
inaugurated to end the lives of these children because the quality of their
lives was so obviously intolerable. In other words, the death instinct may
function as the lure to mental death when the subject has an inkling that
his life scenario is subjectively too difficult to endure (Grotstein, 1985).

"IMAGINATIVE EMPATHY"

Imaginative empathy is the innovative term Dr. Kainer employs for a special kind of attunement to her analysands. The term issues from a

sublimated aspect of projective identification and implies the therapeutic process whereby the analyst is able both to imagine ("image" as a verb) and to empathize ("trial vicarious experience") the analysand's personalness. The "cure" in psychoanalysis, according to Dr. Kainer, is the analysand's experiencing of the analyst's imaginative empathy which is felt like a healing balm. Part and parcel of this cure is a parallel process whereby the analyst is able to help the analysand "exorcise" the bad "precursor objects" with which he or she once identified, This "exorcism" can devolve into an unworkable delusional transference situation if there is too little basic trust in the therapeutic alliance. It requires the sustenance of the holding/containing/attuning environment where the analysand always feels safe in becoming more and more known.

Dr. Kainer has written a healing text, one in which hitherto differing schools of psychoanalytic thought can be bridged in order for clinicians to gain access to differing camera angles on their patients' dilemmas. After all, what do we offer our patients for cure if not appropriate perspective models for them to superimpose on their own constricting models? Psychoanalysis may in fact be considered as a marketplace for model exchange. The creation of bridges between existing models only enlarges the leverage of existing models. Dr. Kainer deserves our gratitude for her model building and bridging, and clinicians and their patients are the beneficiaries of her laudable work.

REFERENCES

Bion, W. R. (1965). *Transformations*. London: Heinemann.

———— (1970). *Attention and Interpretation*. London: Tavistock.

Bollas, C. (1979). The transformational object. *International Journal of Psychoanalysis,* 60:97-107.

———— (1987). *The Shadow of the Object: Psychoanalysis of the Unthought Known*. New York: International Universities Press.

Grotstein, J. S. (1985). A proposed revision of the psychoanalytic concept of the death instinct. In *The Yearbook for Psychoanalytic Psychotherapy*, ed. R. J. Lange. Hillsdale, NJ: Lawrence Erlbaum Associates, pp. 299–326.

———— (1997). Integrating one-person and two-person psychologies: Autochthony and alterity in counterpoint. *Psychoanalytic Quarterly,* 65:403–430.

Ogden, R. (1994). *Subjects of Analysis*. Northvale, NJ: Aronson.

———— (1997). *Reverie and Interpretation*. Northvale, NJ: Aronson.

Spitz, R. (1945). Hospitalism: An inquiry into the genesis of psychiatric conditions in early childhood. *The Psychoanalytic Study of the Child,* 1:53–74. New York: International Universities Press.

Preface

Any book, whether fact or fiction, is composed of imagined truths. The power of its truth is found in the coherence of the narrative—whether a patient's narrative, or one of an imagined character, or the narrative of one's own life. My construction of the inner world of the patient and my reportage of what was constructed between us is such an imagined truth. In those cases where the reportage was done independently both by the patient and by me, I have been struck by the concordance of minds. How can we possibly achieve knowing the mind of the other? Even after many years of attempting such knowing, I am still in awe of the process. It has been a great privilege to know others in this way, to gain a body of knowledge, and to give this witness to what has been learned. I hope that it proves of use to others.

The paradox of preparing a book such as this is that it is a long and inherently solitary task that can come to fruition only through an involvement with many others—both those in actuality and those who have existed only in my thoughts. My precursors of the psychoanalytic ideas are noted in the book itself. They provided me with the basic material to newly fashion my own observations and analytic experiences.

Other figures of mind have played a different part. Their ideas are not present per se in this work, but their creative strength is—such literary and philosophical figures as Mary McCarthy and Hannah Arendt, and the example of their sustaining literary relationship. The brilliant biographies of the latter, as well as that of Anna Freud, by Elisabeth Young-Bruehl, were a special source of inspiration for presenting intellectual material with great care.

Important analytic figures—Esther Menaker, the late William Menaker, and Edith Weigert—hold a special place in my formation and learning. There have also been many colleagues who, at different periods of my work, have shared in the pleasure of ideas and the excitement of thinking, and I am indebted to them. I have been lucky in my psychoanalytic colleagues and have greatly appreciated the input of James Barron, Katalina Bartok, Monica Callahan, Harold Eist, John Gedo, Arnold Goldberg,

Susannah Gourevitch, James Grotstein, Susan Hadler, Virginia Hendrickson, Peter Kramer, Joseph Lichtenberg, Jancis Long, Paul Ornstein, Alberto Pieczansky, John R-Love, Jill Scharff, Rosemary Segalla, Damon Silvers, and Robert Stolorow, among others, who have connected with my thoughts or, at telling moments, helped me clarify them through the interchange. From other fields closely connected with my own, I have been grateful for the collegiality and encouragement of two eminent scholars, the art critic Donald Kuspit and the philosopher Thelma Z. Lavine.

The working out of the ideas of the text came in many stages, each necessary to its formation. Members of the Philosophy of Psychotherapy seminar of the Forum for Psychiatry and the Humanities read the proposed work and offered detailed and valuable commentary. The Division of Psychoanalysis of the American Psychological Association, the Conferences on Self Psychology, and the American Academy of Psychoanalysis and the Washington School of Psychiatry all provided forums for the earlier presentations of my ideas. My students in the Advanced Psychotherapy and the Supervision Programs of the Washington School of Psychiatry, and those of the Washington Society of Psychoanalytic Psychology, were invaluable collaborators. My patients have been both the subjects of my investigations and my teachers. I have enormous gratitude for the privilege of knowing them and their often great courage and determination.

In the preparation of the actual text, I am indebted to the expert editorship of Gloria Parloff for chapter Two, and for the final preparation of the manuscript by Van Dashner. Only Thomas Wolfe with Maxwell Perkins, and Kafka with his Max Brod, have been as lucky as I in having Jon Frederickson as an unflagging intellectual and editorial companion for the entire manuscript. Its flaws are mine, but its strengths were enhanced by him. The encouragement of Stephen Mitchell and Lewis Aron, the Relational Series Editors, and the help of Eleanor Starke Kobrin and Paul Stepansky of The Analytic Press were experienced on both a personal and professional level.

I have been especially sustained by the warm and witty friendship, patience, good will, and intellectual stimulation of Catherine Kirschner, Gordon Kirschner, Clara Aisenstein, and Ron Blanken. Barbara Meade holds a special place for her devotion to books, her interest in this one, and her encouragement of my writing for many years. Finally, to S. Kainer, Eden Kainer, and Stephen Kadlecek, my tender gratitude for serving as models for taking on very difficult creative tasks and seeing them through.

ROCHELLE G. K. KAINER

Part I

Creating the Self

The theme of identification, and its great significance in the formation of the ideal and pathological aspects of the self, are developed in the chapters of this first section. One's active pursuit of the *ideal self* rests on conscious and unconscious identifications in the service of *becoming*. Similarly, the formation of the *pathological self* rests on the powerful regressive pull of our objects of attachment. These chapters explore how the *bad object* and the *ideal object* exert their force, highlighting the dialectical tension between the power of the need for attachment and the will toward self-creation within the individual.

Chapter One

Found Objects

On the Nature of Identification

> *Found objects are invitations to flights of fancy. They challenge us*
> *to invent, to expand the borders of what are considered the*
> *proper components for an interior. . . . Each found object is the*
> *unique expression of its interpreter. It is as individual as you or I.*
> —MARIO BUATTA, *Found Objects*

The paradox of the self that we create lies in the duality of its chance and determined nature. The taking in of our objects creates a dialectical tension that is always at work within the self. Identifications—unconscious as well as conscious—form a large part of the self in both its pathological and its ideal aspects. The triumph of the ideal over the pathological forms the basis of the *transcendent self* and brings us to the therapeutic task.

This chapter sets out a general theory of the role of *identifications* in making that which is outside of the self part of the self-structure. Freud held that a libidinal attachment is never abandoned; lost objects are taken back through an identification with them. Klein's focus was on the destructive; identifications are forged through the instinctual envy of the good object. Fairbairn, shifting from the instinctual to the object relational, said that we internalize the object experienced as both exciting and rejecting. If early libidinal attachments are indeed immutable, my thesis is that identification with the bad object is the echo of an intense object-relationship, born of disappointed love which has turned to hate. The "shadow of the object" (Freud, 1917, p. 249) lingers on adhesively in the psyche and forms the core of the pathological self. Pathological identifications are characterized by a loss of freedom and choice.

In contrast, in identifications forming the nonpathological self, the will-to-form the ideal self (Rank, 1932) stimulates partial identifications with the *admired object* (Jacobson, 1964), identification with *likeness* (Kohut, 1984), and identification with the *ideal object* (Kainer, 1996). They comprise our object of identification[1] for individuation, growth, and the fullest experience of self. Like their counterpart in art, our objects of identification are "found objects," used for the purpose of creating the self. We relate to them as to a Duchamp[2] "Readymade" (see chapter two): taking them in, imbuing them with subjective meaning, and appropriating them as our own. Never entirely finished with its artwork, the self contains both its failed parts adhesively clinging to the bad object and those parts which are more freely chosen and thus more successfully realized.

The identifications made with our pathological objects, and those made with our ideal objects, are of special interest because of their dynamic interplay in the creation of the self. In our pursuit of the ideal self,[3] there is a struggle with internalized pathological objects—still powerful because they serve defensive or relational needs (or both) and have become adhesive (Meltzer, 1975) because of that. They were once our objects of survival. Attachment to these bad objects generates a continuous, lifelong internal dialectic between the forward push of the ideal and the regressive pull of the pathological.[4] The longing to realize the ideal self fuels the search for therapeutic transformation; transcending the regressive pull of the pathological self constitutes the therapeutic task.

The unconscious aspects of pathological identification arise from a great need to deny and suppress the dangerous emotions stimulated by the bad object. In addition, however bad they may be, they can also elicit unconscious pity because of an identification with their pain. We often retain, through identification, their worst features. These identifications with our objects become the bedrock of our emotional life.[5] By the nature of their power, adhesive identifications become the subject of analysis— and the object of the longing for transformation, and of becoming (see chapter two).

THE PRECURSOR OBJECTS OF IDENTIFICATION

The effects of the first identifications made in earliest childhood will be general and lasting.
—S. Freud, "The Ego and the Id"

Freud: Lasting Love

The important place I give to identification in the life narrative[6] has its roots in some of the ideas of Freud, Klein, Fairbairn, Jacobson, Schafer, Racker, and Kohut. I will briefly trace those of their thoughts which directly bear on the ideas here. The relevant thread in Freud's thought is embedded in the critic Harold Bloom's comment, in a lecture he presented, that psychoanalysis is a theory of love. Freud (1917) made clear the power of attachment to our object of love—that we "never willingly abandon a libidinal position" (p. 244). Should the object be lost, a narcissistic (i.e., ego) identification with the object can "substitute for the erotic cathexis" (p. 249).

This "law" of love is closely related to Freud's use of the metaphor of the energic laws of physics. Total energy (in this case libido) cannot be lost—it can only be transformed.[7] If the libidinal cathexis to the object itself is weakened, its free energy is transformed into an identification with it. The result of a "narcissistic identification with the object" is that "in spite of the conflict with the loved person the love-relation need not be given up" (p. 249). Thus, in Freud's theory of instincts, the energy associated with loving the object remains even if the object is lost. Although psychoanalytic theory has evolved beyond an energic instinctual model, there is no doubt that we stay attached to our early objects, both in actuality and through an identification with them affecting our internal world.[8]

Love and Narcissistic Identification

Freud's theory of libido is itself an example of the relationship of love to a narcissistic (self) identification. He himself never abandoned it. It was his uniquely creative discovery and most lasting love—despite all other significant changes in the development of his thinking. His historic breaks with Jung, Adler, and Rank were rooted in their challenge to this (his) heart of psychoanalysis. Freud was always identified with, and can be identified by, the narrative of his creation. Freud exists as "Freudian" theory.

In this famous passage—which presaged the development of the superego—Freud (1917) outlined his narrative concerning the persistence of attachments born of love:

> An object-choice, an attachment of the libido to a particular person, had at one time existed; then, owing to a real slight or disappointment coming from this loved person, the object-relationship was shattered. The result was not the normal one of withdrawal of the libido from this object and a displacement of it on to a new one, but something different . . . the free libido was not displaced on to another object; it was withdrawn into the ego . . . [and] served to establish an *identification* of the ego with the abandoned object. Thus, the shadow of the object fell upon the ego and the latter could henceforth be judged by a special agency, as though it were an object, the forsaken object [p. 249].

Freud (1923) later added, *"The character of the ego* is the precipi-
tate of abandoned object-cathexes and . . . it contains the history of those
object-choices" (p. 29, italics added).

Internalized as the ego ideal, each small turn of the self is critically
and inexorably measured against it. Not only does the self contain the
residues of all that we have lost and internalized, we now stand vulnerable to harsh self-criticism in the shadow of all the objects with whom we
have identified. Freud's idea is overwhelming to contemplate, yet, in the
light of the powerful struggle between self and the internalized other seen
clinically, it rings true.

Jacobson: Partial Identifications on the Way to Becoming

> *Identifications cannot be created out of nothing. They involve
> selective reorganization of already existing wishes, behavior,
> patterns, capacities, viewpoints, and emphases. . . . It is the
> reorganization itself . . . that is the novelty in identification.*
> —ROY SCHAFER (1968, p. 147)

Continuing the theme of the power of love and attachment in relation to
the development of identifications, Edith Jacobson (1964) had an understanding of its more conscious—and less adhesive—aspects, those bearing on the formation of the ideal self (see chapter two). Although Jacobson
remained focused on the framework of drive theory, she made an important contribution regarding the development of the self in relation to its
objects. Speaking of a young child's advance in the object world from
symbiotic attachment to ego autonomy, she was describing a later stage
of development beyond that of Mahler's (1968, pp. 7–31) infant's developmental progression from normal autism to normal symbiosis to sepa-
ration-individuation. Stern's (1985) infant research corrected the
Mahlerian perception, and that aspect of Jacobson's theory does not fully
represent the fine-tuning of this later work (pp. 18–19).

Nonetheless, Jacobson's narrative is very useful and evocative. She
sensed how we emerge from our embeddedness in our earliest objects
and begin to create a self that not only reflects these objects, but also that
is separate and distinct from them. The young child, in creating its identity, has both a sense of the future and a wish for a "realistic likeness" to
the love object. These are achieved through a "selective identification":

> In fact, the ego cannot acquire a realistic likeness to the love object
> unless admired traits of this object become enduringly introjected into
> the child's wishful self images. . . . [They] reflect the traits actually
> taken over from the object of identification, so that a likeness between

object and self images can now be experienced on a realistic basis . . . .
[These selective identifications] are a prerequisite for the establish-
ment of ego ideal and ego goals, i.e., of realistic goals regarding the
future [p. 51].

Thus, Jacobson advanced drive theory to include a concept of self
forged by selective identifications with loved and admired objects of attachment. These admiration-based identifications preserve the available
love and strength of the object.[9] These selective (partial) identifications
represent a developmental compromise between either remaining symbiotically attached (in the object's thrall) or, alternatively, destructively
breaking the symbiotic ties "by way of aggressive, narcissistic expansion
and independent ego functioning" (p. 50). Her work suggests that partial
identifications can lend a nonpathological fluidity to the sense of self.
Identifications with what is admired, while strong, are not "adhesive," as
are fear-driven identifications. The fluidity reflects the greater ease
between holding on to, and letting go of, the other.

Jacobson's *self* goes beyond Freud's (1923, p. 15) *ego* as the mediator
of id impulses with reality. We now have a self that can be seen as self-
determined rather than merely being driven. It is a self that functions as
an organizer of one's individuality and growth and has the potential for
balancing the paralyzing identifications made with the "bad object."

Theories as Found Objects: The Examples of Jacobson and Klein

In addition to their developmental role in the formation of identity, partial identifications (selection of what is admired) play an important role
in thinking and creativity, as in the example of my identification with
some (but not all) of the existing ideas in psychoanalysis. For example, I
may make a partial identification with Freud's (1915) idea that we never
give up an object of love and use it as a building block for the development of my own theoretical position, without symbiotically merging with
his entire body of thought or becoming a "Freudian."

Jacobson and Klein *were* Freudian by virtue of their time and place
in history but nonetheless were not so merged that they could not make
important advances and, in the case of Klein, radical ones. Klein (1946,
1952) revolutionized Freud's concept of the superego with her belief that
it exists from birth and is crucial to the powerful projective and introjective
processes taking place between mother and infant. Klein, however, in
contrast to almost all of Freud's other followers, never abandoned the
death instinct. She continued to identify with it and be identified by it.

But Jacobson never gave up the superego as Freud conceived of it—

as "heir to the Oedipus complex," that is, as a function of the renuncia-
tion of instinctual impulses. Jacobson's ideas on the object-relational aspects of the development of the self are, however, a distinct push toward
present-day thinking. Klein's and Jacobson's advances reflect a mixture
of attachment and individuation in relation to their most important precursor figure and object of identification. The strength of the work of
these writers lies in their grappling with the pull of the theory in which
they were steeped and the push of the vision of their own originality (see
chapter two). Their identification with Freudian thought was not absolute and reflected their individuality. Their attachment to Freud was maintained, but redefined by them—allowing for greater intellectual freedom.

Selective Identifications and the Transformation of Self

There is a parallel need for fluidity and freedom in the analytic situation,
but the conditions for achieving it differ from those in the situation with
the precursor. The selective identifications made by the patient in search
of the transformational analyst are also admiration based, but the need
here is not solely to take on the traits of the admired object, but to have
the analyst capable of identifying with them. Klein and Jacobson did not
actually need Freud to identify with them to achieve their creative freedom in the intellectual realm (although they might have had fantasies
about that), but the patient needs the analyst to do so in the emotional
realm. In the hope of being more fully known, there is a radical need for
the therapist's "I" to be the same as the "I" of the patient.

    In the therapeutic situation, in order for the analyst to be able to
identify with the patient, there must be a capacity to make a "concordant
identification" (Racker, 1957). That is, the analyst must be able to identify with the "self-component of the patient's internal object relationship" (Ogden, 1986, p. 152). As Racker (1957) notes, "The concordant
identification is based on introjection and projection, or, in other terms,
on the resonance of the exterior in the interior, on the recognition of
what belongs to another as one's own ('this part of you is I') and on the
equation of what is one's own with what belongs to another ('This part of
me is you')" (p. 134).

Kohut and Selfobject Sameness

Like Racker, Kohut (1984) had special insight into the nature of identification, which culminated in his observations on twinship, or alter ego
selfobject, function, that has direct relevance here. I agree with him that

there is a human need for a shared identity that is separate from the selfobject need and experience of affirmation and approval (mirroring).

For example, he described returning home from a foreign country as "the experience of feeling strengthened by the presence of alter egos. The support that our self derives from being in a milieu of alter egos, from the nonverbalizable experiences of sameness, of identity, arise whether or not we get any actual help from those whom we feel are like us" (p. 227).

These twinship, or alter ego, identifications are crucial when one is undertaking difficult creative tasks. I especially include the analytic task among them and have previously likened it to an act of artistic creativity in which the analyst is muse and identifies with the patient's attempts to restructure the self (Kainer, 1990)—especially its pathological parts. Identifications based on sameness (concordance, twinship) are a necessary beginning to the working out of the most damaged parts of the self. One must be known to the other, and that is why the analyst must be able to identify with the patient.

IDENTIFICATION AND SELFOBJECT NEED

But who will call me Vicky?
—QUEEN VICTORIA *upon the death of Prince Albert*

Advances in psychoanalytic thinking strongly suggest the expansion of the meaning of loss of the object to include the loss of its selfobject function.[10] When Prince Albert died, Victoria lost Albert as object (in Freud's sense), as well as the Albert who served an important selfobject function for her (in Kohut's sense). For Victoria, the part of the loss she was expressing was not about Albert per se, but about her experience of a loss of part of her self as she was known only by him. Similarly, Margaret Mead, upon Ruth Benedict's death, is reputed to have said that Benedict was the only one who knew all of her work, Mead's word echoing the longing for one's existence to be acknowledged through being known by the other.

It is not only the object that is lost, but that part of the self which was known by the object. Also lost is the selfobject experience of strength and completeness. Selfobject loss is *not* overcome solely through identification with the lost object and the redirection of libidinal energy; it is a matter of finding a *new selfobject source* for one's strength and cohesiveness. The selfobject need for alter ego likeness in the analyst goes beyond the egoism of Freud's (1914) "narcissistic object choice." What is sought in the analytic undertaking is the selfobject experience of strength for the difficult task of rebecoming.

On Beginning the Analytic Task

The following clinical vignettes are examples of partial identifications made at the initial phase of treatment. These entry identifications act as pathways to a deeper resonance between the unconscious worlds of the patient and the therapist. Even if these identifications seem to require a leap of imagination on the part of the hopeful patient, they have to be based in some reality of the therapeutic situation, either palpable or unconsciously communicated. They are the necessary precursors of the process that will become, if the mental qualities of each allows, the interpenetrating mix between analyst and patient that will be safe for them both to enter in the analytic encounter. They are the "identifications that precede projection" (Tausk, 1919) and the precursor of the creative use of projective identification that may follow. Neither delusional nor the project of wishful thinking, they are a function of the introjective and projective empathic resonance present in a meaningful clinical exchange.

CLINICAL EXAMPLES

Patient 1: You are my "I": A mature European woman with great yearnings to fulfill her intellectual promise made an initial appointment by telephone. At the first meeting she told me that, after making the appointment, she had come by my house, which was not far from her own, to "see what it was like." After seeing it, she said that she "knew it would be all right."

Patient 2: I am you: A young woman interviewed another colleague as well as me in her search for a therapist. My colleague lived in a beautiful house in a historic part of town. When the young woman came to see me and I inquired about her previous analytic explorations, she replied, "Oh, to Dr. X I had a house transference and to you I have a book transference!"

Patient 3: Conflicting identifications: A young woman seen early in my practice confessed years later that she definitely did not like me at first and "couldn't stand" my style. I asked her, if that were so, why she chose to work with me. She replied, "Oh, I sensed you would know more about what was wrong with me than anyone else."[11]

Her hope was based on her unconscious resonance to the underlying "good fit" rather than the discomfort of stylistic differences. She did not risk voicing or acting out her distaste at the time, preserving her hope for the goodness of the work to come.

Patient 4: Identification precedes projection: A young professional woman with a fear of her hidden psychotic part tells me, several years after beginning our work, that her first reaction to my furnishings was a thought that "You [the analyst] were crazy" but kept that thought to herself. Years later, on the occasion of buying an antique chair, she suddenly realized that it was similar to the one I had in the entry room. Some time after our work was complete, I saw her home. It was artistically pleasing, with many unusual and original touches. Her initial disidentification with my furnishings was a disavowal of her artistic self, unconsciously linked in her mind with her mother's psychotic parts. The projection of her fear of her "crazy" self onto me was made possible through her unconscious identification with my artistic part. "Projection must be preceded by a stage of identification" (Tausk, 1919, p. 542), and "There is no projection without identification" (Grotstein 1985b, p. 132). Her first thought about my "crazy" furnishings expressed both her fear of the craziness of her own artistic leanings and her relief that they would be understood by me, also "crazy" in that way.[12]

Patient 5: The initial assessment made by the patient can be very rapid: A mature woman with many years of prior therapy began work with me and steadily carried out significant and long-postponed professional goals. During the early phase of our work, she surprised me by relating that before she began our work she had interviewed Dr. P but had decided "not to work with her."

I knew Dr. P to be a very experienced and intelligent clinician and asked my patient why she had not undertaken treatment with her. She replied, "Oh, I could tell that she had too much pain, and I *knew* I would start to take care of her like I did my mother—and I had to get on with other things." Her uncanny reading and rapid rejection of Dr. P's internal world represented a disidentification with it. In her years of previous therapy, she had already worked through the identification with the pathological part of her mother. Breaking that aspect of her emotional tie to her was necessary to going on with her further development. In rejecting Dr. P, she was rejecting the reconstruction of her old internal object relationship of the child caretaking the mother-in-pain. Instead, she chose to identify with a therapist who she also uncannily assessed was more identified with her *strivings*.

In rejecting Dr. P, she was also attempting to overcome the identification she had made with her own mother-in-pain—becoming that "I." This identification was now internalized and recreated with her own children. Working through the emotional tie she maintained to her mother by being the mother-in-pain to her own children constituted a major theme of our extensive work.

In addition to the hope for transformation implicit in these identifications, the initial interview also contains what Ogden (1989) has called "the leading transference anxiety" (p. 183). I share his thought that

> in the initial interview I listen from the outset for the patient's "cautionary tales"—that is, the patient's unconscious explanations of why he feels that the analysis is a dangerous undertaking and his reasons for feeling that the analysis is certain to fail.
>
> The patient unconsciously holds a fierce conviction (which he has no way of articulating) . . . about the specific ways in which each of his object relationships will inevitably become . . . disappointing. . . . In this belief, the analysand is of course both correct and incorrect.
>
> The analyst . . . serves as the container for the patient's fears about beginning this relationship, as well as the container for the patient's hopes that internal change is possible and the pathological attachments to internal objects can be altered with sacrificing the life of the patient [pp. 181–182].

I believe that one of the leading transference anxieties is the dread of not being known in all one's parts, both the ideal and the pathological. There is an "inarticulated anxiety" that the strivings of the ideal self will not be recognized or that the frozen pathological parts will be ignored by either the patient or the therapist. This fear of stirring up the demons of one's bad objects and object relationships is shared by both analyst and patient.

PATHOLOGICAL IDENTIFICATIONS

> *Love and Hate are necessary to Human existence . . . . Love is the passive that obeys Reason. Evil in the active springing from Energy.*
> —WILLIAM BLAKE, *The Marriage of Heaven and Hell*

The strands of thought of my narrative regarding *pathological identification* are to be found in Freud, Klein, Fairbairn, and Kohut. They begin with Freud's idea of "love turning to hate," take us through Klein's identification with the "object of envy" to Fairbairn's "exciting and rejecting object," and conclude with Kohut's "selfobject" failure. Each is a significant contribution regarding the sources of pathological identifications made with the bad object with (what I have found to be) great clinical utility. Because I am conscious of an ideal of preserving the good of the past and transforming it for present use (see chapter two), I shall give some details of the ideas of these thinkers.

Freud: "Love into Hate"

Freud (1915) thought that one vicissitude of an instinct is *reversal* and that, in particular, love can reverse itself into hate. It is a common human experience. In a metaphoric way, the libidinal energy of love is transformed into the energy of hate. What remains constant when love turns to hate is the attachment of the object (Freud's "libidinal cathexis"). If Freud was correct about never abandoning a libido position and maintaining the cathexis through an *identification* with an object—and that hate is a reversal of love—then the internalization of the hated (bad) object is also fueled through an identification with it. This is how we ourselves take in and become the bad object.

The best known example of becoming the bad object is one's "identification with the aggressor" (A. Freud, 1937). Becoming the bad object (i.e., containing the bad object as part of the self) is not limited to one who is psychotic or borderline. The phenomenon exists more subtly in the neurotic personality as well. Even if not blatant, pathological identifications can be inferred through an person's life narrative, problems of affect, issues of self-esteem, and interpersonal difficulties.

Disappointment with archaic objects—often caused by the object's early and continuous selfobject failure—can add to the virulence of the hate for the object, who is experienced as malevolent (see example in chapter three). Hate for the object works in the same way as the loss of the object; they are both internalized through identification. I further believe it necessary to make the distinction between the dynamics of *internalizing the bad object* and the effect of *selfobject failure* as two distinct entities affecting clinical treatment, which I discuss further in chapter four.

"Mrs. Klein": Love and Hate

The most complex psychoanalytic exposition of the "energy" of hate is to be found in Melanie Klein's work, which is essentially her dialectic with, and complement to, Freud's theory of love. It is less widely understood that her view of hate (as discharge of the death instinct) also contains the belief that it is in the service of the life force. The clinical goal is to have split-off destructive forces worked through to a better integration with the life force, thereby allowing greater stability of self.

There is, however, sometimes a clinical problem with hate and envy if they are understood only as by-products of the patient's instinctual self, having nothing to do with the analytic interaction. The current (intersubjective) understanding of hate is a step forward, as I discuss in chapter eight. The "death instinct" projections of the patient's "aggressive object relations"—as Klein (1946, p. 8) referred to projective identification—can be seen as creative attempts to have the therapist understand what the patient's inner world of hostile objects is like so that they may be transformed.

Looked at this way, the patient must be able to unconsciously recognize and activate the hostile objects of the inner world of the therapist and identify with them as their "I." To be successful, the identification must be mutual, which is a function of the degree of comfort the analyst has with that aspect of his or her own mental makeup. The process is not unlike Bion's (1965, pp. 62–63) description of the infant's struggle to make its inner world known to the mother who is able to receive the projective identification. Properly used within a therapeutic setting designed to contain these disturbances, the transformation of pathological internal object relationships becomes possible (as in the example of Patient 6, which follows later).

Whereas Freud understood identification as a way of preserving the erotic energy of the life force for a love object who was no longer a "good object," Klein understood identification as a way of preserving life in the face of the force of the death instinct. Klein was talking about a process that she felt was in operation from birth. While Jacobson (1964) was describing identification as an ego process important to the formation of self ideals, Klein was describing an even earlier superego phenomenon that is vital to the evacuation of stimuli too indigestible to contain for psychic life.

The Lingering Shadow of the Object

We are heirs to Fairbairn's (1954) paradigmatic shift that we are object seeking rather than pleasure seeking. What is longed for is the relationship with the object, not merely libidinal discharge through the object. Fairbairn (1954) evokes the most experience-near sense of the lingering power of the bad object. He described that object as both "exciting and rejecting." The imagery is of the figure who fires the child's imagination, fantasies, and longings.

Although Fairbairn linked the exciting and rejecting object to the imagery of the breast and penis of the preoedipal and oedipal periods respectively, it should not be left there. The rejection by the object comes not only through its failure to satisfy "libidinal" excitation, but also through its failure to meet selfobject needs. For example, the "exciting and rejecting breast" is the failure of the maternal object to meet the selfobject needs of the infant's bodily self (see chapter seven).

Similarly, the feeling of rejection from the exciting oedipal object does not come so much from the child's failure to possess it as from the exciting object's selfobject failure to provide a sense of strength and co-hesion. How and why this occurs for any one individual is the "found object" aspect—of what the self makes of the givens—and determines the course of the analytic work.

THE ANALYST'S ROLE IN THE TRANSFORMATIONAL PROCESS

The unconscious of the therapist is as vital an aspect of the unfolding analytic scene as is the unconscious of the patient.[13] The previous ex-amples illustrated the psychic "scanning" of the therapist by the patient who hopes to reach, and be reached by, the analyst's unconscious capaci-ties. The partial identifications (in Jacobson's sense) made with the real-istic traits of the therapist offer a sense of twinship for the patient that acts as a pathway for profound mental interconnectedness. It is at this level of interpenetration of self and other that introjective and projective processes function as the creative interplay of the therapy.

These experiences can result in the transformational moments (Kainer, 1993a) that directly affect pathological identifications and en-hance the formation of the ideal—i.e., "true," "cohesive," "integrated," "biophilic," "creative"—self that one knows at some level are capable of attainment. It is here that the dialectic of the two parts of the self, the pathological and the ideal, meet to form the third, the *transcendent self*.

Clinical Example

Patient 6: A "Complementary Identification" with the Pathological Self: This clinical example illustrates the major role I assign to identifi-cation in its object-relational and self-psychological aspects. The coun-tertransference here is in the nature of a *complementary identification* (Racker, 1957), in that the therapist's unconscious identification is with that aspect of the patient's ego that is identified with the object

Entering treatment with a long-standing depression, Ms. A expressed confidence that I would not be "bothered" by her "psychotic parts." An intelligent professional woman, she was plagued by an inability to ex-press her thoughts, even at times by not being able to think. I sensed that at some level she wished help with her intellectual functioning. This ses-sion occurred after a long initial period of work during which her depres-sion lifted.

The hour began with my usual "So-o-o?"—our ritual starting signal. Although ordinarily she remained silent for a time after this opening moment—sometimes gathering her thoughts and often retreating for a while into herself—she immediately responded this time with an identical "So-o-o?"—catching my exact tone and inflection. I experienced it as mocking.

After a while, I asked her if she knew why she had mimicked me. Once she gathered that I felt attacked, she was clearly upset, particularly because she had no conscious intention to attack me. On the contrary, she said she was feeling pleasant and loving just before saying that, conscious only of being happy to be here.

My first, and conventional, analytic thought was that perhaps she was having difficulty holding on to a good feeling and unconsciously provoked me in order to return to the familiarity of a depressed mood. Whether or not this was true at some level, it was not relevant to the dynamic being enacted between us. It would also be a technical error to insist on that particular interpretation—or *any* interpretation—that failed to be concordant with her "I."

Her good mood reflected the lifting of her depression and the positive aspects of her maternal object relationship, which had been present in our work. It was now safe, and it was now time, to get to the destructive pathology—the attacking mother that she carried around within her and her split-off, attacking self. My "So-o-o?"—an identification with my own analyst—was the signal to raise the curtain on this important drama. She now experienced me as the attacking mother. In processing it, we came back many times to this fruitful moment when she was able to convey to me the destructive element of her attacking maternal object. I *felt* angry like her mother, I *became* her mother, I *was* her mother.

Ogden (1985) has said, "[The therapist] is coerced into seeing himself only as the object represented in the internal object relationship. More accurately, there is an attempt to make the recipient's experience congruent with the way in which the internal object (aspect of the ego) *experiences itself* and perceived the self-component of the internal relationship" (p. 151).

In my own narration of the projective identification of this enactment, however, I give less weight to the therapist's being coerced, which may lead to a defensive, hostile, nontherapeutic enactment with the patient. *Rather, we both unconsciously seized on the clay of the material at hand to fashion the relevant internal object relationship that was badly in need of transformation.*

She seized the moment and *I* responded with narcissistic injury, using both elements to understand *her* internal world. That this was relevant to her particular inner world comes from my knowledge that I have not become injured when other patients have teased me. I experienced teasing differently in other cases where it did not have the (mother's) mocking quality. Only in this case did its quality have the potential for becoming meaningful to a particular (her) internal object world.

Her seizing on my "So-o-o?" was not to disrupt the good feelings she had achieved in our work together. She could use my ritual opening as a "found object," and precisely because she had achieved the lifting of her depression. In my complementary identification (becoming the mother's "I"), she was able to reexperience the phenomenon of her mother's inexplicable hostility to her.

Indeed, her mother often verbally, and sometimes physically, had abused her. During the next period of our work, she reported being fearful of my attacking her, and I found myself trying to lessen her fear of me. It was clear that she had tapped into my capacity for hostility and was now using it to work out one of the most problematic aspects of her internal world. We could begin to directly address the meaning of her mutism in learning situations and its relationship to the hated, hateful—and pitied—mother.

Notes

[1] Edith Jacobson (1964, p. 51) first used this term, and Roy Schafer (1968) similarly defined it as "someone who is important, impressive, or emotionally significant to the subject at the time he is taking as a model" (p. 159). Their development of the theory of identification has been especially meaningful in the present work.

[2] Marcel Duchamp (1887–1968), father of the Dada movement in art.

[3] By ideal self, I mean all that represents the best level of functioning of which one is capable, which already exists within the self.

[4] This is essentially the Manichean duality of good and evil that Laplanche and Pontalis (1973, p. 101) think characterizes Melanie Klein's view of the death instinct. My emphasis on the struggle with good and evil is on transcendent longings versus the regressive pull of the pathological. It is the dialectical struggle inherent in the therapeutic task.

[5] In chapter 7, I also raise the question of the possible relationship of genetic and constitutional factors in forming identifications.

[6] Schafer's (1968, 1981, 1984) seminal work on the life narrative and the role of identification in internalization has been important to the formation of the present work.

[7] In Freud's (1914) "first duality," libidinal cathexis (energy) was seen as a fixed entity that could be channeled into either the sexual instincts *or* the ego instincts. It makes sense in this schema to view the total energy (which, according to laws of physics, cannot be lost) as redistributed between the two. In Freud's (1920) "second duality," he grouped the sexual instincts and the ego instincts together as part of one "Life Force" that struggled in opposition to the "Death Instinct."

[8] See Ogden (1986) and Schafer (1968) on the internal object and the meaning of internalization.

[9] These crucial needs that we have for our object became the cornerstone of Kohut's (1984) later theory of the selfobject function of the idealizable object.

[10] Rowe (1994) is essentially correct in his view that "Kainer's (1990) concept of selfobject has a paired meaning in that selfobject refers to the experience of the functions provided by the object and to the experience of the object providing the needed functions" (p. 13). See chapter 10 for further discussion.

[11] As Schafer (1968) notes, "identifications may conflict with each other, and, in any given set of circumstances, one identification may be experienced as alien to the immediately dominant subject self; it may then take on a demand character in relation to that self; consequently, the me-ness of the temporarily alien identification may be obscured" (pp. 17–18). (See also example of patient 4 in this chapter.)

[12] For a further discussion of "good fit" between patient and therapist and the working out of psychotic residues, see chapter 6.

[13] Loewald's (1960) work presaged the current movement away from a "one-person" psychology based on individual instincts to the effect of the interconnectedness of self and other in the clinical moment expressed here and previously in the motivational psychology of Lichtenberg, Lachmann, and Fosshage (1992), and in the intersubjective psychology of Stolorow et al. (1987).

On Falling in Love with a Work of Art

Identifications in the Creation of the Ideal Self

In 1913 I had the happy idea to fasten a bicycle wheel to a kitchen stool and watch it turn . . .
—MARCEL DUCHAMP, "Apropos of 'Readymades'"[1]

It is as important to understand the nonpathological identifications made in the creation of the ideal self as it is to know one's pathological identifications, because each defines the self and determines the life narrative. Self-ideals and the ideals of the self are the inner and outer workings of the ideal self. In the previous chapter, the ideal "found object" of identification was the *other*. In this chapter, I discuss the identification of the ideals of the self through the "found object" of art—in this instance, the novel *The Makioka Sisters*, by Junichero Tanazaki.

IDEALS OF THE SELF AND THE SELF-IDEALS OF THE ARTIST

An artwork that is loved reflects the ideals of the self and is loved for that very reason. The artwork also contains projections of the self-ideals of the artist. For example, in the opening quotation, the driving force of Duchamp's now famous bicycle wheel enactment was a projection of his unconscious artistic ideal. At the time of the "happening," he was not yet aware of his intention to revolutionize the world of art. In his recollection of the events following the incident of the bicycle wheel, we can see how his intention unfolded:

> In New York in 1915 I [then] bought at a hardware store a snow shovel
> on which I wrote, "In advance of the broken arm." It was around that
> time that the work "Readymade" came to mind to designate this form
> of manifestation. A point which I want very much to establish is that
> the choice of these "Readymades" was never dictated by esthetic
> delectation [pleasure, enjoyment] [Duchamp, 1973, p. 141].

Duchamp continued:

> This choice was based on a reaction of visual indifference with at the
> same time a total absence of good or bad taste . . . in fact a complete
> anesthesia. One important characteristic was the short sentence which
> I occasionally inscribed on the "Readymade." That sentence instead of
> describing the object like a title was meant to carry the mind of the
> spectator towards other regions more verbal [p. 141].

That the "Readymades" in and of themselves gave him no great aesthetic pleasure and were not projections of an aesthetic ideal was exactly
the point of the deconstruction toward which he was moving. The "happy"
quality of the 1913 event was linked to his unconscious recognition that
something of great importance to him was being expressed by the act
itself and was not due to the content of the work. Duchamp's ideal that
art be seen and made in a new way was unconsciously projected into that
1913 act—and subsequent ones. The ideal of seeing things in a new way
has its parallel in the therapeutic undertaking.

THE ROLE OF THE SPECTATOR:
PARTIAL VERSUS TOTAL IDENTIFICATIONS

My own "happiness" with Duchamp's act comes from an appreciation of
his use of his witty imagination for a serious purpose. Identifying with
Duchamp's humor is a partial rather than a total identification with his
art, unlike the case of the video artist Shigeko Kubota, who is

> a painter and sculptor involved in the 1970s with the neo-Dada Fluxus
> group [who] did her first video piece, "Video Chess" in 1975, inspired
> by a visit to the grave of her idol, Marcel Duchamp. Since then she has
> conceived her sculpture in terms of video, creating worlds that reflect
> her own life and her interest in nature as well as Duchampian jokes
> and ironies [Glueck, 1996, p. C28].[2]

The difference in our response is also an example of the important
role of the spectator in the act. As Duchamp later said in 1957: "the cre-

ative act is not performed by the artist alone; the spectator brings the work in contact with the external world by deciphering and interpreting its inner qualifications and thus adds his[3] contribution to the creative act" (Duchamp, 1973, p. 140). Duchamp's awareness of the role of the spectator echoes my deep interest in the parallels between the psychoanalytic and the creative processes (Kainer, 1990). The spectator of an artwork and the analyst as spectator are similar; both must bring their active imaginations to the productions of the artist/patient in order to complete their meaning. The tenet holds both for the engagement with art and in the clinical exchange.

A crucial distinction of the analyst as spectator, however, is that what the patient produces is almost never completely independent of who the analyst is as object. The artist's actual production is usually more independent of the spectator, although, as Duchamp said, the spectator figures in its final evaluation. I believe that the analyst not only makes a "contribution to the creative act" of the analysis, but also influences and shapes it as well. For example, another analyst might well have found a different Anna O from the one analyzed by Freud, and the Freud whom Anna O encountered might have been different from the Freud created by another patient, since the patient shapes the analyst as well.

Even if we account for the influence of culture, time, and aesthetics, a response to art is also a function of the spectator's individual mental makeup.[4] Having strong likes, dislikes, or simply lack of interest in what another may be passionate about suggests that a process of "identifying in" must first take place in order for one to love a work of art, just as it does with our objects.[5] A concordant identification with the "I" of the artist pulls us in to the work and furthers the imaginative process of falling in love with it. A self-analysis of my response to *The Makioka Sisters* illustrates this idea in detail.

SELF-ANALYSIS AND THE ANALYSIS OF ART

Freud's (1928) note of caution that psychoanalysis must "lay down its arms" when it comes to analyzing the poet, and, by implication, the artwork, has been honored only in the breach. His words serve as a reminder of the difficulty of the task rather than as an injunction. In the actual history of psychoanalysis, the advice has been breached not only by Freud himself, but early on by Rank (1932) and by Freud's later followers. It continues in our own time with further contributions from other schools of thought.

Similarly, since Freud's own historic self-analysis, psychoanalysis has had several notable examples (Guntrip, 1975; Little, 1990), and increasing attention is being paid to it (Barron, 1993). However, there has been little actual attempt at self-analyzing one's response to a work of art. Recently in a symposium on "Finding the Self in a Work of Art: Projective Phenomena" participants from psychoanalysis, the visual arts, and literature analyzed their responses to works that had profoundly engaged them. Their data identified for me three sources of an artwork's projective pull that the spectator finds within it: the *ideal object* (Kuspit, 1996), the *lost object* (Spitz, 1996), and, as in the following case illustration, the *ideal self* (Kainer, 1996).

ON FINDING AND LOVING THE MAKIOKA SISTERS

I came upon the novel *The Makioka Sisters* by Junichero Tanazaki, a Japanese writer who was previously unknown to me and not well known outside his country. The book was a "found object" in both a literal and figurative sense. I recalled that it had been made into an arthouse film that played only briefly and I had missed. Given a general appreciation of the Japanese aesthetic and the relative infrequency of the local showing of its films, I regretted not having seen it. Thus, the book caught my eye.[6]

To my surprise, I became immersed in it in a way I would not have predicted, having no special interest in or knowledge of the time and place—the pre-World War II era in Osaka, Japan in the 1930s. On its surface, it is a novel of domestic life. Such a novel could hold some interest for me, but *not* to this degree. I found that I couldn't wait to get back to it each day and became totally absorbed in it. It finally led me to undertake a scholarly and personal journey. Like Duchamp's bicycle wheel fastened to the kitchen stool, the novel became a "happy idea," and I had no conscious knowledge that I was engaging with something of great importance to me—what turned out to be a glimpse of my ideal self.

At Home with Tanazaki: The Pursuit

Although I first read *The Makioka Sisters* only for the simple pleasure of a seamless, beautifully written novel, I was also fascinated by Tanazaki's account of the psychological and aesthetic details of family life. When I finished it, I quickly tracked down the movie and, after viewing it, organized a seminar to have an excuse to see it again with my colleagues.

At first this activity took place as unanalyzed enthusiasm, but the intensity of the pursuit itself began to interest me. I wished to learn why I found the novel so compelling. My search led me to Tanazaki's other fictional works available in translation,[7] as well as his memoirs of child-

hood written when he was in his 70s (Tanazaki, 1955–56), and the scholarly literature that was available in translation (Kato, 1979; Ito, 1991;
Keene, 1994; Haver, 1996). I came to know the projections of Tanazaki's
self-ideals through analyzing these works and slowly began to recognize
myself in them.

The eloquent beauty of the novel is self-evident, but I did not know
when I began that Tanazaki is thought of as "possibly the greatest Japanese
novelist of this century" (Ito, 1991). There surely would have been wider
recognition for him in the West had his candidacy for the Nobel prize in
Literature been more timely; it was not to be awarded to a Japanese writer
until 1968, much after the World War II era and just beyond Tanazaki's
lifetime.[8]

However, the level of my personal involvement could not be accounted
for only by the quality of the work. Looking back now to that time when
I was also beginning my own book, I understand that I had forged a twinship with Tanazaki through his novel. Hidden in it was my ideal self mirrored by someone whose personal history bore a strong correspondence
to my own, despite the differences in culture and gender and the time in
which we lived.

The Makioka Sisters: The Story

The text of *The Makioka Sisters* concerns the rituals and domestic trials
of a once very affluent business family attempting to marry off Yukiko,
the third of four sisters. By tradition, her unmarried state was preventing
the marriage of her younger and nontraditionally minded sister, Taeko,
who already had a serious, self-chosen beau. Taeko lived on her own as a
financially independent doll-maker and was most eager to resolve her
highly charged love life. By custom, however, she could not do so until
the older Yukiko married.

Yukiko, on her part, was silently determined not to marry any of the
unsuitable hyperactive "modern" businessmen that her two older married sisters were duty bound to present for her approval. The tension of
this plot spans almost the entire novel. It seems unlikely that this theme
should hold more than a passing interest for a contemporary Western
feminine consciousness. Nevertheless, a process of identification was
taking place as I read on.

"Identifying In"

Identifications were possible first because of Tanazaki's unexpected refu-
tation of my stereotype of Japanese culture. It came as a welcome surprise

that there was not one "obedient" woman to be found among the major characters.[9] Tanazaki's loving portrayal of this world of women was entirely different from the view of the subjugated woman often encountered in the "phallic narcissism" of such more familiar work as that of Yukio Mishima (Ito, 1991, p. 95)."[10] Even in Tanazaki's other works, which are more concerned with his image of the woman as femme fatale than as maternal ideal, it is never the woman who suffers in love.

In their individual ways, each of the Makioka sisters knew exactly what she wanted and went about getting it with great self-determination, as well as the approval of the author. Even the reticent Yukiko—who most represented the traditional Japanese woman in demeanor, dress, and artistic accomplishments—was stubbornly impervious to the pressure of both her biological clock and her obligation to marry. In what were the most comic scenes later depicted in the film, she simply silently refused to be paired off with whatever wrong man of the moment was frantically vying for her approval. It never came.

She became totally mute as the men tried to get her to speak on the telephone. She remained silent throughout the many dinner "matches" arranged by the families. Instead, she quietly perfected the art of her calligraphy and samisen and devoted herself to the care of her little niece. She did not relinquish her feminine role, rather she expressed it only as she saw fit.

The resolution of Yukiko's narrative directly contradicted the psychoanalytic interpretation I gave it while reading the text—that Yukiko was passive-aggressively resisting her familial duty in order to carry out her underlying intent never to marry. I was wrong. Near the end of the long book (and charmingly depicted in the film) the sisters finally bring to the table not another modern manic businessman (possibly to pump up the fading Makioka business fortune) but a tall, lean, graceful aristocrat who matches her completely in his perfection of the arts and languid style—and has studied aerodynamics as well! Yukiko's tiny smile of assent appears at last. In the film they are next shown at the train station—a radiant couple being pelted with flowers as they depart for Tokyo.

It was not that Yukiko intended never to marry. Rather, with an admirable strength of purpose, she did what was right for her while still carrying out her obligations. Her love was contingent on finding a man who represented the graces and learning as much as she did, and she achieved an even more serene love in her arranged match than her younger sister had in her completely self-chosen one. I consciously identified with Yukiko's use of her strong will to carry out her own definition of the good.

This idyllic resolution of the mating problem also reflected Tanazaki's ideal. After two previous mismatches, he finally achieved a very successful and lasting marriage to the "charming and graceful" Matsuko. Her "theatricality matched his," and they established a personal artistic haven that included a household "totally overwhelmed" by her three sisters. As Yukiko might have said—had she ever spoken—Tanazaki himself said of his own good match with Matsuko: "This was no less than what I wanted" (Ito, 1991, p. 187). He had found his ideal in Matsuko. In the novel, he projected this self-ideal.

Identifying with the Pulls of Past and Present

Despite the novel's old-fashioned story of the arranged marriage, it was interspersed with many contemporary elements. Although the novel is set in the 1930s, the Makioka sisters went out frequently, hunting down restaurants in pursuit of the perfect sushi, by now an easy-to-identify-with pastime. They went as often to the "Western" theater as they did to Kabuki. The youngest sister, Taeko, was the very model of a modern independent feminist—whose trials were treated not unsympathetically by the author. There was enough of the cosmopolitan "West" interspersed with the traditions of the "East" with which to identify. The intrinsic order and craft of the East that he detailed was also appealing.

The juxtaposition of East and West was achieved through the narrative device of frequently shifting the setting from Tokyo to Osaka and then back again, which Tanazaki made mesmerizing. Tokyo was the "Western" present, and Osaka the "Eastern" past, and the back-and-forth movement between them represented the task of reconciling the conflict of past and present on many levels. It went on and on.

Tanazaki also portrayed the struggle of past and present as the classical yearnings of Yukiko holding up the progress of Taeko's modernist leanings. I associated to another work—that of the Egyptian Nobel Prize winner Naguib Mahfouz (1956), who also portrayed the struggle of past and present as between two women. As Mahfouz said it more literally:

> The juxtaposition of the two women appeared to illustrate the interplay of the amazing laws of heredity and the inflexible law of time. The two women might have been a single person with her image reflected forward to the future or back into the past.
>
> In either case, the difference between the original and its reflection revealed the terrible struggle raging between the laws of heredity, attempting to keep things the same, and the law of time, pushing for change and a finale [p. 203].

On both the personal and the cultural level, Tanazaki was mourning the loss of a world that no longer existed. The coherent, ordered, traditional world he created in *The Makioka Sisters* was his ideal construction of a way of life and a culture that had been destroyed. Under the "inflexible law of time," the past was no more, and the novel was his elegiac remembrance of it.

The identification with Tanazaki's determination not to let a past culture be totally obliterated is in operation in my own work. It reflects a need to preserve the timeless truths found in the past culture of psychoanalysis and to reconcile further this past with the inexorable push of knowledge gained in the present.

In his life as well as his art, Tanazaki found his personal solution to the conflict of past and present by embracing the traditional after a period of "infatuation" with things Western. Not coincidentally, this shift also exactly met his artistic needs. His was never to be the life of the Tokyo "salary man"—the type of man of business Yukiko consistently rejected in the novel. Like Yukiko, Tanazaki "always remained an artist true to private vision" (Ito, 1991, p. 2). Tanazaki commented that, after his marriage to Matsuko and the setting up of their exotic household, "I resolutely avoided Tokyo manners and sought to be drawn to Osaka ways. Though *I was not fully aware of this at the time*, somewhere beneath the surface, the exoticism a Tokyo native [himself] feels toward Osaka people played a part in my attitude toward the three sisters" (in Ito, 1991, p. 187, italics added).

Thus, these two powerful chords of recognition—Yukiko as the quietly strong-minded woman with great needs for artistic expression, and the struggle of past and present—were the initial elements of the identifications that drew me into the work and further into the world of the author's "I." The novel's text and subtext and his other works in translation, as well as Tanazaki himself as he was depicted in the scholarly literature and autobiographical writings, allowed me to name Tanazaki's self-ideals—and this understanding led me to further identify my own.

NAMING THE IDEALS OF THE SELF

Like Duchamp's bicycle wheel enactment, the reading *of The Makioka Sisters* was a first step toward carrying the mind of this "spectator towards other regions more verbal." The naming of the following ideals reflects the projective and introjective process between myself as spectator and Tanazaki as author, and the importance of the artwork as a conduit of our joint imaginations. Although they appear clearly stated here, they were until then part of the "unthought known" of my psyche.

The Artistic Preservation of the Ideal

The Makioka Sisters was written during Japan's austere war years of the 1940s, but Tanazaki's setting in the pre-War 1930s completely removed the war from the novel's concerns. He did so because his powerful artistic aim was to make the real world into a fictional one. In that fictional world there was no war, only an ideal way of life of aesthetic sensibility that he knew would be no more. In its seamless focus on the interior domestic and psychological world of its characters, Tanazaki's obedience was to the power of his imagination, which was far stronger than the press of his present reality.

The suppression of present reality was in effect a denial of its value, a point not lost on the military censors who banned the work's serialization. While the novel was not directly critical of Japan's militarism, it had as its ideal a world that was destroyed by it (Ito, 1991, p. 191). In fighting back against the reality of the present destruction, Tanazaki employed my ideal weapon of choice—that of art, not war.

As also projected into the character of Yukiko, Tanazaki patiently held on. He simply kept on writing until the end of the war released him from the censors. His ideal of the "good" was expressed through the use of his imaginative powers to build a world that would endure beyond the one being destroyed—and he succeeded! In a way, Tanazaki brings to mind the works of my favorite early German expressionist painters (Beckman, Dix, Jawlensky, Kirchner, Nolde, Schmidt-Rottluff), who similarly used their imaginations to find solace in a destructive environment. Tanazaki had created a space protected from his culture's militarism by recreating a nonwarring past. The painters—"bogged down" (Kuspit, 1997, personal communication) in their Germanic present—gained distance from it by turning to primitive art and an explosion of a powerful self-expression.

Like Tanazaki, these were artists whose work placed them outside of the mainstream of art, but not of their culture. They served as silent critics of the destructive. Hitler referred to these giants as *Kunzwege*, or "art dwarfs" (Barron, 1991). There is ironic pleasure in the knowledge that the greatest of their works were exhibited as "Degenerate Art" in 1937 by the Nazis. Acts of imagination are always acts of risk, and they are especially admirable when they also reflect moral courage.

The Ideal of Imagination

The Makioka Sisters was so vividly drawn by Tanazaki that its resemblance to the Tanazaki household seems uncanny. This mixture of art and life was so great that Keene (1994), upon attending Tanazaki's funeral, reported a "startling experience when I saw the four sisters of the novel before my eyes as one after the other they offered incense at the altar." Keene's confusion of art with life goes on: "When I learned of Tanazaki's death in 1965, I rushed to a nearby post office to send a telegram of condolence to Mrs. Tanazaki. I knew that her name was Matsuko, but in my state of shock over the news, I unintentionally addressed the telegram to Sachiko, using the name of the character in the novel who closely resembled her" (p. 179).

However, Matsuko Tanazaki herself said that the novel, although resembling the actual Tanazaki household, was "fiction in every way" (Ito, 1991, p. 189). The "world depicted in the novel has been transformed through the act of writing," making it more radiant and harmonious (p. 189). All of Tanazaki's created worlds, even those which actually resemble the real one, are acts of imagination. His powers of imagination were well recognized, and he himself said that "he could not create anything that was not of the imagination."

The fictional world he builds in the novel extols the ideal and makes understandable the relationship of the ideal to the real. I believe that the press to employ the imagination to overcome reality through the construction of the ideal also reflects a longing to make the ideal a reality. The need to transcend reality through the creation of the ideal is neither a delusion nor a form of pathology. It is a creative realization of the wish to refashion a lesser reality into something more. Tanazaki's novel, as an imaginative act, is an act of transcendence. This same quality can be seen with equal power in therapy, when patients use their imagination in the creative process of analysis to convey and transcend their pathology.

The Ideal of the Sensual

Tanazaki was by all reports, including his own, a hedonist. His hedonistic aims were accompanied by an aesthetic sensibility and a love and great appreciation for life. Keene (1994) recalled a visit to the Tanazakis: "I was occasionally invited to dinner by Mr. and Mrs. Tanazaki. Tanazaki's gourmet tastes seem to have been known throughout Japan, and I got the impression that whenever someone caught an unusually fine fish or harvested unusually delicious fruit, the first thought was to send it to Tanazaki-sensei [master]" (p. 179).

Through his novel one gets the sense that these gifts not only served as a mark of the honor in which Tanazaki was held, but also came from the giver's understanding that Tanazaki, above all others, would savor its perfection. His aesthetic sensuality extended to his writing, which was always graceful and elegant. At one point in the film of *The Makioka Sisters,* the director caught this aspect of Tanazaki by creating a breathtaking color montage of the resplendent kimonos that the sisters were trying to decide amongst for the annual viewing of the cherry blossoms. It was a visual portrait of Tanazaki's ideal of art as the beautiful and his self ideal of "my life for art."[11] In this novel in particular, it is artistic sensuality rather than erotic sensuality that predominates.

Tanazaki could also find a sublime aesthetic in the unlikely place of the traditional Japanese toilet. In his *In Praise of Shadows* (1933), his evocation of its darkness and the scent of cedar boughs was so inviting that Keene (1994) was disappointed that the bathroom he took pains to inspect on his visit to Tanazaki's Kyoto home "was of gleaming white tiles" (p. 179). It turns out that, while sincere in his praise of the traditional toilet, Tanazaki admitted this rare preference for West over East.

The Ideals of Playfulness and Irreverence

An important aspect of *In Praise of Shadows* is its intrinsic humor, although not readily apparent in its somber, lyrical tone. Tanazaki has a unique knack of being genuinely appreciative and faintly irreverent at one and the same time. He did not make broad jokes like Duchamp. His subtle and mischievous humor came from his juxtaposing exquisite form with improbable content.[12]

Nowhere does his mischievous side put the reader to a greater test than in Tanazaki's (1931–32) *The Secret History of the Lord of Musashi*. A macabre novella set in the 16th century, it is essentially a bizarre tale of a young boy, the son of a defeated feudal lord, who witnesses the custom of taking the severed heads of those felled in battle, removing their noses, and otherwise making them ready for a victory display. He is drawn to this ritual, and the desiccations become the focal point of the boy's erotic obsession, as well as an instrument of revenge for his father's defeat. The boy grows up to be Lord Musashi.[13]

In exemplifying Duchamp's point about the importance of the role of the spectator and the important place I give to identifications, a comparison with my reaction to this novella with that of Haver (1996) is useful. I thought the novel might be a parody of what Haver has called the early Japanese "Era of Warring States." While Haver also found the work parodic, it was not this aspect that most interested him. He responded to it with a thoughtful and complex Lacanian treatise on the symbolism of the phallus, castration, erotogenic sadomasochism, homosexuality, death, and the intersection of one's public life and secret desires.

I simply found the novella comic, despite its macabre content and somber tone, but much less interesting than *The Makioka Sisters*. I agreed with the assessment that Tanazaki had a "rather macabre sense of humor" where "one can almost hear the author's cackle of glee in the background (McCarthy, 1989) and gave it no further attention. In this work, Haver's "I" was closer to Tanazaki's than to mine in giving meaning to the obsessional aspects of the erotic.

In terms of an ideal, it seemed to me that in *The Secret History*—with its legacy of warring manifest in Tanazaki's own time—Tanazaki (1931–32) was probably satirizing his culture's long-standing obsession with the samurai warrior mentality. *The Makioka Sisters* reflected his elegant and indirect censuring of his culture's destructiveness which I share. Similarly, *The Secret History* reflected his subtle censure of those aspects of his culture's character that perhaps were the very source of its destructiveness. However, I was less drawn to Tanazaki's "naughty boy" erotic interests in the book than I was to the part that was expressive of him as a morally strong man.

I had no difficulty in fully responding to his more sophisticated humor in *The Makioka Sisters* when the "Tanazakian sense of the ridiculous" (McCarthy, 1989) was aimed at his culture's obsession with ritual itself. I could take hearty pleasure in the passage: "Each spring finds [the husband] out in the yard throwing stones at the sparrows to keep them away from the young shoots in the lawn, a practice that always causes his family to remark that *'the time for the throwing of the stones has come'*" (Tanizaki, 1943–48, p. 83, italics added). Questioning the dubious givens of any existing culture appeals to me and relates to the ideal of the voice of the mother.

The Ideal of the Voice of the Mother

Although my identificatory interest may be greater in the psychological realism of *The Makioka Sisters* than in the macabre eroticism of *The Secret History*, the latter also contains an element of serious play that constitutes a challenge to authority. In parodying the warrior and the warrior nation, or even his culture's obsession with ritual, Tanazaki was essentially challenging the "Word of the Father" (Lacan) that has dominated his culture. His irreverence was directed against the destructive and outworn aspects of its authority. Tanazaki's perspective was a shift from what one would expect of a man from his culture.

Closely related to Tanazaki's disidentification with his culture's militaristic and phallic narcissism is his appreciation of women. His portrayal of women also represents a significant cultural shift, for his novels go far beyond the "traditional Confucian and Buddhist attitude . . . that they are inferior creatures, scarcely worthy of serious attention" (Tanazaki, 1931–32, p. x). The woman in all aspects of her femininity, including her strength, is the theme of much of his work. It is exactly Tanazaki's serious attention to the psychology of women that is unique, and it was no coincidence that the classic work he chose to translate until perfect—*The Tale of Genji*—was written by a woman.[14]

This aspect of Tanazaki parallels the culture of psychoanalysis. The inexorable movement away from the phallocentric origins of psychoanalysis has challenged the word of the Father. It was succinctly captured in Joyce McDougall's (1995) comment, "I think it is perhaps less Lacan's 'word of the Father' than it is the 'voice of the Mother' that affects the infant." It is a movement with which I can identify, and a shift that time makes necessary. Ito (1991) described Tanazaki's feminism as "simply a person who 'favors' women" (p. 13). Tanazaki projects admiration, caring, respect, and desire for the Woman even in the novels where the ideal of the erotic femme fatale is the focus.

An Ideal of a Man's Love for a Woman

In *The Makioka Sisters,* Tanazaki's "most detailed portrait of a woman" occurs. It is particularly in his portrayal of the second oldest married sister, Sachiko, that a chord of recognition is struck. She is a totally feminine woman whose traits are admired and cherished by a man. Her admired femininity came through clearly in the text and was noted by Ito (1991):

> As she responds to various events, Sachiko reveals not only her capacity for affection and sympathy, her respect for tradition, her refined sensibilities, and her intense femininity, but also her class prejudices, her pride and her dependence on those around her. Tanazaki's loving portrayal endows Sachiko with a human complexity unseen in his previous portraits of idealized women [p. 194].

It was the way in which Tanazaki detailed her character, as well as her husband's response to her, that was so satisfying. Sachiko was a woman who was deeply understood by the writer. Whether Tanazaki was portraying her as frantically making matrimonial arrangements for the resistant Yukiko, planning for the family's dining out, or selecting just the right kimono for the cherry blossom viewing, he displayed a fond acceptance for the anxiety such domestic preoccupations would naturally have for this kind of woman. There is no doubt that Sachiko's efforts were all toward the building of a rich interior world. These efforts were appreciated by Sachiko's husband in the novel, as were similar efforts by Tanazaki in his own life with Matsuko. The woman as truly appreciated, with the further possibility that the appreciation will be mutual and equal, is a contemporary feminist ideal I share.

Thus I could identify with—and project into—a work that portrayed the "theatrical" woman loved by the amused husband. Tanazaki's own self-projection into the novel was of a man who, it was said, "had been married most of his life" (Kato, 1979, p. 200). The portrait of Sashiko was by a man whose love and awe of the mother (Tanazaki, 1955–56) became the love and admiration for the wife (Kainer, 1988). In his other novels, his idealization of the woman is an erotic femme fatale. Even in those works, however, if anyone suffers for love it is the man. The absence of the stereotype of the masochistic woman from all of Tanazaki's work, including women of erotic obsession, was gratifying.

The Ideal of Craft

Closely related to the love of the sensual is the ideal of craft, for each makes much of the details. Tanazaki's ideal of craft is evident in all his writing. He undertook a modern translation of Lady Murasaki's epic 11th-century classic *Tale of Genji* three times until he was finally satisfied. In his first translation, he voluntarily excised portions that the military authorities might find objectionable—parts having to do with Imperial incestuous behavior (Ito, 1991, p. 186). However, he undertook another entire translation of the very lengthy work twice afterwards, until it met with his satisfaction. He called the final translation "a pleasure of old age."

In Tanazaki's (1955–56) memoir *Childhood Years*, he said: "For a time, as one means of improving my style, I excerpted the best passages from a variety of classical works and then tried to incorporate them in a new work of my own" (p. 181). This passage is directly relevant to an identification with the classics in my own field, but I also identify with that part of his "I" which needs to improve its style. The beauty of Tanazaki's writing contains an ideal. Similarly, my parallel ideal in psychoanalysis is for both its preservation as a classic and its improvement as a craft.

Certainly Tanazki's artistic courage, his great powers of imagination, his aesthetic sensuality, his dedication to the perfection of craft, and his wish to conserve the past were his self-ideals embedded in the novel to which I *unconsciously* resonated. My immersion in the book was the literary equivalent of the "reverie" characteristic of empathic immersion. He is a playmate for the mind's imagination and a gifted artist who diligently perfected those gifts. But an even older ideal in him is the capacity for a man to cherish a woman. One could fall in love with a work of art in which these ideals have been projected.

SHARING THE "I" OF THE AUTHOR: THE LOSS OF PLACE

Another point of identification that unexpectedly emerged from the research on Tanazaki may account for a part of the shared "I" in reading the novel. I strongly resonated with his sense of a lost past and his wish to preserve it. His past included a climactic loss of place for him, as it did for me. Although from different times and cultures, in a broad sense we were both children of the "shitamachi." That is, both of us came from a world of small neighborhoods of shopkeepers and artisans embedded in cities of "major importance and vitality" (Ito, 1991). We each were displaced from those worlds: he from the old Tokyo destroyed by the great earthquake of 1923, and I from the richness of New York, not through a natural disaster but as part of a life narrative.

Although moving by choice, as I did, and having one's city destroyed, as Tanazaki did, differ, we both suffered disruptions of place and the loss of a vital cosmopolitan world marked by artistry and individuality. In Tanazaki's words, "the *shitamachi* of Tokyo" became "a city now changed beyond recognition" (Ito, 1991, p. 7). Neither of us seems to have had much fondness for the replacements of our lost worlds: modern corporate Tokyo for him, and contemporary political Washington for me. For each of us, the world that was lost has been retained as a longed-for ideal— one that we each in various ways have tried to recreate.

Tanazaki took comfort in removing himself to the old cities of Osaka and Kyoto and imagining the traditions of that life in *The Makioka Sisters*. I instinctively relocated to what was later designated a historic neighborhood. I now understood the meaning of my search for places that retained visible signs of their past history, just as Tanazaki held on to the past in both his art and his life. Visually and artistically, we were like refugees seeking to reestablish the lost clan.[15] I identified with his being "an immigrant from Tokyo" who "searches for a sense of home" (Ito, 1991, p. 112). We both needed to reconnect with a lost place, a lost way of life, and a lost past. His need became the theme of his great novel, and mine the theme of psychoanalysis, which is also about finding the lost part of the self and creating a new home for it.

A photograph of Tanazaki in his last years which I particularly like is of a beaming, benign figure, possibly plump and certainly playful. It is my ideal of having "gotten it right" in aging.[16] Perhaps behind the ideal of playfulness is the transcendent hope that one can retain the spirit of the

child. To preserve the child, to keep and replenish its imaginative capaci-
ties, to nurture its potential, that too is the ideal of psychoanalysis with
which I identify.

Notes

[1] From Duchamp's October 19, 1961 talk at the Museum of Modern Art, New York
(see Duchamp, 1973).

[2] One of her "jokes" is a sculpture in the form of a robot that is a perpetual
fountain, a man urinating into a bucket. A monitor in his forehead carries images
of the video pioneer Nam June Paik, Ms. Kubota's husband (Glueck, 1996). The
work may be an example of art imitating life, the power of identification, or yet
another tolerant and good-natured husband, proud of his wife. As of this writing,
they are still married.

[3] In Schafer's preface to the 1990 edition of his classic 1968 work, *Aspects of
Internalization*, he notes: "I would no longer use the pronoun *he* to refer to men
and women alike. There is no compelling stylistic reason to persist in a convention that has been shown to be one facet of the subjugation of women in our
world . . ." (p. xxiii).

[4] Finding a work to be a "work of art" already implies the existence of an "ideal."
A widely recognized work of art has identificatory appeal for many individuals.

[5] The German film *Maybe, Maybe Not* incisively captures the meaning of "interest"—or its lack—as it functions in sexual preference.

[6] A special form of identification, a shared "I," occurs when a book one loves is
made into a film that the filmmaker clearly also loves. Examples are the film of
Anaïs Nin's *Henry and June* and Hubert Selby's *Last Exit to Brooklyn* (see Kainer,
1991).

[7] *Naomi* (1924); *Some Prefer Nettles* (1928–29); *Arrowroot* (1930); *The Secret
History of the Lord of Musashi* (1931–32); *A Blind Man's Tale* (1931); *A Portrait
of Shunkin* (1933); *Captain Shigemoto's Mother* (1949); *The Key* (1956).

[8] However, Tanazaki was not without recognition. "In 1949, he received the Imperial Award for Cultural Merit, and in 1964 was elected to honorary member-
ship in the American Academy and Institute of Arts and Letters, the first Japanese
writer to be so honored" (from the introduction to Tanazaki's [1931–32] *The
Secret History of the Lord of Masashi*). He died in 1965.

[9] With the exception of the one woman servant, a characterization that reflected
the reality of class differences in the society.

[10] Mishima was better known to the West than Tanazaki. Unlike the latter, Mishima
"was an unsophisticated aesthete rather than a psychological writer" (Kato, 1979,
p. 287). He is well known for his militarism, body-building, and well-publicized
death by the ancient ritual suicide of *seppuka*—self-disembowelment—as he is
for his novels *Confession of a Mask* (1958) and *The Sailer Who Fell From Grace
with the Sea* (1965), among other writings.

[11] A similar ideal was conveyed in Ingmar Bergman's film *Fanny and Alexander*.
After his autobiographical portrayal of the repressive effects in his boyhood of

his maniacally religious stepfather, the finale of the film is marked by an explosion of color on the occasion of the birth of twins celebrated by a family of theater people. It unmistakably conveyed the power and triumph of art for Bergman.

[12] Which at one point involved helping with the correct rematching of his "quiet, domesticated" first wife, Chiyo, with another fellow writer, Sato. Tanazaki had actually been in love with Chiyo's sister, "a quick-tongued and assertive woman who ran a restaurant in Tokyo" but she was not available. They "sent their friends and associates an announcement which said in part: 'At this juncture, we three have come to a joint agreement whereby Chiyo will divorce Junichiro [Tanazaki], and marry Haruo [Sato].' Worded in a formal, sinified epistolary style, the statement exhibited a wild incongruence between form and content" (Ito, 1991, p. 134). Seidensticker, in his introduction to *The Makioka Sisters* (Tanazaki, 1993) said, "It was one of the most delicious and eccentric happenings in the literary world of the day, and indeed all through the modern century" (p. x).

[13] The theme of erotic addiction is never too far in many of Tanazaki's works other than *The Makioka Sisters*.

[14] Lady Murasaki, b. circa A.D. 978, d. not known. *The Tale of Genji* was written approximately between A.D. 1001–1020.

[15] For a particularly well-written account of trying to recreate the lost identification of the past, see Young-Bruehl's (1982) biography of the political philosopher Hannah Arendt as refugee.

[16] Contrast this with the portrait of aging as projected by novelist Philip Roth and artist Pablo Picasso, in chapter nine.

Chapter Three

Sadomasochistic Identifications

The Formation of the Pathological Part of the Self

By reason of its empathic character, pathography[1] implies the special energy—the energy of identification—with which psychoanalysts have pursued artists.

—DONALD KUSPIT

In the previous chapter, the ideal self as expressed by the ideals of the self were presented as important to the structure of the self. There is a self we have the longing to fulfill, and the capacity to do so. There are also parts of the self that are well, nonpsychotic,[2] nonautistic, enduring, connected, playful, thoughtful, resilient, and creative. The pathological parts of the self of concern in this book—its sadomasochistic tendencies, its lingering psychotic and autistic residues, its unbearable bodily tensions are juxtaposed with this more ideal self and exist in a dialectical tension with it.

In the struggle between them, both the ideal and the pathological parts of the self must come to be known; each is a factor in determining the life narrative as well as the analytic undertaking. The transcendent force of the ideal self makes the regressive pull of the pathological all the more unbearable and contributes to the suffering of the neurotic personality.[3] This suffering is particularly acute in sadomasochistic pathology, where there is a longing for transcendence over masochistic tendencies.

The extensive body of literature on sadism and masochism contributed by different schools of thought speaks to its erotogenic, object-relational, and self-psychological dimensions (Kainer, 1993b). The previous work most relevant here is the relationship of sadomasochism to separation and creative will (Menaker, 1979), and the narcissistic structure of sadomasochism (Stolorow, 1975; Kohut, 1979; Gear, Hill, and Liendo,

1981). In this chapter, sadomasochism is taken beyond it erotogenic roots and the repetition compulsion of Freud's (1915, 1924) death instinct, to explore its role in self-defeating behavior and pathological relationships.

The case of Mr. X, to follow later, illustrates how the formation of a sadomasochistic identification with the bad object was a function of the narcissistic injuries sustained through the object's failure to meet selfobject needs. Narcissistic injury is an affective signal that the needs of the self are not properly being met. Severe narcissistic injury shapes character structure and contributes to the determination of who we become. To illustrate further, I use biographical material from the life of Franz Kafka, whose sense of narcissistic injury was a significant factor in his art as well as his life, and then present the case of Mr. X.

THE ETIOLOGY OF PATHOLOGICAL IDENTIFICATIONS

In the preceding chapter, my ideal self was shown as formed, but not yet fully named prior to the (self) analysis. The ideals of the self were discovered through an identification with the artist's work, but the artist himself had no actual role as an object of identification in their formation. An identification with an artist's work differs from an identification made with an archaic object.[4] In the latter case, there are additional factors of attachment and dependency that more strongly affect selfobject need and increase the potential for selfobject failure. These disturbances contribute to the formation of pathological identifications.

Selfobject Failure

Discoveries concerning selfobject needs and selfobject failure have come from self psychology, whereas object relations theory has concerned itself with the nature of internal objects and the dynamics of internal object-relationships. By treating these findings as separate schools of thought, we miss the significant natural relationship between one's internal object world and the sense of self. One profoundly affects the other, and both are affected by the need for maintaining attachment to our objects.

Whether or not attachment is instinctual (Bowlby, 1969, 1980), we have ample clinical evidence to believe that attachment to our actual objects leaves us particularly vulnerable to their selfobject failure. For example, objects who cannot be idealized means that the necessary selfobject experience of vitality and strength cannot be found through them. Their selfobject failure then leads to a rejection of the object, but attachment to that object is still maintained through an unconscious identification with it, which is often an adhesive one. One internalizes the very traits that reflect the disturbed—and disturbing—aspect of the object. One *becomes* the bad object by taking the "I" of the bad object as the "I" of the self. This view echoes Freud's (1917) thought that, through identification, we never totally abandon an object that was once the object of love (see chapter one). We do not choose it, but we adhere to it.

Selfobject failure is inevitably experienced as profound loss. Not only is the good of the bad object lost, there is a loss of the sense of a cohesive and well self owing to the selfobject failure. The loss furthers a search for compensatory figures, particularly for the selfobject need of idealization. The loss may be temporarily overcome through hating the bad object, which lends strength and pseudo-cohesiveness through its energy. But this attack on linking does not yield the strength gained from connection and true individuation. Furthermore, in a nonpsychotic state, hate is soon counterbalanced by reparative longings and relational needs, which spur the replacement of these rejected objects through an unconscious identification with them.

In the case of Mr. X, his adhesive sadomasochistic identifications were the outcome of a struggle to maintain an attachment to his objects despite their overwhelming failure to meet his selfobject needs—particularly those of idealization, mirroring and containment. I am adding *selfobject containment* as a primary need present at birth and an earlier selfobject need than mirroring, idealization and twinship. Selfobject containment refers to the basic requirement for the caregiver to regulate bodily tensions and psychic excitations through their capacity to experience these self-states. It is a further link of Bion's (1957) work to the formation of the self. (See chapter seven for further discussion.)

Although the energy of love was transformed into the energy of hate, he remained identified with, and embodied, the pathological aspects of the objects who had profoundly failed him. The identifications served to keep him connected, albeit pathologically.

SADOMASOCHISM

Erotogenic Roots

The most literal expression of sexualized sadomasochism is the familiar "S & M" of bondage and domination, both in fantasy and acted out. This kind of behavior is a concrete example of Freud's (1915) erotogenic sadomasochism, illustrating the instinctual energy of sexual and aggressive drives that is the bedrock of his theory. In this eroticized form of sadomasochism, there is often no real other in the relational sense, only an "other" who functions as the object fulfilling the instinctual aims of excitation and discharge. This object is highly interchangeable with others who are willing to serve the same function. In this case, the sexual dominates the relational. In Freud's erotogenic sadomasochism:

> (a) Sadism consists in the exercise of violence or power upon some other person as object.
> (b) This object is abandoned and replaced by the subject's self. With the turning round upon the self the change from an active to a passive instinctual aim is also effected.
> (c) An extraneous person is once more sought as object; this person, in consequence of the alteration which has taken place in the instinctual aim, has to take over the role of the subject.

Freud adds:

> Case (c) *is what is commonly termed masochism*. Here too satisfaction follows along the path of the original sadism, the passive ego placing itself back in phantasy in its first role, which no in fact has been taken over by the extraneous subject [pp. 127–128, italics added].

Although the foregoing quote primarily describes erotogenic sadomasochism, Freud's model also has use for understanding sadomasochism in its other forms. His concept of sadism in obsessional neurosis is particularly relevant to one aspect of Mr. X's case:

> In [obsessional neurosis] there is a turning round upon the subject's self *without* the attitude of passivity towards another person: the change has only got as far as stage b. The desire to torture has turned into self-torture and self-punishment, not into masochism. *The active voice is changed, not into the passive, but into the reflexive middle voice* [p. 128, final italics added].

What Freud meant here is that the quality of suffering characteristic of the obsessional condition is masochistic suffering, coming not at the hands of another, but administered by the self.[5] One is now actively sadistic toward the self rather than passively masochistic in the hands of another. The suffering coming from self punishment, however, is as great as the suffering inflicted by another.

Freud (1924) later conceptualized "moral masochism" to designate masochism that is "chiefly remarkable for having loosened its connection with what we recognize as sexuality" (p. 165). Menaker's (1979) classic work on masochism as a defense reaction of the ego in the service of attachment further removed it from the sexual and brought it closer to the object-relational. Freud may or may not have been correct when he called sadism and masochism primary instinctual phenomena, but there can be no doubt that there is a self-reflexive, nonsexualized sadomasochism that is directed against the self and frequently observed in patients.

SELF-REFLEXIVE AND RELATIONAL SADOMASOCHISM

In addition to self-defeating sadomasochism, there can also be pervasive and persistent sadomasochistic interactions with others. In the familiar latter case, one unconsciously "finds" the object who can complement one's own masochistic or sadistic aims. Gear et al. (1981, pp. 389–407) best captures this *relational* aspect of sadomasochism when describing "the masochistic agent's" effect on the "sadistic patient" and the "sadistic agent's" effect on the "masochistic patient." This dynamic operates between individuals in smoothly reciprocal movements, with each one unconsciously knowing the part he or she must play in relation to the partner. In this chapter, sadomasochism is discussed in both its self-reflexive and its relational (i.e., interactive) forms in the case of Mr. X.

THE RELATIONSHIP OF SELFOBJECT FAILURE TO SADOMASOCHISM: THE CASE OF FRANZ KAFKA

An important factor in the formation of sadomasochism is that of selfobject failure. The latter gives rise to the experience of hatred for the object because of the often severe narcissistic injury selfobject failure provokes. In the case of Franz Kafka, the catastrophic mismatch between the emotionally fragile but strong-willed genius son and the selfobject failure of idealization experienced with his father, Herrmann, is well known in literary history (Pawel, 1984). Kafka was especially appalled by Herrmann's business-driven, loud, crude demandingness. He felt demeaned by his father's mocking, bullying, shaming, and total lack of comprehension of his very different, extraordinary, and difficult son. At age 36, Kafka (1919) wrote his classic "Letter to his Father," an extensive accounting of the narcissistic injury of failed idealization and mirroring.[6] Its theme of annihilation is captured in the following passage: "However it was, we were so different and in our difference so dangerous to each other that, if anyone had tried to calculate in advance how I, the slowly developing child, and you, the full-grown man, would stand to each other, he could have assumed the you would simply trample me underfoot so that nothing was left of me" (p. 141).

His sense of injury at the selfobject inadequacy of his father remained with him throughout his life. In an ironic identification with his obtuse father, Kafka could never really understand (accept) that his father was simply a not very intelligent man who was mostly bark and no bite (Pawel, 1984, p. 19). Rather, he experienced his father as a superior force who at any moment might crush him. Although his injuries were real, Kafka may also have needed to hold on to them as the fuel and subject for his writing. This theme of the damaged self was woven into his great works of fiction, which were made all the more autobiographical through his living out a life of suffering.[7]

Kafka's favorite (maternal) uncle, Siegfried Löwy, a country doctor and a bachelor (as Kafka was to remain), was a better object of identification—as an ego ideal and as a compensatory father figure.[8] Later, the devotion of the writer Max Brod as friend and editor kept Kafka's artistic self alive.[9] The selfobject experience of these figures, plus his unswerving creative drive, enabled him to carry out his artistic ideals. However, his ability to sustain a love relationship with a woman other than through letters was severely impaired. His lack of strength for marriage was considerably fueled by his awareness of his physical frailty.

But his attitude toward marriage was also affected by his aversion to his parents and their marital relationship. Kafka never lost his revulsion for his father, nor his bitterness toward his mother for her preoccupation with his father's business affairs. Kafka's feelings may or may not be a variant of oedipal difficulties, but they certainly express narcissistic injury. In pronouncing his mother his "father's devoted slave" and his father "her devoted tyrant," Kafka (1919) suggests that his image of the marital relationship as sadomasochistic may have foreclosed his own ability to take on the problem of marriage.

Nearing the end of their long courtship by voluminous correspondence, Kafka finally wrote to his fiancée, Felice Bauer:

> Now consider what changes your marriage to me would bring about, what each of us would stand to gain and to lose. I would lose my for the most part terrifying loneliness, and gain you. . . . You, on the other hand would lose a life with which you are almost wholly satisfied. You would lose Berlin, the office you enjoy, the girl friends, the small pleasures, the chance to marry a healthy cheerful good man, to have beautiful and healthy children [letter dated 6/16/13, Pawel, 1984, p. 294].

And

> Writing is the one good feature of my being. . . . How will you put up with a marriage in which the husband . . . comes home from the office around 2:30 or 3, eats, goes to bed, sleeps until 7 or 8 in the evening, has a quick snack, takes a walk for an hour, then starts writing and

writes on until 1 or 2 in the morning. Could you really put up with that? [p. 295].

Although determined to carry on his writing, Kafka was not a tyrant by nature, and he refused to be one by identification. He was astute in his assessment of the "Kafkaesque" nature of what a marriage to him would be like. He also refused to identify with his parents' pursuit of material security. Like them, Felice had an ideal of a comfortable material world and a longing for prosperity and conventional normalcy. In refusing Felice, the writer-driven son refused this identification with his business-driven father and refused to become the object of another's marital torment. This the long engagement was foreclosed. When Felice married another man with whom she had two children, Kafka was genuinely happy for her. Both were spared what would most likely have been a union where each would suffer.

After other intense love affairs also conducted by letter, it was only in the last two years of his life that he finally moved out of his parents' home with the much younger Dora Diamant, with whom he hoped to emigrate to Israel in a growing identification with his heritage. The fatal nature of his illness intervened, however, and she became his willing care-taker. Ironically, she did not have as strong feelings about sharing Kafka's art with others, and after his death, supposedly at his direction, she de-livered a serious blow to the preservation of his remaining work. It was only Kafka—the man and artist with whom she had a personal relation-ship—who was ideal to her. Kafka, the "universal man" and immortal artist, was of little concern (Pawel, 1984, pp. 436–447). To Kafka the man, now dead, her destruction of his work could no longer come as a narcissistic injury. Against Kafka the immortal artist, it may have been her act of revenge for the narcissistic injury of his abandoning her through death.

Narcissistic Injury and Art

I have previously observed that the greater the strength of will toward individuation and self-expression—which is particularly active in cre-ative personalities—the more susceptible the individual is to narcissistic injury (Kainer, 1977). A child with gifts that set him or her apart from others may have multiple selfobject needs that are harder for any parent to meet in their entirety. (This is an issue in the case of Mr. X.) It is certainly true in the case of Kafka, whose creative will and exquisite hypersensitivity could never allow him to make peace with his father's very real deficiencies.

However, Kafka was also able to transcend his injury and rage artistically. He used his self-experience in acts of literary imagination. For example, his sense of being crushed by his father became the "insectification" of a man in Kafka's (1915) *Metamorphosis*. The protagonist, Gregor Samsa, awakens one morning to find himself transformed into a giant bug—a dung beetle—and thereby becomes alive. Perhaps the profound appeal of this work lies in its imaginative portrayal of the human spirit that is forever being overpowered but proves itself indestructible.

This theme is a significant one in his fiction, and the very act of writing was a signifier of his own refusal to be crushed. Kafka was finally overpowered, however, and was crushed by poor health at an early age. While not crude like his father, he was unfortunately not robust like him either. Despite the elder Kafka's eventual decline in old age, unlike Kafka, Herrmann lived out his time. Franz Kafka died at 40. He had always lived under the shadow of his own physical mortality.[10]

Identifying with the Good of the Bad Object

There was, however, an extraordinary identification that the asthenic son made with his dominating, in-the-world, economically obsessed father. Kafka's image is of the quintessential brooding, suffering, and most interior of 20th-century man and artist (Karl, 1991). It is less known that, after enduring the tortures of law school, he held a position with an accident insurance company in Prague, where he served for 14 years (p. 689). Simultaneously, while working nightly on his fiction, Kafka also made a genuine contribution to pension reform in Prague![11]

While his legislation may have reflected a rebellion against Herrmann's harsh treatment of his workers and Kafka's identification with their suffering (p. 237), nonetheless he occupied an important place in the real world, as well as an extraordinary place in the world of imagination and letters. Each was as great a success as anything his father had achieved. Both father and son were self-made men, without childhoods and without fathers. Perhaps Kafka's successes reflected a son's attachment to, and identification with, the father he longed to love.

THE STORY OF MR. X

Every effort at liberation or individualization involves a dialectic with countervailing attempts to prevent disengagement from the general terror of mankind.

—FRANZ KAFKA

The sense of having a damaged father, and being damaged by him, is also prominent in the case of Mr. X.[12] For both Kafka and Mr. X, the damage foreclosed their sense of themselves as strong. In Kafka's case, he felt himself too weak to take care of those he would love, and in the case of Mr. X, life was on hold until he could prove himself to be a man among men. Both of them held to an ideal of the good father who could be a source of strength. For Kafka, the ideal was of a strong father who was also loving; that ideal may have stimulated his later pursuit of his Jewish forefathers. In the case of Mr. X, he pursued the loving father who could *also* be strong. They each longed for this missing piece of their internal-object world.

Mr. X came to treatment when a young man because he repeatedly found himself defeated in his professional and artistic aims, despite his ambitiousness, intelligence, talent, and capacity to get on well with others. However, after college he became stuck and felt helpless. Like Kafka, he would also fall deeply in love and ultimately be unable to sustain the commitment. Unlike Kafka, whose creative will was always paramount, Mr. X's pursuit of his art kept being sidetracked.

In the conduct of his life, Mr. X was closest to Freud's (1924) description of an individual who, in his hidden masochistic impulse, "must do what is inexpedient, must act against his own interests, must ruin the prospects which open out to him in the real world and must, perhaps, destroy his own real existence" (pp. 169–170). He had already given evidence of acting against his wishes, and his difficulties bore an uncanny resemblance to his father's frustrations in the business world. He fit Schafer's (1984) description of a man pursuing his father's failure, as an idealization [of] entrenched psychical suffering. Mr. X's unconscious identification with the "I" of his suffering and failed father was a key factor in his difficulties, and this sadomasochistic dynamic became the focus of our initial work.

He had identified with the pathological aspects of a father with whom he had experienced early and severe selfobject failure. He consulted with me because he had heard that I "gave artists a fair shake," and he had the unspoken hope that the same would be true in his case. This selective mutual identification (see chapter one) created the analytic connection and also proscribed the limits of our work. Mr. X's artistic limbo was the self-reflexive part of his sadomasochism in which his sadism was "turned round upon . . . [his] own ego" (Freud, 1915, p. 127), taking him down in masochistic self-defeat. His sadomasochism was also expressed interactively. He persistently engaged in two kinds of pathological relationships: he was masochistic toward the men in his business life and subtly sadistic with the women he loved.

Masochistic Identifications and Paternal Selfobject Failure

Although Mr. X felt tenderness and pity toward his gentle father, he had also disastrously experienced him as passive, lacking in vigor, and defeated in the workplace. Paradoxically, his father's effete qualities created as much anguish and anger for Mr. X as Herrmann Kafka's noisy aggression had for his son. A vivid image for Mr. X was of his father coming home from work each night and lying exhaustedly on the couch. This posture was maintained even when Mr. X was being bullied by his older and more motorically aggressive brothers and truly needed adult intervention. His father failed both to protect him from his actually dangerous surroundings and to help him contain his feeling of terror.

Mr. X was not able to take his father as an object of identification for his considerable intellectual and artistic ambitions. These existed in the men on his maternal side, but here again Mr. X was not as fortunate as Kafka in finding a good object among them. Mr. X's grandfather and uncle were intellectually and artistically gifted, but his grandfather, although very successful, was an overly dominating patriarch. His uncle, effete in the extreme, was also no help with his masculine identity as Kafka's Uncle Siegfried had been for him.

Mr. X's uncle was able to develop his art, but only by marrying a dominant woman who ran his life, enabling him to retreat from the world. Becoming overly dependent on a woman (as his father and uncle had) did not accord with Mr. X's ideal self, and, as he reflected years later, his uncle "was no model for anything," despite his artistry. Unlike for Kafka, artistic expression alone was not enough for Mr. X. He also needed to succeed in the competitive business world of men in the way his father had not. I had the sense that this was not so much oedipal rivalry in the classical sense as it was an act of reparation for the ineffectual father whom he pitied.

His ideal self included being successful in business as well as artistically creative and having a relationship of equality with a woman. The overarching ideal was to have all these aspects of his self coexist. That was his Tanazakian ideal. Rather than this being grandiose, he actually had the ability to achieve each and all. For a long period in our work, however, he remained an "artist manqué" in every respect.

Mr. X had experienced his father as dominated by his socially superior mother, who was from a prominent and talented family. Like Kafka, Mr. X saw his parents' relationship as sadomasochistic—with his father in the demeaned position. It foreclosed his own marriage to a very beautiful young woman whose prominent family more than welcomed this gifted and personable young man. They would gladly have eased his struggle in life, certainly financially and professionally and possibly artistically. His ambivalence won out. Although very attracted to her, Mr. X realized—like Kafka—that it could put him in danger of repeating unhealthy aspects of his parents' marriage, as the poor boy married into the wealthy family.

Mr. X was also fearful that this young woman had halted her own intellectual and professional development and was placing all those aspirations in him. He worried that she was prematurely turning to marriage as her vocation, and he reluctantly ended the relationship after we began our work. His later choices included women who themselves had professional ambitions of their own, which seemed a better balance for him.

Both Kafka and Mr. X had been unable to find in their fathers a good enough object from whom they could gain strength, and both felt their vulnerability. However, unlike Kafka, Mr. X had a need for a strong father which led to attempts at restoration through compensatory figures who ranged from simply inadequate, like his uncle and the men in his adult work life, to catastrophically traumatic. As a young boy, Mr. X turned to the "father figure" of an intellectually gifted teacher who recognized his gifts and mentored him. This charismatic man turned out to be a pedophile who also preyed on the young boys in his charge (and many years later was successfully prosecuted). Mr. X desperately wanted the enrichment of the attachment and endured the sexual part with a sense of its being against his will and without pleasure. It reinforced his identity of victim, was to play an important part in the analytic narrative.

It also set his pattern of masochistic submissiveness. This submissiveness later translated into enduring work environments where his own will and interests were again sacrificed in order to stay close. For example, Mr. X. could not take advantage of a prestigious graduate fellowship awarded to him after college. Instead, he was driven to stay on too long with a series of employers who were struggling to make their business ventures a success. He would "pull all nighters" in the service of their current mission. He gave them the help his father had needed, as if all the king needed to be victorious were the aid of the valiant prince. His own further schooling and creative work were put on hold, and these persistent masochistic choices continued for a long time into our work. The "prize" for him—graduate school and art—were always just out of reach, and his love life was always on hold.

Sadistic Identification and Maternal Selfobject Failure

While his father failed to be an adequate protector and source of inner strength on which to build his masculine and professional identity, his mother was also a complex source of his self-defeating and sadistic pathology. Her identification with his artistic talent was gratifying, but it was contaminated by her unconscious envy and distaste. For example, in a transparent rejection of the patriarchy of her dominating father, she chose as her love object a man completely his opposite and dominated him. This gentler, but more passive and less gifted man provided Mr. X with the dubious image of a woman's object of desire as a man who was unsuccessful in the world, a nonartist, and the weaker marital partner.

Although the combination of his grandfather's professional and artistic success came closest to Mr. X's own ideals, he was sensitive to his mother's unconscious ambivalence. He was left with her duality: the rejected grandfather who was successful but not beloved, and his unsuccessful father who was a loving man but a disappointment. He was confused as to how to be a man in relation to a woman and how to be a man among men. Freud's well-known puzzlement, "What do women want?"—and Brecht's image, in *Threepenny Opera*, of a man devouring others in response to his questions, "What keeps a man alive?"—became *his* questions as well. He had taken on his mother's conflicts as his own.

His mother's "I" included the ego of the bad object (his grandfather). Although she had overtly rejected the narcissistic aspects of her own father, she still had them as an internal image of her own, with which Mr. X now identified. For example, although it would be against his ideal to be a tyrannical man, he would express a deep narcissistic longing for his girlfriends not to desire any of his time or attention for themselves, but to be completely adaptive to his needs. If they loved him, they were to have no will of their own, and he was often sadistically withholding. However, he was not comfortable in this role and needed to experience himself as loving as much as he needed to feel himself powerful. He disavowed his narcissism, but this inner conflict of desires created uncertainty and delayed his taking his place as either an artist or as a man with a woman of his own.

A more powerful example of his direct identification with his mother was his response to his father's decision during his adolescence that the family move once again so that he could try yet another business venture. Mr. X's mother was depressed at the prospect. It came at a time when Mr. X was about to enter a special high school. There was an unthinking and disastrous decision not to let Mr. X live away from home to attend the school but force him to relocate with them to a town that had no such opportunity. His despair and frustration were so great that he made a serious suicide attempt.[13]

My interpretation at the later time of our work was that the profound despair driving him to that act, in addition to its being a response to the crushing blow to his aspirations, was an identification with his mother's increasing depression at her husband's dysfunction and business failures. Mr. X loved her, hated her, was bound to her, had to escape from her, and adheringly identified with her. In an interview some years after our work was completed, he said that he had found the interpretation meaningful in working through feelings regarding this act of self-destruction. It had helped him to understand the nature and depth of his attachment to this woman he thought he only hated, and it lifted the guilt and fear he had about his act. He had not been able to separate from her through the power of his hate alone. He had to also understand the force and nature of his disavowed love for her.

Part of his rage at her stemmed from her failure early on to protect him from his brothers' attacks, as well, indeed as instigating them. As the youngest child, he proved to be the natural heir of her family's intellectual and artistic gifts, which had not become evident in her older sons. She seized on his giftedness as a source of great narcissistic pride but also used it as weapon against his less gifted and "less refined" siblings, whose noisy aggression she loathed. She stirred his brothers' envy of him as the crown prince—perhaps as a repeat of her envy of her own brother's talents—and then failed to protect him from its fallout.

Typical was his scornful remembrance of his mother's "refined" tea-drinking ritual and the way in which she held her hand and the cup. He associated this posture to those times when he needed help with his siblings' rivalry. His rage was a reaction to her unmistakable message of "a plague on both your houses" to her fighting sons, whom she continued to ignore while drinking her tea! It was a serious abandonment for him that duplicated his father's failure to protect him and added to his perception of himself as a victim.

More important to the development of his sadism, however, was her latent psychotic residues, which led to her inappropriate sexually seductive behavior toward him in dress and manner. For example, she might appear before him in a revealing nightgown or would stroke his back, too low and too often. In some ways, her psychotic intrusiveness and its result seemed a contemporary version of Kohut's (1979) Mr. Z and his mother. Like Mr. Z, Mr. X had to give up some of his own masculinity to keep the identification with his father and sustain the alliance with his mother. While she was disturbingly sexually inappropriate, she was also more emotionally available than his overwhelmed and absent father was, and he needed her.

As a child he had experienced her proper lack of concern for his safety—in tandem with her improper sexualized attention—as sadistic attacks. He related that even now she could still display some of that sexualized behavior toward him, along with being "all right" in other ways. He could tolerate her behavior without collapse. Our work had enabled him to understand, accept, and better metabolize the effects of his mother's psychotic aspects. He was luckier than Kafka, for he finally was able to find forgiveness for his disturbed and disturbing parents.

Her behavior not only had been a source of rage, it had added to his confusion regarding his identity, both as a man and as an artist. The associations to his artistic side were both feminized (through identification with his mother and effete uncle) and sadistic (through his grandfather). An example of his confusion was his statement that he had succeeded in spending one weekend, not at the office rescuing his boss, "but the way a woman would." That is, "self-contained" and not heeding or needing others—devoting himself entirely to his creative work. It was this imperviousness and self-sufficiency that he ascribed to women. I was struck by this because it is often the fantasy that women have regarding men.[14] The working through of his blinding awe of women helped him become more connected to his art.

THE ANALYTIC ENCOUNTER

I was amazed, amazed at the fourteenth century . . . the opposite of ours: a time when everything . . . remained within and played itself out . . . without any real prospect of finding external equivalents for its . . . condition.
—Rainer Maria Rilke (letter to Lou Andreas-Salomé, 3/1/12)

It became clear during the course of our work that the problems of being an artist and finding his proper partner were not to become resolved until he first "proved himself" in the workplace. I have found the "proving" of one's self true of other sons whose fathers had met defeat on that particular battleground.[15] There is in the son a pull to disidentify with the father in this matter and be successful. At some level, the father's default becomes the son's debt of honor.[16] For Mr. X, proving himself as a man among men involved first working through the residues of repressed psychotic terror as well as eventually finding a way to internalize a strong father. The first was accomplished in our own analytic work, and the second eventually took place beyond it.

The Selfobject Containment of Terror

Uncovering the elements of his psychotic terror came later in the work, for it was masked by the more conscious fear of his brothers and his anger at his mother's psychotic seductiveness. In conjunction with the demonic betrayal by his teacher and spiritual mentor as a young boy, they all left him with a sense of the world as an evil place. His terror existed in juxtaposition with his abundant good humor, optimism, and affable disposition. His sense of evil arose from a deeply religious awareness of its possibility.

He finally became anxious as he spoke about the "craziness" of the persecutory feelings he was experiencing. I sensed that we had entered the realm of his psychotic anxiety and that he was very frightened by it. When I entered the room the following session and saw his stricken look, I must have connected to the religious part of his "I," and greeted him with, "Can we talk Devil here?" "Please" was his relieved response. We worked through these psychotic residues by sharing and naming them every time they arose. It took courage on his part because of feelings of shame for being "scared" of things. More emboldened, he readied himself to venture further "out of the house" and "into the world."

Finding Iron John and the "Groupobject" Experience

In my response to him as the positive part of his mother's "I" there had been a strong connection between us from the beginning of the work. My subjective experience of him was as an intelligent, creative, personable, and decent lad. The work we created together was conducted in the reflected glow of this capacity for fondness in my mental makeup. However, I was a new and better object (Loewald) for him than his mother had been: there was an appeal of minds rather than sexual seduction; I had a correct assessment and appreciation of his capabilities; he was relieved of the burden of taking care of me; and I even drank my tea in a way that evoked his mother, but without using it as a distancing mechanism! Perhaps, and most important, I knew that, despite his talents, he desperately needed help.

There was an aspect of his pathology that was begun in our work on his psychotic anxiety and completed beyond it. It added a dimension not accessed in the individual therapy. He entered a phase in our own work of trying to locate strong, loving, but tough enough masculine objects with whom he could identify. It came in the heyday of the 1980, popular men's movement, led by its guru, the poet Robert Bly. I strove to keep an open mind. His search went on for what seemed to me a very long time. I blurted out to him one day, possibly from a state of weariness and a *literal* attempt to create a concordant identification: "Look, I'm Iron John," and, equally unhelpful, "You'll just have to be your *own* good father."

I must have had the manic belief that he could form an identification with my masculine and aggressive strivings or, failing that, provide his own! With his more sober intelligence, he did not believe in my magic, but he was forgiving of my flaws. That also may have marked a greater acceptance of his own, and he soon joined a men's therapy group.

What he accessed in the group was something not as available in either my mental makeup or in the structure of the individual analytic work. He could more fully identify himself as a victim among fellow victims. Paradoxically, he gained strength from this group of males as a member of their tribe and began to directly address his fear of his own aggression and that of other men. As he reported in our later interview, he then tackled some rough situations.

In particular, he confronted his mean brothers and his childhood seducer with the attitude, "What the hell, they're not going to let me get hurt!" taking the strength of the men in the group along with him. His aggression was not as available in the maternal matrix of our own work because he "couldn't risk losing" me. Although it was unnecessary, his anxiety in this regard was overdetermined and persistent. Given his history, it was easier for him to access his hostility as part of a male "groupobject" experience (Segalla, 1996) than as a maternal "selfobject" function.

In a later interview, he reviewed the developments after our work had ended. Our analytic work had essentially dealt with his masochistic tendencies and the psychotic aspects of his anxiety. Now, in the group, his identity as an abused victim was more firmly established and creatively used to help him transcend it. He was able finally to effect an ingenious solution to his competing needs. He worked out a plan that enabled him to be financially self-sufficient and enter an excellent long-postponed graduate program. He was moving along toward his rightful and appropriate place as leading the artistic organization started by his grandfather, which would allow him to develop his own artistry. There was also a promising relationship in the works.

Furthermore, now that he was freer of their sadistic and masochistic introjects, he was able to connect with his parents instead of physically running away while remaining in psychic bondage to them. He no longer needed to escape from them and enjoyed seeing them as a part of his new academic schedule that brought them together frequently. His former sadomasochistic attachments to them were pseudo-attachments that foreclosed genuine connection. He always wanted to be free, and he always longed to be close. Hate no longer bound and fueled him.[17]

SADOMASOCHISM AND THE SENSE OF CATASTROPHIC INJURY

Mr. X's validation of himself as victim in the group went beyond my experience of him as one who suffers and provided the necessary tools for the ultimate release from his sadomasochistic identifications. My own mental makeup was less empathically tuned to the self-state of victim. I experienced his injury as the suffering of a sensitive person who is in anguish because sounds are louder, experience is lonelier, the will to form is greater, and injury to one's narcissism is more likely. In his experience, he is not only one who suffers, but one who has been injured and left damaged.

However, even if my mental makeup could have allowed me to better identify with the self-as-victim, he still needed to have this part of his self validated through identification with others who experienced themselves similarly. Otherwise, it was as though he had been injured in a terrible accident that no one except those similarly injured could understand. His was first the suffering of a victim, not of an artist, and it had to be so acknowledged. The power of the groupobject identification helped to lift the addictive-like adherence to a pathological self-view. The group's identification of him as a wounded soldier helped him, in turn, to be heroic in confronting the bad objects in the face of his fear. It was a necessary adjunct to my experiencing him as an "artist manqué." Both parts of him needed to be understood and contained.

Notes

[1] Kuspit (1993) notes: "Freud's term for his inquiry of 1910 into the unconscious of Leonardo was "pathography" (p. 561). He quotes Spitz as saying: "Pathography implies writing about suffering, illness or feeling, with important overtones of empathetic response on the part of the author for his subject" (p. 561). In this sense, I see the analytic undertaking as a pathographic study of the patient with the further aim of working through the pathological states.

[2] Bion (1957) noted "Patients ill enough, say, to be certified as psychotic, contain in their psyche a non-psychotic part of the personality . . . a prey to the various neurotic mechanisms with which psycho-analysis has made us familiar, and a psychotic part of the personality which is so far dominant that the non-psychotic part of the personality with which it exists in negative juxtaposition, is obscured" (pp. 267–268). This book is concerned primarily with the subtle psychotic features in the neurotic personality (see chapter six).

[3] I am mindful that, for some people, the pathological *is* the "ideal"—as when destructiveness toward self or other is at the forefront of one's way of being in the world. It has not been my experience with those seeking treatment in whom there is, or there can be created, a hope for transformation. The ideal there is of transcendence of pathology.

[4] The selfobject need for sameness (Kohut's twinship) may be met by finding oneself through a work of art, but the mirroring expectation is not present except perhaps in fantasy (J. Frederickson, personal communication). However strong the identification with, and idealization of, an artwork may be, there is a difference when these selfobject needs are found through an actual other. This difference in these projections might be further explored.

[5] Freud (1915) stated that the characteristic turning of active into passive—which would require an object outside the self—does not operate in the obsessional condition.

[6] In this 45-page letter, Kafka (1919) painfully detailed the narcissistic injury experienced at the hands of his father, whose child-rearing methods Kafka described as "abuse, threats, irony, spiteful laughter and—*oddly enough*—self pity" (p. 151, italics added). I have noted that unconscious pity for the bad object stimulates attachment. Kafka here was expressing his surprise that such a bombastic personality could even be capable of being vulnerable. Consciously at least, the father was a one-dimensional ogre. Although it was probably likely that the letter was read by his mother—whom Pawel (1984) thought was the actual target of Kafka's scorn—it was never sent to his father. Kafka considered it his one major literary accomplishment for that year, and it was later published as such. This letter and the voluminous correspondence with each of the women he loved also served a selfobject function of cohesion for Kafka's emotional and artistic needs.

[7] Kafka had what was called "an autobiographical impulse" (Hayman, 1982, p. 1).

[8] Described as "eccentric, diffident, book-loving . . . [and] the only relative beyond the immediate family with whom Kafka maintained lifelong close ties. The crusty Uncle Doctor, with his broad range of interests, rational skepticism, and wayward sense of humor was . . . perhaps the only adult figure in K's childhood who, in his undemonstrative way, conveyed something akin to paternal sympathy and understanding. . . . He killed himself on the eve of his deportation to Terezin [the concentration camp] in 1942" (Pawel, 1984, p. 116).

[9] Kafka's twinship with Brod was legendary and mutual. Brod is remembered for his relationship to Kafka and not as a prodigious author in his own right. Having ignored Kafka's instructions to burn his manuscripts after his death, Brod fled Nazi Germany with his single suitcase containing them. Without this act, their publication by Schocken Books in America could not have taken place and they would have been irrevocably lost. Unlike Dora Diamant, Brod fought for Kafka's place in literary history.

[10] Perhaps this was an unconscious identification with the childhood deaths of his next two younger brothers. These events appear to be unworked through by the parents, who went on to have three daughters. The early loss of two children may have contributed to Herrmann's psychotic despair over Kafka's delicate, finicky nature and Julie Kafka's overdetermined concentration with business matters outside the home. Kafka's death was due to tuberculosis of the larynx, the result of pulmonary weakness.

[11] Excellent accounts of Kafka can be found in Hayman (1982), Pawel (1984), and Karl (1991).

[12] For reasons of confidentiality, I have omitted the specific details of Mr. X's life narrative, which is otherwise accurate. I am deeply grateful to him for his permission to present his story, and his help in preparing his psychoanalytic "biography"—as well as rich experience of our years of work together.

[13] There was a similar point in Kafka's life when his father wanted the writer to take over his latest business venture, running an asbestos factory. He wrote of his suicidal despair to a friend, who alerted the family. It was Kafka's mother who responded the most intelligently, and he was no longer pressed into this service.

[14] Anais Nin's (1959) *Spy in the House of Love* deals with the fantasy that women

have about a man's relationship to lovemaking that is undertaken without attachment. Thus, "Sabina . . . opened her eyes to contemplate the piercing joy of her liberation: she was free, free as a man was, to enjoy without love. Without any warmth of the heart, as a man could, she had enjoyed a stranger. And then she remembered what she had heard men say: Then I wanted to leave. . . . That was the meaning of freedom. Freedom of attachment, dependency and the capacity for pain" (pp. 49–50).

[15] Schafer (1984) notes men's "idealization" of their father's failure, which persuasively dictates the life narrative.

[16] I have thought that Thomas Jefferson's ambivalence toward slavery—as opposed to a natural rejection of it—was connected to his inheriting his father's enormous debts in England, which he then considered his own. This pressure may have affected his astonishing perception that the slaves, who were vital to his solvency, were people who were "endowed with a good heart but inferior intelligence." There would have to have been a very strong force that would allow a man of his caliber to confound lack of intelligence with what was the result of the lack of formal education denied to them. There is historical evidence that one of his slaves (a woman) who *was* literate, wrote to him when he was on one of this frequent travels and with great literary eloquence gave him the details of the events at home. His denial was overdetermined.

[17] As Hartmann, Kris, and Loewenstein (1946) said regarding attachment to the love object and identification: "the child identifies with the parents in a new way in order to escape the conflict between love, hate and guilt and the torments of anxiety" (p. 33).

PART II

The Collapse of the Self

The next four chapters explore a major theme of the book, that of the nature of the factors that weaken the structure of the self. Post-Kleinian and post-Kohutian thought are interwoven throughout to better examine a collapse of the self signaled by states of narcissistic injury, compulsive eating, psychotic anxiety and rage in neurotic personalities, and the mind–body issues of depression. There is a particular emphasis on the interplay between underlying pathological structures and how the self is experienced. The theme of adhesive pathologenic identifications is again carried through in this section.

Chapter Four

Narcissistic Injury and
Its Relation
to Paranoid/Schizoid Collapse

You were so huge, a giant in every respect. What could you care for our pity or even our help?
—Franz Kafka, Letter to his father

The constructs of *narcissistic injury* (Kohut) and *the paranoid/schizoid position* (Klein) have been central to the development of self psychology and object relations theory. Although these constructs have been well explored within the confines of their respective schools, I want to discuss the way in which they relate to each other in the clinical encounter.

Within the ongoing dialectic of psychoanalytic theory, Bacal and Newman (1990) began bridging self psychology with object relations theory, and Mitchell (1988) observed the *relational* common denominator of these two schools of thought (i.e., they are both a "two-person psychology" in contrast to the "one-person psychology" of instinct theory). However, my focus here on narcissistic injury and paranoid/schizoid collapse is not as they refer to two similar (or disparate) schools of thought, but, rather, on their descriptive powers. Having the common denominator of rage, these are two modes of affective experience in which there is a preponderance of unconscious *shame* in the rage of narcissistic injury, and a preponderance of unconscious *anxiety* accompanying the rage of a paranoid/schizoid collapse.

My understanding of narcissistic injury began with Kohut (1972, 1977, 1984), and my exploration of a paranoid/schizoid collapse originated with the work of Klein (1946) and Fairbairn (1940).[1] For the most part, Klein's expositions of the mental states she described as "positions" (i.e., the depressive and paranoid/schizoid positions) have been discarded by non-Kleinians (esp. Stolorow, 1996, personal communication). Even for those employing Klein's ideas, the problem is that "although Klein introduced the concept of the positions as a way of moving beyond the notion of a phase or stage, I think that she did not fully appreciate the importance of her contribution. She very often lapsed into treating these positions as developmental phases and on those occasions ran into considerable theoretical difficulty" (Ogden, 1994, p. 197).

Also, Ogden (1986) has noted, "Melanie Klein was interested primarily in mental contents and as a result left relatively unexplored the implications of her theory for a psychoanalytic conception of fundamental background states of being" (p. 68).

I would add that Klein's "positions" are not only states of mind (Bion, 1957), ways of processing information (Grotstein, 1981), and background states of being in the world (Ogden, 1989), but they also describe one's mental and emotional state of being at a given moment in time. In that respect, these "positions" are describing *experience-near* phenomena and are of greater use to self psychologists than has been realized. Thus, this chapter reflects my understanding of a collapse of the self into a "paranoid/schizoid position" as an experience-near phenomenon and shows the role of narcissistic injury in this experience.[2]

One feature common to both narcissistic injury and paranoid/schizoid collapse is the element of unpredictability and surprise that often greets their eruption. Although both frequently appear in borderline and psychotic personality organizations, they are also part of a neurotic structure as well. It is not the experience of narcissistic injury or a paranoid/schizoid collapse that is pathognomic per se, but rather the inability to recover from it. For example, while almost no one is free of the experience of a narcissistic injury, the condition of chronic narcissistic rage is an ominous one (see Kohut, 1972).

Similarly, the *experience* of a paranoid/schizoid collapse is the same in the neurotic personality as it is for someone with more extensive pathological organization. Lack of recovery from these experiences more than the experience itself is the greater difficulty.

THE EXPERIENCE OF NARCISSISTIC INJURY

In its most benign form, narcissistic injury occurs as a wound to self-esteem. Although an almost unavoidable experience in one's relational life, it can further evoke a temporary self-state of fragmentation and loss of a sense of cohesion. Like a slip of the tongue, it is part of the "psychopathology of everyday life"—ordinary, but fraught with significant individual meaning. Even as a transient flare-up, it can evoke retaliatory rage. It can be the precursor of a paranoid/schizoid collapse.

Narcissistic Injury and Narcissistic Rage

In one of his most important papers on the psychology of the self, Kohut (1972) distinguished narcissistic injury from other forms of "mature aggression." Its singular quality of *revenge* makes it unique in the "role which aggression and hatred play from the beginning of life" (Klein, 1946, p. 4). Kohut (1972) separated out the revenge aspects of narcissistic rage from the theoretical issues of the death instinct (Freud, 1920; Klein, 1946), and described the relentless need to redress a wound to the self as the need "for undoing a hurt by whatever means, and a deeply anchored, unrelenting compulsion . . . which gives no rest to those who have suffered a narcissistic injury. . . ." (Kohut, 1972, p. 338).

Ahab's deadly pursuit of the great whale who has severed his leg (in Melville's *Moby Dick*) is the quintessential literary expression of the catastrophic thirst for revenge for damage that cannot be either forgotten or forgiven. It is an essential consequence of an assault to one's bodily (narcissistic) integrity.

This fictional account is also an accurate portrayal of how injury affecting bodily integrity (e.g., accidents or ill health) is simultaneously experienced as an assault on the psychic self. Similarly, a wound to the psychic self (through an insult or deflation), creates an uncanny parallel to the reaction evoked from an experience of injury to the bodily self. One's cohesive sense of narcissistic integrity is a function of a self that can recover from being wounded both physically and emotionally.

Although seemingly less pathologic than the affective state of paranoid/schizoid collapse, the persistence and frequency of narcissistic injury can be the signifier of deeper pathology. Clearly, a minor puncture of self-esteem in which one feels "miffed" differs from a blow-out of the self that requires an annihilation of the other to avenge. Kohut (1972) described *chronic narcissistic rage* as "one of the most pernicious afflictions of the human psyche" (p. 638).[3] Similarly, evidence of a "continuing hostile disposition" (Gedo, 1989, p. 419), as in the following case of Ms. A, signifies a pathological underlying structure. Rage is a factor in both marcissistic anger and paranoid/schizoid collapse, and it is sometimes difficult to determine its origins through observation alone.

The Case of Ms. A

Ms. A was part of an ongoing colloquium whose members were asked to introduce themselves at the beginning of a new segment, comment on their learning experience thus far, and express their hopes and interests to the new instructor. Several members asked about my integrating schools of thought, which their previous instructors seemed to have indicated I would do. I felt uneasy contemplating the enormity of the task and, believing they had misunderstood what they were told to expect, I replied, "Oh, that sounds overwhelming. I think what they meant is that I will integrate certain theory with clinical practice."

It was then Ms. A's turn to respond. I was startled by her sour comment: "I'm only here because of the collegial contact!"

At the time, I did not connect her remark to my own, which I only later learned had relieved the group's anxiety about what may have been expected of them if I attempted a massive integration—but made her very angry. I thought at the time, "Uh-oh," and experienced her response as a gratuitous attack on the instruction, past, present, and future. I became wary of her and cautious about my responses. I knew that at some level I had clearly unfavorably excited her, and I was quite conscious of not wanting to be a "rejecting object" in turn (Fairbairn, 1954).

Over the next few weeks she was technically present, but not at all there. She quietly exhibited odd behaviors that I can now better identify as attempts at autistic self-soothing (Tustin, 1986), such as retreating into the hood of her jacket or frequently leaving the room.[4] I caught some agitation and depression out of the corner of my eye. She did seem to take comfort from physically being with the group who, amazingly, did not "notice" or visibly react to her behavior. I seemed to be the only one affected by her. She proved herself correct in her assessment that she was just there for the collegial contact, as she neither did the readings nor joined in the discussion. Something kept me from experiencing it as a narcissistic injury.

I was encouraged when she later volunteered to present a case during a discussion of Melanie Klein, and I had the fantasy that she was now in the "depressive position"—making reparations for her attacks! She presented a case of a disturbed person who could not tolerate regular therapy sessions. I sensed that she had hoped for the admiration of the group regarding her clinical sensitivity and her capacity to let the patient work out her own therapeutic method.

However, the group proved uncomfortable with aspects of the case, including its unconscious parallels with Ms. A. The suggestion of hospitalization—for her patient—was made, in which I did not join. She was visibly disappointed and injured by their negative reaction and went back into her withdrawn mode. As this group was neither a clinical nor a supervisory group, there was no appropriate way to process it beyond quietly containing it.

My strongest feeling was one of anguish at the wasted opportunity of her not doing the readings, and I had the thought, "The trouble with killing off the bad object is that you lose the benefit of its love." I wasn't entirely sure what I meant by that, but clearly she evoked regretful feelings about my own residues of hostility and capacity for rejection. What I did observe, however, was that containment can have its own good effect. Later in the semester, one member asked if we could do "sadomasochism"—knowing that it was a particular interest of mine and members of the group. Having regained my spirits, I manically replied, "Sure. We can even do the psychotic core!" There were some gasps from the group, and I said, "No, no, we'll make it user friendly. You'll love it!" For the first time Ms. A murmured agreement.

Discussion

> *Evidently the final opinion . . . will not be the same when the facts are viewed in the light of a belief that the patient is normal as it is when the belief is that the patient is mentally disturbed.*
> —WILFRED BION, "Transformations"

All that was actually observable in this extraclinical situation was that Ms. A was angry at whatever failure in me she perceived at our initial meeting, and she subsequently withdrew from the aversive (Lichtenberg, 1989) encounter. We cannot be certain of the source of her rage and the nature of her withdrawal and what they signified in terms of her dynamics, internal object relationships, or selfobject needs. Was her withdrawal an example of an expression of rage following a narcissistic letdown, or did it signify a paranoid/schizoid collapse, a combination of both—or something else? My cautious reaction to her, plus her own subsequent behavior, lends some weight to my belief that she suffered from an underlying personality difficulty to which I tried to be attentive.

Previous experience had taught me that, although groups do indeed manifest the psychotic features of their members (Bion, 1957), they can also house members who seek a therapeutic experience in learning situations such as this one. Ms. A's opening remark had not been merely a sarcastic comment. I responded with selfobject containment because I unconsciously experienced her attack as a signifier of a wish for help.

The dynamics of the group helped to create this. When the group attempted to assign me an "overwhelming" theoretic task handed down from their previous classes, their "misperception" of what was to be undertaken this period also was a projective identification communicating the unspoken message: "You will be the one to put it [her?] all together. You will integrate and make coherent what is now in bits and pieces." When I at first demurred, Ms. A may have experienced this as the thwarting of her longing to have "sanctuary and coherence" (Britton, 1992, pp. 102–113). My demurral angered her as a failed promise hinted

at by the previous instructors. That I seemed to be the one most reso-
nant to her disturbed part indicated that "in theory" I was to be the
therapeutic object of transformation. My disclaimer had made me into
a bad object.

Gedo's (1989) emphasis on the importance of "the effects of prior
structuralization on the regulation of behavior" is useful here. We do not
actually know what created Ms. A's "continuing hostile disposition" and
her subsequent behavior. My conscious resistance to becoming the bad
object may give us a clue. For, if revenge is the most salient characteristic
of narcissistic rage, the unmasking of the bad object is the most salient
feature of those prone to paranoid/schizoid collapse.[5] I resisted becoming
one, although Ms. A. may have been structurally disposed to make me so.
However, there is also evidence that not only was she predisposed to experience me as the bad object, she was also looking for the object of
transformation. At some level, I heard this.

THE EXPERIENCE OF A PARANOID/SCHIZOID "COLLAPSE"

Ogden

Ogden's (1986, 1989, 1994) observations on the meaning of the "bad object" in a paranoid/schizoid collapse are important here. In particular,
Ogden (1986) noted that in the clinical situation:

> When a borderline[6] patient feels angry at and disappointed by the thera-
> pist, he feels that he has now discovered the truth. The therapist is
> unreliable, and the patient should have known it all along. What had
> previously been seen by the patient as evidence of the therapist's trust-
> worthiness, now is seen to have been an act of deception, a mask, a
> cover-up for what has become apparent. The truth is now out, and the
> patient will not deceive himself or be caught off guard again. *History is
> instantaneously rewritten.* The therapist is not the person the patient
> thought he was; he is now discovered to be someone new. Each time I
> have arrived at this juncture in a therapy, I have been freshly stunned
> by the coldness of the patient's renunciation of shared experience. *There
> is an assault on the emotional history of the object relationship.* The
> present is projected backward and forward, thus creating a static, eter-
> nal nonreflective present [p. 62, italics added].

It is important to understand that in the patient's mind at the moment of collapse, one is not *like* the bad object, one *is* the bad object.
This collapse is not limited to "delusional" (i.e., psychotic) or borderline
patients. It is the state of mind of *anyone* experiencing this collapse. The
less disturbed the person, the more quickly the "delusional" moment is

overcome. If, in addition, the bad object is a source of humiliation, the defense of flight may be necessary as in the next case.

Narcissistic Rage and Paranoid/schizoid Collapse: The Case of Ms. B

The following incident took place in the analytic therapy of a woman after many years of our working successfully together. She had been placed in my care as a "highly regarded and difficult patient" by a departing colleague who had worked with her for several years. All went well for a long time during which she made steady gains in her life. She became a home owner, completed an advanced degree in her field of study, and slowly attained confidence and satisfaction in her field, where she evidenced skills of diplomacy and organization with her coworkers. She had considerable ability to humanize a very competitive work setting.

Her personal love relationships, however, were tortured arenas of her vulnerability, and her love of any man with whom she was seriously involved could not contain her hate and foreclosed an intimate relationship, in which "hate" is a natural part. Her relationships always ended with her anguished termination.

She was the daughter of an intelligent but very difficult and controlling father, whom she disliked but with whom she maintained connection through matters of money. She was also the daughter of an "incompetent" mother, whom both she and her father scorned. He had divorced Ms. B's mother, and Ms. B had emotionally disowned her. A troubled sibling had not survived beyond young adulthood.[7]

Ms. B was prickly, and I was always careful with her. As an example of the "diplomacy" one had to exercise: although getting her advanced degree was of great importance to her, she resented any hint that I had interest in it. I had no difficulty understanding her need to feel she was accomplishing it for herself only—and not feel it as my narcissism or will—as she had with her autocratic father. When I lapsed simply through my enthusiasm, we could make use of processing my empathic failure.

Her intelligence, organizational skills, and methodical ways were such that it always startled me when she made poor choices about finances and imposed great stress on herself. Her dysfunction had a quality that I did not fully understand. It was clear, however, that she strongly identified with her father's style of financial management, which included his using money belonging to her. Although a successful professional (as she now was), he compulsively took on more financial and home projects than he could manage, which often left him in a state of financial need. She was scornful of him but nonetheless had the same tendency. Her

mismanagement was especially significant because she was contemptuous of her mother's poverty as a sign of her ineptness. Ms. B, as well as
her father, lived on a high level of "being broke" and were as poverty
stricken at that level as the mother was in actuality.

The collapse in the therapy came during a recurrence of financial
strain in which, following a romantic collapse, Ms. B was now maintaining household expenses she could barely manage and voluntarily assum-
ing the support of a housemate, a vulnerable young woman whom she
could not bear to ask to share the costs. (In hindsight, she was reenacting
her mother's earlier struggles to provide for her, perhaps without adequate
funds or support from Ms. B's father.)

At the time, I understood none of this and was able to experience her
only as unwilling to address the problem by simply adding a housemate
who *could* contribute. Instead, driven by her own internal logic, she wished
me to agree to her not paying for her therapy for an extended period of
time. Balking at what I experienced as the "irrationality" of her refusal to
make the needed adjustment in her domestic situation—and the inap-
propriateness of her proposed solution with me—I replied: "This makes
me crazy!" Although true, my response was a serious technical error in
which there was a failure to adequately contain all the elements of her
experience. In reacting to her as if we were engaged in a literal interpersonal situation, I had failed to receive the communication housed in the
enactment. I also impugned the caution I had so carefully nurtured with
her over the years of our work together. These failures pushed the work
beyond her endurance.

Her reaction was to resist any effort I made to process her injury and
rage, and, refusing even another session, she abruptly broke off the years
of work. The haughty withdrawal born of narcissistic injury was merged
with the cold persecutory rage of a paranoid/schizoid collapse. She had,
as Ogden would say, unmasked me at last as an unreliable, unfeeling
object. The work became a holocaust in which the history of the years
of our fruitful joint effort was obliterated. There was to be no further
dialogue.

Discussion: Shame in Injury and Collapse

> The shame . . . [the] object-related humiliation. . . .
> —Andrew Morrison, *Shame*[8]

Most certainly my negative response to her inflicted the psychological injuries of "ridicule, contempt, and conspicuous defeat" (Kohut, 1972,
p. 638) that are particularly provoked in those raised with contempt. I
treated her as her inadequate mother had and took on the persona of the

contemptuous father. Her rage was a defense against the shame I stimulated in her, which was transformed through projection.

Thus, "the source of shame is changed from inner failure and defect to external callousness [of the therapist]. It's not my failure, desire, or need, but your scorn or lack of reciprocal concern, that makes me feel this way" (Morrison, 1989, p. 126).

It is not only because she was "shame prone" (Kohut, 1972, pp. 643–644)[9] that she reacted in this way, however, and certainly her pathology was not the sole source of the difficulty. The very nature of my response reflected a certain coldness toward her complex feelings, and my refusal created a "retaliatory rage toward the unresponsive therapist/object" (Morrison, 1989, p. 125).

I was frustrated in my understanding of this part of her pathology. Her inconsistency *was* too irrational for my makeup, and I expelled it in an attack on her. The subtext of my words was, "How can one so smart be so lame-brained?" My reaction was a departure from my usual careful way of responding to her underlying fragility and reflected my idealization of her competency. I had erred on the side of seeing her as less disturbed than the money difficulties signified. I had responded to her as if all she had to do was "shape up" or "be reasonable" to solve her problems.

She reacted catastrophically because this was not a fight in which two equals could resolve their differences about money in the context of their "mature aggression" as they got in each other's way. The battle was between the overwhelming forces of contempt, on one hand, and the shame and humiliation of weakness, on the other. That is never a fair fight, and she fled.

Shaming the Internal Object Relationship

In the projection of noxious stimuli owing to narcissistic injury, "one commonly used means of expunging shame is through a massive expression of rage aimed at the 'offending' object (either the unresponsive selfobject who fails to mirror or to accept idealization, [or] the rejecting object of attachment) . . ." (Morrison, 1989, p. 102). Ms. B's financial problems gave rise to a "*selfobject* need and hunger [that] may itself come to represent a falling short of the imposed ideal of self-sufficiency" (p. 85, italics added). My refusal of her need exposed one source of her shame: her failure to live up to her ideal (and my own) of self-sufficiency.[10]

There were other sources of shame beyond the stimulation of unmet selfobject need. When exposing her as incompetent and needy (like her mother), I was also rejecting her solution to use "my money" as her father would hers. I was scornful of the identification she had with him in these matters.

These (pathological) internal object relationships are crucial components of the self, and I attacked its fragile structure. The shame of likening her to her mother was compounded by my *interruption of the symbiotic identification with her father*. When she discarded her mother as an object of identification earlier in her development, her father became an important compensatory figure for her. Narcissistic collapse is most acute when it involves the compensatory figure whom one has turned to for relief from the selfobject failure of the primary object. He had been her sanctuary, which I had invaded in an unforgivable trespass.[11]

Father and daughter had shared an active contempt for the marginalized mother. In identifying with her father's haughty arrogance, she used contempt as the same defense he did against his own ineptness. Morrison's (1989, p. 105) depiction of contempt as the "projective identification" of shame is exactly right in this case. My selfobject failure now presented her with the overwhelming task of taking back in the projection of contempt and owning the shame of her own ineptness. She was not ready to do so.

Furthermore, she took flight because "in a paranoid/schizoid mode, the experience of loving and hating the same object generates intolerable anxiety, which constitutes the principal psychological dilemma to be managed" (Ogden, 1989, p. 19). She hated me—her wounding and humiliating object—and she could no longer maintain her love in the face of the anxiety her hate created. As she had her mother and her partners, she once again left her object of attachment. As well as it served as an antidote to shame, her cold rage also saved her from the catastrophic anxiety of having to hold love and hate for the same object. Bacal and Newman (1990) suggest that "schizoid defenses serve to prevent deep involvement, and paranoid defenses build a protective aura of suspicion and hostility around the self to keep potentially injurious objects at a safe distance" (p. 245).

I had both injured her and made her anxious, and, for the purpose of our work, the wound was fatal.

The Case of Ms. D: Unintegrated Narcissistic Pathology in a Neurotic Personality

This final example illustrates the collapse of the self due to the injury inflicted by the analyst where recovery *was* possible. Ms. D helped reconstruct the event, and her notes are included.

Ms. D had also been in treatment for several years prior to the incident. She was the child of a pathologically narcissistic mother who would "forget about her" and abandon her when she [the mother] wanted to pursue her own interests. However, her mother was an exciting as well as rejecting object and would frequently engage with her in colorful artistic outings, lending a feast or famine quality to maternal attention and care-taking. In turn, Ms. B identified with her mother's artistry and was herself now inconsistent in the quality of her own care: dressing thoughtfully and very beautifully, but eating thoughtlessly and recklessly.

Furthermore, although deeply committed to the analytic process, she sometimes had difficulty "keeping things in mind" (Britton, 1992). If her attention was elsewhere, as during a vacation break, she could "for-get" our next appointment in a disconnected manner. When she would thus drop me from mind during the early phases of our work, I under-stood it as a residue of a pathological identification with her mother, who had obeyed only strong signals of stimulation and gratification that drowned out whatever was less compelling at the time. These lapses were fruitfully used, rather than derailing the work.

There was a "good fit" between us that allowed the work to flow. The strength and regularity of the attachment also helped to modify the in-tensely anxious, "panicky" state in which she had first presented her-self.[12] While Ms. D was not prickly in the same way as Ms. B had been, her extreme sensitivity could make negativity, criticism, or rejection unbear-able for her. As the work progressed however, her capacity to remain consistently connected and to tolerate rejection was markedly increased.

But the misery of her helplessness in mastering the complicated dy-namics of her food addiction, coupled with her temperamental "resis-tance" when she tried to do so, was a recurring theme in our work. When she became especially fearful of the harm her unchecked eating was cre-ating, she made what soon became a short-lived attempt to "do some-thing" about it. Like many people caught in this cycle, she had only a limited awareness that "dieting" did not work to permanently reverse her complex physical and emotional disorder.[13]

My empathic lapse and the "collapse" of the work were stimulated by a renewed attempt at weight loss, this time stimulated by the appeal of the sympathetic concern of her internist. It involved a new drug and a nutritionist. Moved by his kindly manner, she was again motivated and wished me to consult with him. I did so, but my optimism flagged when she immediately reported reacting unfavorably to his nutritionist. I found this an ominous sign. The collapse in the work came shortly after.

Ms. D's Recollections
(Ms. D's notes are interspersed with my own.)
Ms. D: I had gone to see Dr. _____ [her internist]—we talked about my [weight] problem. I remember feeling despairing and vulnerable, and the conversation seemed to "inspire" me to do something. I

remember asking R [me] to speak to him vis-à-vis the resistance problems (or my "psychological profile"). Something made it seem okay to ask that my two doctors speak to each other if we were to get into a more successful effort to help me. R told me she had called him and that he seemed to be a nice guy. I met with the nutritionist once and did not have a strong positive feeling about working with her. She didn't "inspire" me at all! Told me nothing I didn't already know. It could be my motivation slipping away. I talked to R about this.

[Her internist *was* sympathetic and well-intentioned, but my "nice guy" reference was an editorial comment revealing a sense that that was not going to be enough at this advanced point in her eating disorder. With little more than the usual fad drug (which they had already determined was not suitable for her medically), and the ominous sign that she already felt an aversion for the nutritionist, the situation did not bode well.]

Ms. D: Then—and this has gotten blurry—I remember something about R saying that she would be in touch with me to schedule an appointment (an extra one?). She didn't call, and I remember thinking, that's odd! She's usually attentive to such things. But, then, I didn't call either to say that, since she didn't, I was calling to set the appointment. I had the feeling that something was wrong. I felt "odd."

She correctly sensed my state of mind. Deeply involved with my own work (like her mother), I was conscious of not wanting to waste time or effort. Therefore, while adaptive to her needs in the past, I identified with her negativity and resistance and went "on strike" toward providing further motivation. My behavior laid the groundwork for narcissistic injury. Her notes for the next session capture it.

Ms. D: This is also blurry. At a session, when we discussed this, R said something about not calling because she was busy with whatever (can't remember what was originally said), and then, at some point, she talked about not having called because "*it was enough.*" She'd gotten frustrated with me, or something like that. But what I heard was some anger with me. Like I had used her, taken advantage, made her do something she really hadn't wanted to do [in calling the internist] [italics added].

While I had been willing to call the internist, I balked at any further effort on my part and put it back on her to provide it. She was hurt by my negativity toward her, and in the next passage she details her feelings of narcissistic injury:

Ms. D: I heard also that she was irritated with me because this seemed like a "false" effort (probably after I "lost it" with the nutritionist). I had experienced it as a sincere effort at the time and so felt hurt by R's response. Maybe we could have talked more about it, rather than her getting personally involved . . .?

Or, to translate it psychoanalytically: rather than my redirecting the projective identification back onto her as if it were a hostile missile! The next passage eloquently expresses her state of mind created by my "frank" expression that I had "had enough."

Ms. D: It felt like there was a breach of the relationship; like her "outside-the-client-relationship" self broke through, and it wasn't friendly! Instead of being my psychotherapist in the predictable way I had grown to expect (being encouraging, supportive, questioning, etc.), she seemed to show some frustration with me—annoyed with my resistance to taking care of myself, perhaps? Or was it that I raised hopes and then dashed them so quickly?

Exactly so. It was similar to the attack I had made in the case of Ms. B, but this time I made a deliberate decision to enter into a tricky realm with her. Although risky, and stimulated by my own needs at the time, it was a response made with more thought and sense of timing.

Ms. D: *I remember feeling very hurt and very confused"* (italics added).

It is the "confusion" that is significant and hopeful. It can exist only in the absence of the deadly clarity of mind that accompanies the revenge of narcissistic rage or the icy withdrawal of self-justification following the exposure of the bad object in a paranoid/schizoid collapse. Although hurt and shaken, she is able to be self-reflective in the next passage (which Kleinians might find to reflect the "depressive [whole object] position").

Ms. D: I took her [RK's] response to me against myself, feeling I was such a hard person to be in relationship with . . . which reminded me of S's [a friend] anger with me, which she expressed as my being so anxious and difficult to be close to, and being so narcissistic and demanding. [We] never really had any friendship to speak of after that, and then she died.

The death of her friend repeated the trauma with her own mother, for which she had regret. She was anxious that my anger with her would also mean the death of our relationship. She does not seek to disconnect here—she fears it.

Ms. D: I felt terribly misunderstood and also very despairing about myself and my behavior. There were touches of those feelings in this interaction with R. The whole thing brought up some dark and awful feelings about myself. It all seemed humiliating. I [put it] off at a distance and went on, thinking that it might all get clear or prove to have been helpful, later on sometime. *Our relationship returned to what it had been before* [italics added].

We went on to successfully work through the injury and temporary collapse.

Discussion

The psychological challenge for Ms. D was to accept that the *perfectly* loving object is not to be found. I challenged her to accept that in the subtext of my words "I had enough," I had become her worst fantasy—the bad mother who turns her attention to her own narcissistic pursuits and becomes annoyed when demands were made on her. That was never to happen again. Ms. D. thought she had found the good (i.e., perfect) mother but she had not. I was not *like* the bad mother—I *was* the bad mother.

My "confession" of my state of mind made her grapple with the phenomenon of someone both loving and hating her and, in effect, further challenging her most sacred fantasy of unlimited goodness. She now had her nightmare in the room. The perfect mother had acted hatefully, and she who was once wonderful now was horrible. Her recovery from the collapse was dependent on her ability to integrate the two because "to live always in the paranoid/schizoid position is to be wracked and torn by impossible demands for a *pure* love and *pure* hate" (Mitchell, 1993, p. 257, italics added).

It is this integration of love and hate that Klein (1952) believed was a necessary condition for a stable self. It modifies the bad object and relieves persecutory anxiety. "The ego, because of its 'lack of integration,' has only a limited tolerance of anxiety" (Laplanche and Pontalis, 1973, p. 299), and anxiety was a pronounced feature of Ms. D's affective structure. The ideal of the perfectly loving object defends against the guilt of having to hate the bad object and the *torments of anxiety* it engenders (Hartman et al., 1946).[14] In the beginning years of our work together, her anxiety was mitigated by the emotionally soothing containment of the connection.[15] The current psychodynamic episode strengthened her mentally as well as emotionally by challenging the fantasy of unlimited love to which *she was addicted* and, more important, asked her to contain both love and hate for the same object.

There is also a subtle aspect to Ms. D's structure that may have helped to prevent a total paranoid/schizoid collapse. Her capacity for autistic self-soothing (constructively through her artistic creativity and destructively with food) suggests that she was capable of creating a psychic re-treat (Steiner, 1993) that served to protect her from falling into a paranoid/schizoid collapse. In this state, as I illustrate in chapter five, there is a withdrawal into the self when persecuted, but there is also a capacity to return to deep connection with others. (See chapter five for a further discussion of Ms. D and autistic self-soothing.) In contrast, Ms. B did not have these self-soothing alternatives available in her mental structure.

FURTHER THOUGHTS

What do the three examples suggest? The case of Ms. A tells us that we can neither predict nor underestimate the potential for narcissistic injury in any given person because we are not privy in advance to the vulnerability and flaws of the underlying self-structure. I was consciously alerted to her disturbance only through my discomfort with the attempt of the group to have me take on an overwhelming task of a massive "integration," quickly followed by her hostile comment. It put me in a watchful, containing mode regarding her. It was probably more therapeutic to err on the side of seeing her as carrying around residues of profound disturbance.

In contrast, in the case of Ms. B, I *underestimated* the extent of her disturbance in the face of her nonpathological parts, which I had idealized. Attempting to ward off the frustration of her seemingly irrational behavior, I entered into premature mortal combat with her pathological internal objects. My dual blows of exposing the fallacy underneath her symbiotic attachment to her father and shaming her failure to meet her ideal of self-sufficiency resulted in a humiliation that could not be borne by so fragile a self-structure.[16] Having no psychic retreat other than a paranoid/schizoid collapse, Ms. B escaped in that way.

I agree with Grotstein (1985b) and Ogden (1989) that a paranoid/schizoid collapse is a defense, and I further believe it to be a defense against disturbing the self's dangerously weak construction. Paranoid/schizoid collapse is more likely to occur in the condition of defending an *emotional lie*. Contempt is one such lie, erected to overcome feelings of shame. Building a self-structure based on the shifting ground of unworked-through shame left Ms. B vulnerable to narcissistic injury. Shame-based narcissistic injury is an incendiary force that sets off the paranoid/schizoid collapse—a condition where the good object (now bad) is annihilated in the service of protecting pathological internal objects. The good object, now unmasked as bad, ceases to exist and can no longer be injurious or a threat.

In contrast, despite my injury to Ms. D (which came from every bit

as serious a prod to the self as in the case of Ms. B), recovery *was* possible. In the case of Ms. D, I was battling her addiction to being only loved
and her intolerance of the aversive. This addiction to experiencing only
the sweetness of love was as harmful to her psychic development as her
food addiction was to her physical well-being. I was asking her to tolerate
feelings of my hate (and by implication her own) so that she could further integrate the hateful feelings within her self-structure and reduce
her anxiety. While difficult, the integration of love and hate (ambivalence)
still does *not* imply the total abandonment of one's internal object world
as it did in the case of Ms. B.

   To be void of objects, as Fairbairn knew, is intolerable to the human
psyche. Thus, the paranoid/schizoid collapse contains a recognition by
the self of one's profound existential isolation, devoid of good objects and
suffering an assault on the pathological ones. Anyone in that condition
can become Nijinsky.[17] Not the Nijinsky who was the choreographic and
performing genius of ballet, but the Nijinsky who, bereft of all objects
both external and internal, took on his final role, for which he is least
remembered. At the age of 29 and empty of all objects, he became the
mental patient he was to remain for the rest of his life. His collapse was
permanent.

Notes

[1] Klein (1946) appended Fairbairn's (1940) construction of the schizoid position
to her own of the paranoid position (i.e., the paranoid/schizoid position). It is in
this position that she postulated the instinctive mechanism of splitting (good
from bad) to deploy the intense anxiety of infancy. Klein was most concerned
with the mental mechanisms of the discharge of death instinct phenomena to
preserve the ongoing sense of life. Although it begins early, it not a developmental position per se, but *a state of being*, in which these mental mechanisms operate.
[2] My use of the image of "collapse" of the dialectic of the self was stimulated by
Ogden's (1986, 1989, 1992a, b, 1994) understanding of the *dialectical interplay*
of Klein's "positions" (i.e., the depressive and paranoid/schizoid positions) as
well as his own concept of the autistic-contiguous position). It is out of this dialectical interplay that our subjectivity emerges, and its "collapse" defines the
mode of our pathological state.
[3] "either in its still endogenous and preliminary form as grudge and spite, or,
externalized and acted out in disconnected vengeful acts or in a cunningly plot-
ted vendetta" (Kohut, 1972, p. 657).
[4] Autistic self-soothing is more fully discussed in chapter five.
[5] For Ogden's (1989) understanding of "experience in a paranoid/schizoid mode,"
see pp. 18–30.
[6] I think it more meaningful for our understanding of this kind of person (or any
patient) to speak of her "borderline" aspects or parts, rather than foreclose the

meaningful interplay of all the parts of herself by the concretization of her as a "borderline" patient per se. There were parts of her that reflected neurotic conflict, psychotic terrors, autistic self-soothing, as well as the ability to carry out her nonpathological and ideal parts.

[7] I have noted a surprising number of incidents in the life of my patients in which a sibling has died young. These siblings were often seen to be in conflict with or "too much" for the parents. The subjective experience was that the ineptness or malevolence of the parent "killed off" the sibling. It provided a fear-based rationale for remaining attached (and identified) with the pathological parent.

[8] Morrison's (1989) work is an important contribution to the self-psychological and object-relational aspects of shame.

[9] Tomkins (1987) identified shame as a basic affective response, and Kohut (1972) identified the shame-prone person as one "who is ready to experience setbacks as narcissistic injuries and to respond to them with insatiable rage [and] does not recognize his opponent as a center of independent initiative with whom he happens to be at cross-purposes. . . . The mere fact, in other words, that the other person is independent or different is experienced as offensive by those with intense narcissistic needs" (pp. 643–644).

[10] Blaming the patient often evokes the intense experience of shame.

[11] It is probably better to conduct a therapy according to a sense of good of "timing, tact and dosage" (as Loewald once said), firmly in place than to lapse into an "Attila the Hun" posture. This courteousness does not negate the possibility of the *constructive* use of the analyst's engaging in mortal combat with the patient's destructiveness.

[12] Britton (1992) relates Bion's "container and the contained" to the need to find sanctuary and coherence through the other. I have observed that being mentally "dropped" by the other early on contributes to states of panic and affect disorders related to basic fears of survival, which persist through life. (See chapter seven for discussion of a severe case of this.)

[13] Short-term "dieting" is typical in the history of most people who are emotionally and physically addicted to food. Brigham (1997) has also noted the "aversion" to regular exercise necessary to maintain a healthy weight as part of the disorder.

[14] This is the same anxiety also faced by Ms. B, who could not tolerate it because of her more depleted internal structure.

[15] The connectedness helped to enhance the small amount of medication that successfully stabilized the panicky feelings of her affective disregulation. (See chapter seven for a case where this was the central issue.)

[16] As Blos (1969) has said, we would rather die than see our ego-ideal die.

[17] Nijinsky, suddenly separated from the maternal objects in this life—mother, wife/mother, and sister/muse (Nijinska), who was crucial to his artistic life—always empty of the good internal father who had abandoned his family early on and, most important of all, cruelly abandoned by the jealous and vengeful father/muse (Diaghilev), simply succumbed to a mental collapse, from which he never recovered.

Chapter Five

Compulsive Eating

Autistic Self-Soothing in a Neurotic Structure

"It is not a matter of mother comforting me—it is simply a soothing sensory experience."
—THOMAS OGDEN, *The Primitive Edge of Experience*

The relationship of the bodily self to the structure of the mind is implicit in Freud's (1923) statement: "The first ego is the bodily ego" (p. 26). And there have been notable further psychoanalytic contributions on the significance of the relationship between mind and body (e.g., Bick, 1968; Meltzer et al., 1975; Anzieu, 1985; McDougall, 1989; Ogden, 1989; Tustin, 1990; Mitrani, 1996). In this chapter, I focus on thinking as it relates to the inordinate craving for food. Disregulated eating is viewed as a multiply determined disorder generated by a mental state of unrelieved psychic tension—and fueled by a progressive physical addiction—leading to food-driven acts of autistic self-soothing.

Further, I suggest that the substitution of sensate thinking for mindful thinking in food-disordered individuals[1] relates to a fundamental disruption in attachment to an object. In particular, the loss of the use of the mind of the good object makes one, in turn, unable to take mindful care of oneself. Attachments are fundamental to transforming the autistic use—and abuse—of food.

THE "AUTISTIC OBJECT" AND "AUTISTIC SPACE"

S. Klein (1980) and Tustin[2] (1981b, 1986, 1990) have called attention to autistic phenomena in otherwise nonpsychotic, well-functioning persons. In an autistic collapse, an *autistic object* is used to create autistic space void of mindfulness. By definition, every autistic act signifies an emotional detachment from others—a retreat to a world of one's own making—

in search of relief and protection.[3] Particularly in food-related episodes one *actively* seeks the temporary, "unalloyed satisfaction" (Tustin, 1986, p. 168) that is possible to achieve only through an act carried out in an autistic mental space that is impervious to the intrusion of the other.

The following nonfood-related example shows how a part of the body can be used as an autistic object for autistic self-soothing and the creation of an autistic space.

Autistic Self-Soothing: Example 1

My observation took place during a three-hour train ride between two major cities frequented by passengers traveling for business and pleasure. Most passengers use the comfortable ride to work or relax without their usual distractions. Seated across the aisle and slightly behind a young woman and her daughter of about five, I could clearly hear them, but my view of the mother was obscured by the high back of the train seat.

They had made a private enclave for themselves by reversing the backs of the seats in front of them. The child then used the seats to spread out her array of books, games, and toys to occupy her for the long trip. I could observe her at her many activities. Approaching her projects with the zest and concentration characteristic of the serious play of a competent child, she drew and wrote with continuous absorption.

She frequently addressed her mother, who responded to her and also spoke continuously. I noticed that the mother's responses did not always reflect what I could see the child was occupied with at the moment. I was awed by the mother's stamina and her seemingly unending capacity to be in a teaching mode. My only view of the mother was the puzzling sight of her elbow rhythmically and steadily projecting out into the aisle.

When I later stood up, I could see that the mother's bent elbow movement was the last stage of the gesture of her *continuous stroking of a strand of her long hair*. It was performed in a repetitive motion while she was simultaneously absorbed in a magazine. She seemed totally unaware of her act. In this exquisitely self-absorbed state, she was actually tuning out the child, which accounted for her inaccurate responses. This self-stroking, as well as her nonstop speech, had autistic features (Hendrickson, 1997, personal communication) in someone who was not autistic in the usual clinical sense.

Discussion
The mother was using her hair for self-soothing. The creation of autistic space for herself was a compromise between her obvious wish to

relax and her need to mother her child. Deprived of the comfortable solitude that particular train trip is known to afford its passengers—and unable (or unwilling) to completely surrender her maternal role—she handled the resulting tension by resorting to ritualized, rhythmic, self-soothing motions that served to give her needed space from the child. Her nonstop talking—while she appeared to pay attention—provided an autistic screen to block out the child.

In this autistic state of self-soothing, *a true connection to the other is missing*. The mother's constant talking helped to camouflage the fact that in reality she was *an absent object* (O'Shaughnessy, 1964).[4] She was not truly in full mental touch with her child. The mother's state was the opposite of Bion's (1965) maternal reverie—an immersion in experiencing the other. However, her creation of autistic space for herself also served to protect the child from becoming a "bad" object, with whom the mother would be angry (or possibly hate) because of the little girl's desire for mirroring attention and exchange. It worked well enough to avoid conflict but was empty of the potential fullness of a true connection.

This example contains all the attributes of an autistic act: the rhythmicity of the physical action, the mother's pseudo-responsiveness, the mother and child fending for themselves in a *self-reliant* mode, and the avoidance of conflict over competing needs. Many of the components of this experience can also be found in food-related autistic acts and are related to the effects of the loss of the use of the maternal mind. In particular, this loss is reflected in a diminished capacity to think; a detachment from the good object, thus paving the way for the substitution of food for the object; and a "black hole" of abandonment in which one, in turn, abandons care of oneself.

THE CATASTROPHE OF THE LOSS
OF THE MATERNAL MIND

Both Winnicott (1950) and Bion (1965) clearly established the crucial role of maternal reverie in metabolizing the needs of the infant and child. Reverie is essentially an act of *empathic emotional thinking* necessary to the infant's survival and to the child's further development. Kohut's description of the selfobject need for mirroring and empathic attunement—in developmental stages beyond infancy—also reflects the need to occupy the mind of another in the service of maintaining self coherence. The following example shows that problems in maintaining one's place in the mother's mind may also lead to problems in thinking itself and a negation of the sense of self:

Problems in Maintaining Thoughts: Example 2

Ms. Q related that until the age of 18 months she had been cared for by her mother and her grandfather during the anxious time her father was away doing "war work." Her grandfather was a compensatory figure for both the child and the mother—mirroring the child and soothing the anxious mother. Catastrophically, when the patient was 18 months old—a crucial period in the development of the self— her grandfather suddenly died the same week her mother gave birth to her sibling. She was briefly sent to be cared for by relatives.

Ms. Q experienced a double loss: the attention paid to her by her grandfather, to whom she was important, and the maternal preoccupation of her mother with the new infant. Furthermore, the mother lost her compensatory figure for the absent husband, and the patient in turn lost that part of the mother who had been made somewhat available to her through the calming presence of the grandfather. The intense anxiety of this period left its mark of demanding hysteria on the mother, and the toddler responsively took on the role of a noncomplaining child. She assumed her own place as a "little helper" who protectively watched her baby brother and diligently obeyed her mother.

During the next few years, the role of the "little mother" intensified as the sibling developed health problems. *Ms. Q had no place in her mother's mind* other than as her narcissistic extension, and no sense of herself as having a separate existence. The most serious outcome of the object losses and maternal criticality and selfobject failure was an attack on her ability to process thought. Her repeated complaint during our work was that intellectual material she was studying "would not stay" in her mind. Despite her love of learning, she never felt mastery over what she studied. It went "right out of her head." Thinking on her own was another activity that her experience with her domineering mother had made her fearful of because it separated them. She was scorned or reviled for expressing ideas or feelings that differed from her mother's. It actually placed her in physical danger of the bullying mother's capacity for retribution. Later mastery of her own intellectual pursuits was inhibited by a fear of disobeying this now internalized omnipotent maternal presence. She had learned to shut off and "not think." It was associated with being good, and safe.

Ms. Q often experienced herself as knowing nothing and had great difficulty articulating what she felt she did know. At a crucial developmental phase, she had lost the use of the mother's mind to metabolize the feelings necessary for the processing of thoughts. Bion (1965) has shown that, without this use of the mother's mind, the infant will be psychotic because feeling states cannot be linked to thoughts. Its loss at a later time—as in this case—can impair the thinking process itself.

Being Dropped from Mind and Attachment Rejection: Example 3

Being dropped from the maternal mind also affects one's ability to maintain a thoughtful attachment to objects. One drops them from mind in an identification with the narcissistic mother's self-preoccupation. The loss of the use of the maternal mind owing to the maternal figure's becoming an "absent object" fosters one's own attachment rejection and paves the way for acts of autistic self-soothing.

My observation in this case was of a chance extraanalytic view of a patient for whom both shopping and eating were autistic and ritualized compulsions. She had told me of her shopping sprees, which, along with her eating of sweets, were out of control. She had as yet found herself unable to take the necessary steps to change her impulsive and indulgent food habits, despite their considerable risk to her health and damage to her self-esteem. Her shopping forays were also taking their toll on her finances and creating family conflict.

In this particular instance, I caught sight of her from a distance in a neighborhood noted for its clothing boutiques. She was walking slowly in isolation down the deserted street. Her abstracted air (not unlike that of the woman on the train) while coming down the empty street lent the scene a quality of an Edward Hopper painting. The emptied outer landscape reflected her inner one. From our work, I knew her to be the child of a narcissistic mother who frequently left the patient home alone in favor of pursuing her own interests. When abandoned in that way, she would experience great anxiety.[5]

Discussion

Her compulsive shopping and eating binges were acts of sensation rather than of mind. They reflected her frequent attempts to find relief from a self-state of intense inner tension suffused with resentment of the demands made on her, in tandem with her own unmet needs for comfort and attention. The shopping and eating were overdetermined because they also mimicked the pleasurable aspects of her relationship to her mother and the latter's capacity for indulgence. Her mother alternated between creating a fused state with her, in which she bestowed art and fun, and the sudden ejection of her from her mind.

In the mother's narcissistic extremes, there was no space in her thoughts for my patient. While the mother on the train was still making a pseudo-connection with her child through her own act of autistic self soothing, my patient's mother was often actually "absent" in both mind and body. This dual absence of the object led to my patient's hatred and rejection of her (O'Shaughnessy, 1964). This in turn left her without a sense of a good internal object who thought about her and took care of her.

Her mother's acts were the background of the patient's autistic behaviors. The mother's dropping her from mind created what Henry (1983, p. 84) refers to as a "hollow" mental state, in what was once a space shared by both. Because of the narcissistic injury of her absence and abandonment, the patient, as a defense against psychic pain, totally renounced the mother and, through haughty withdrawal (Kohut, 1984), deliberately emptied her own mind of her. The "hollow space" was now filled with the remnants of the relationship—the food and shopping—which became autistic residues of self-soothing. Like the relating of the mother on the train, these activities were acts of maternal pseudo-caretaking.

OGDEN: THE AUTISTIC-CONTIGUOUS POSITION

When empty of the internal image of a caretaking object, many compensatory autistic acts reflect attempts to reduce tension by creating mental space that does not rely on others. *In this space, there is no absent object, bad object, disappointing object or selfobject failure. Satisfaction is attained entirely autosensuously.* As Tustin (1990, pp. 40–41) described autistic children, they seek refuge in a sensation-dominated world filled with "soft" (comforting) shapes and "hard" (protective) autistic objects. Ogden (1989, 1994) added this sensation-dominated mode to Klein's formulation of the paranoid/schizoid and depressive modes of experience; he calls it the *autistic-contiguous position.* The role of the bodily self is central in this mode of experience. Thus:

> Sensory experience in an autistic-contiguous mode has a quality of rhythmicity that is becoming continuity of being; it has boundedness that is the beginning of the experience of a place where one feels, thinks, and lives; it has such features as shape, hardness, coldness, warmth, and texture, that are the beginnings of the qualities of who one is [Ogden, 1989, p. 54].

I believe that the autistic-contiguous position is a more primitive state of being than the paranoid-schizoid and depressive positions, because the latter are states of self that call for a mental relationship to an other. There *is no other* as we know it in the autistic-contiguous mode, just the self in relation to the nonanimate object's "feel" and "shape"—its "hardness" and "softness." As part of a fluid dialectic of the self, it can have constructive and self-nurturing aspects by providing needed soothing, such as losing oneself in music. However, this self-soothing may have—as in the case of food- or substance-dominated responses—pathological consequences. There can be a collapse of the self into an autosensuous mode of experience just as there can be a "collapse" into the paranoid-schizoid mode (see chapter four). The self-structure is weakened at such times.

Someone in the grips of a compulsive eating disorder suffers a continuous collapse into an autistic-contiguous space, with less and less room for the mind to be otherwise occupied. Food is used as an "autistic object" (as a shield) and as an "autistic shape" (for comfort). Food becomes the protective object for autistic self-soothing through familiar mouth, tongue, and psychophysiological sensations. People matter less as a source of well-being. Ogden's (1989) description of an autosensuous world free of (human) objects is relevant because the use of food-as-object relates to both the missing *real* object, and the abandoning, absent, or bad *internal* object. There is no one there—externally or internally—either to soothe *or* to further disregulate oneself. It is *an omnipotent place* where the attachment to a human object is replaced by an all-encompassing attachment to food-as-object, with a potential for destructive consequences.

AUTISTIC SELF-SOOTHING AND THE "BLACK HOLE" OF ABANDONMENT

The loss of the use of the maternal mind has a catastrophic effect if it comes about through loss of the object itself—for it can never be replaced—and can be redeemed only if one comes to occupy space in the mind of a well-meaning other. When this does not take place, it may affect the capacity for sustaining life itself as is illustrated in the case of Ms. F, who retained a "*black hole*" within her. Tustin described this as "an elemental form of depression, such as Winnicott called psychotic depression and Bibring, who stressed the feelings of helplessness, called "primal depression" (in Grotstein, 1990, p. 383). The "black hole" is a place of existential "meaninglessness, hopelessness and chaos." The capacity to experience a black hole is an "inherent imagery which is released by experience, particularly catastrophic experience" . . . the "black hole" is always potential experience" (p. 380).

I share Grotstein's view that one such experience—perhaps the worst—is of "an infantile catastrophic response to object loss [in which the] primary *narcissistic* loss . . . is indistinguishable from an *object loss* . . ." (p. 381, italics added).[6]

That is, in this extreme state, there is *a loss of the sense of self* that accompanies the loss of the object. I believe that the "primary narcissistic loss" comes from losing one's place in another's mind. If one is dropped from thought early on, there is a diminished and emptied self—with something *always* missing—that lingers on. This loss is not automatically redressed through the replacement by caretakers, unless the child also occupies a favorable and cherished place in their mind. It is only the latter circumstance that allows the child to internalize and identify with a relationship involving an object who wishes one well and takes good care. Without it, one is essentially alone in an empty world, as in the case of Ms. F.

The History of Ms. F

Ms. F became an orphaned child at the age of 18 months, literally owing to the death of her mother and figuratively owing to the psychological abandonment by her father and later her stepmother. Early maternal attention to her states of being was containing enough to avoid her becoming actively psychotic, and her intellectual level was high. She did not suffer from a "paper-thin, two dimensional mental state" but, rather, a mental state that had been "hollowed out" as in patients who "once possessed a containing space and then lost it . . ." (Henry, 1983, p. 84).

The loss of the use of her mother's mindfulness for caretaking and soothing proved catastrophic because it was never replaced by the mind of either her alcoholic father or her limited stepmother. The experience of herself as an abandoned orphan was rekindled many times throughout her life. She raised herself instead, using food to fill the parental void and ease her tensions. She was scarcely aware of the *physical addiction* that had progressed as a result of her continuous collapse into a food-driven autistic state.[7] She eventually lost the capacity to "think" in any other mode when she experienced a need for soothing.

Ms. F had suffered the many-headed Hydra of compulsion: alcohol, spending, and food—all attempts at self-soothing. During the long course of our work, she was in good recovery from all but the food. She had a genetic predisposition for manic-depression, which in her father led to his self-treatment with alcohol. It overwhelmed his thinking and turned him into a nasty and maudlin presence. He perversely blamed her for his unhappiness and alcoholism and, having no other to believe in, she believed him.

Although she too turned to alcohol at the adult onset of her own manic–depression, her greater knowledge enabled her to seek proper medication. At the time we began working she had long-term sobriety and maintained a strong attachment to the AA program and to her sponsor. After many years, there was a significant reversal of the compulsive buying that had previously sent her into progressive debt and humiliating bankruptcies.

Her food compulsion was the hardest of all to overcome because it also reflected a physical addiction that increased over the years, and she ultimately succumbed to the fatal effects of her great weight.[8]

She sporadically made inroads in regulating her food, but she could not set up the treatment conditions necessary to giving up this form of self-medication, which was reminiscent of her father's inability to reverse his self-medicating with alcohol. Ironically, her AA sponsor was her "eating buddy", and they would greatly enjoy their food outings together. They both shared the same *mindfulness* regarding alcohol, and *mindlessness* regarding food. She refused to get a sponsor whose mindset could share the task of changing her eating habits. She feared abandoning her food.

When her AA sponsor, who was a much-loved "old-timer" in the program, died from the effects of smoking, it devastatingly rekindled the loss of her mother. She again lapsed into a hollow mental place and entirely gave up the hopeful attempts to regulate her eating she had been capable of before that. She began to refer to herself as being in a "hospice mode," even before becoming physically ill, and her own morbid descent followed soon after.

An Emptied World

The devastating effects of early loss of the object are well documented (see Edelman, 1994; Harris, 1995). The "black hole" here is not just the empty self of narcissistic depletion (Kohut, 1971), but a "frenzied neediness" (Grotstein, 1990, p. 382). Death and dead objects were built into Ms. F's inner world even before the losses of her mother and all those that followed. Her parents had lost their first child before she was born. They then divorced, later remarried, and had Ms. F in an attempt to balance death with life. Only when she was a mature adult did she become aware of the older dead sibling, and then through a distant relative, for her father had never told her.[9]

She had only the dimmest memory of her mother, who succumbed at an early age to breast cancer. There was no mourning possible at this stage of Ms. F's development, and she carried it with her as well as absorbing the effect of the unmourned grief on her parents. Later, her stepmother proved unable to properly care for Ms. F, who remembers best the ill-fitting clothes her stepmother made for her and how she locked the food cupboards to keep her out. A most vivid memory was of her stepmother fleeing the home during one of her husband's alcoholic rages; she took with her only their young son (Ms. F's younger stepbrother) and left Ms. F to her fate with this out-of-control man. These model scenes (Lichtenberg, 1989) of her life narrative spoke to her certainty that she had no father and never had a mother.

Ms. F broke down in college and attempted suicide. She was hospitalized and briefly treated. She was saved only by the faculty's recognition of her fine intellect and managed to obtain a good education and scientific training. The father's death actually came as a relief to all the family members. She worked at maintaining what was to be a largely one-way involvement with her indifferent stepfamily and managed to make her workplace into a better one. She was much loved there as a caring leader. However, she internalized her father's image of nonrecovery, and food became her most reliable and sought-after containing object.

Further Thoughts on Ms. F

With the loss of the mother, who was the center of her existence, a part of herself also died at that time, even though her life went on. What faded from her sense of being was the internal image of the mother who was alive to soothe and protect her. Ms. F was missing both this internal image and an actual mother to soothe her when bereft.

The early death of a mother breaks the link in the chain of connection to the continuity of life for a young child. There is a loss of the caretaking, maternal "I" with which to identify. Ms. F could neither mate nor mother, despite her deep yearnings. She tried unsuccessfully to care for a difficult foster child but had to return her to the agency. She was not even able to take over as designated "stepmother" of her late sponsor's cat. There was no mothering in her to call upon, and she was unable to transcend her own history. She could not attach to a new sponsor just as her stepmother had not been able to attach to her. Ultimately, she could not take proper care of herself.

All further attempts to regulate her food "died out" after her AA sponsor died. She was further desolated by setbacks at work that had also been a source of sustenance to her. Despite also receiving the best of what present-day pharmacology had to offer, she was on a downward path. Her body began to collapse in a series of injuries from falls related to being off balance as a result of her heavy weight. She required surgery and recovered from it surprisingly quickly. She came back to therapy and returned to work in a very short time. Along with her pathology, she also had a courageous capacity for a going-on-being in the face of damage, both physical and emotional.

Autistic Eating

For many years, the soothing rhythm of our twice-weekly sessions had been built into maintaining her psychic life. Although the therapy was life sustaining in one sense, in another sense it was a form of "psychodialysis" (Gear et al., 1981, p. 393). Therapy helped her to maintain herself rather than enabling her to change after a certain point. Change could come about only if she could suffer the pain of giving up the food, and that she could no longer do, despite her longing for it.[10] Over time, the physical addiction had taken hold as a narcotic, and she could not let go of it. It was simply too powerful, and its power was even greater than her attachment to me. I learned to monitor my concerned "interest" in her brief attempts at controlling her eating, for she virulently resisted my own need for her to do so. She experienced my presence in this not as encouraging her to get help to eat satisfyingly and correctly, but as my wanting to deprive her of food as her stepmother had. At these times she emptied her mind and locked herself in the insensate mindlessness of an autistic space that I was not to invade. Her most significant transference terror came in the depressive mode of thinking, when she feared my disconnecting from her because of her "badness," her being unable to conquer her addictive eating. I understood that this was a source of (a rekindled) terror for her, and I sought not to stimulate it in the service of my own will and selfobject need for her recovery from the addiction.

My genuine and sustained interest in her was at best good "foster care." In her internal world, there was no mother caring for her. My psychic presence never completely filled the void left by the death of her mother and the aftershocks of her subsequently traumatic life with her "no-mother" stepmother. She fought her "black hole" and the Nirvana Principle[11] with great dignity and as best she could. The powerful hidden food addiction of autistic self-soothing was stronger.

The early loss of the object through death or absolute abandonment, as in the case of Ms. F, results in the loss of the mind of the other for metabolizing and regulating tension. But, as in examples 2 and 3, being dropped from the mind of the other—dropped from the other's thoughts—also impairs the ability to exercise mindful thinking in regard to caring for oneself.

THINKING IN AN ADDICTIVE MODE

Recovery from addictive eating is dependent on the capacity to be *mindful* of caring for oneself. Most people who recover from addictive forms of overeating must sustain attentive thought to it, usually for life. This mindfulness also requires thinking that is not delusional. For example:

> After an extensive discussion of weight loss and dieting between two now middle-aged classmates at a alumni reunion, they proceeded to the buffet lunch line. After each of them made their selections, they seated themselves together to resume their conversation. One alumna, who continued to manifest the same considerable weight problem she had as an undergraduate years earlier, compared the choice of fruit made by the classmate who had made significant progress. Deliberately pointing to the Napoleon resting on her own tray the overweight alumna said: "I allow myself this on my diet!"

The omnipotent statement that she had made a *choice* was an attempt to deny the fact that she actually had absolutely *no* control over her decision. It was as if the "sensible eating" statements made just moments before by this very intelligent and capable woman—who had had outstanding professional achievements since her college days—had not been uttered. The conversation and previous thoughts had been "dropped from mind" as soon as she spied the sweet, and it exerted its addictive pull.

In this state of inordinate desire, she had no mind as such. Her thought processes were as inanimate as the dessert. Instead, there was a mindless forgetfulness, and the substitution of omnipotent thought for thinking. By her lack of mindfulness (Langer, 1989), I would say that she was instead "thinking" with her mouth, tongue, and salivary glands. Thoughts without mind (in Bion's sense)—or nonthinking thoughts, as I call them—is the state of mind I believe that characterizes the autistic-contiguous mode of experience.

Another clear example of the kind of thinking that dominates in an addictive state appears in the eponymous text of *Alcoholics Anonymous* (Alcoholics Anonymous World Services, 1976).[12] It is an often quoted "tale" that is appreciated because of its incisive depiction of an addictive mindset, and it is a reminder that it can be activated even after many years of sobriety and control. The story is told as, "The Whiskey in the Milk."

Acknowledging that he was an alcoholic who had been, and could still become, violently intoxicated and was now working as a salesman for a concern he formerly had owned, "Jim" relates his story:

I came to work . . . I remember I felt irritated . . . [and] had a few words with the boss, but nothing serious. Then I decided to drive into the country and see one of my prospects. . . . On the way I felt hungry so I stopped at a roadside place where they have a bar. I had no intention of drinking. I just thought I would get a sandwich . . . I had eaten there many times during the months I was sober. I sat down at a table and ordered a sandwich and a glass of milk. Still no thought of drinking. I ordered another sandwich and decided to have another glass of milk.

Suddenly the thought crossed my mind that if I were to put an ounce of whiskey in my milk it couldn't hurt me on a full stomach. I ordered a whiskey and poured it into the milk. I vaguely sensed I was not being any too smart, but felt reassured as I was taking the whiskey on a full stomach. The experiment went so well that I ordered another whiskey and poured it into more milk. That didn't seem to bother me so I tried another. . . .

Whatever the precise definition of the word may be, we call this plain insanity. How can such a lack of proportion, of the ability to think straight, be called anything else? You may think this an extreme case . . . [but] this kind of thinking has been characteristic of every single one of us [pp. 36–37].

Although the substance here is alcohol, such stories are often quoted by those in recovery from an addiction to food. There are myriad examples, but each serves as a caution against the tendency to "forget" and thereby relapse into thoughts without mindful thinking.

KEEPING THINGS IN MIND

Attachment and Nonautistic Eating

Whatever its origin, overloading on food eventually builds up a physical addiction as well as a psychological one.[13] One cause of the high rate of recidivism in those who return to overeating is the failure to keep the physical and emotional pitfalls "in mind." Acts of thinking and rituals of practice are needed to replace the mindlessness of the autistic addictive state, which—like the "whiskey in the milk" thinking or the "black hole of abandonment" feeling—always has the potential for activation.

Breaking through the autistic barriers of eating disorders is also a function of reawakening a capacity for attachment that has been lost through a rejection of the lost, absent, or bad object. The attachment of shared minds restores or builds the ability to "keep things in mind." It is not necessary to experience a loss such as Ms. F's , to have a black hole of elemental depression and resort to autistic self-soothing. The *absent object* who drops one from mind can quickly become the bad, nonsoothing object (example 2). A retaliatory "attachment rejection" of others follows and is characteristic of the state of autistic eating.

This (often willful) *rejection of attachment* carries with it a concomitant loss of the ability to use thought to inhibit destructive actions.[14] All those such as Ms. F and others similar to her literally could not "rethink" their addiction, although they hated their excess weight and at some level were aware of its dangers.

The Case of Ms. E

The following case example illustrates the relationship between *attachment and the capacity to be mindful*. Ms. E fought her way out of an impoverished, semimigrant childhood. Now geographically separated from her remaining family, she was only remotely connected to her mother and sister, toward whom she nonetheless had positive feelings. She had moved away when she cast her lot with a shady businessman, a Runyonesque character with whom she lived and worked. Her link with this sociopathic man created a lifestyle of dodging creditors and being on the run. Her considerable inventive skills were crucial to his business ventures, however, and he repaid her devotion with his fidelity. They had an unspoken pact based on their mutual "overlooking" the severe flaws of his character and those of her physical appearance. They were both outcasts, but with her help he had thus far managed to avoid being an outlaw as well.

She knew she should leave him but found herself unable to do so and sought treatment when she became depressed. As her depression lifted during the course of our work, she began to think about her disorganized physical habits, which contributed to her serious overweight and chaotic, junk-filled home. She felt the urge once again to tackle her eating disorder, but chose not to return to Overeaters Anonymous (OA). She had experienced that organization as not sufficiently "warm enough" to break through her shyness and isolation.

A likable, intelligent original, she decided to "apply principles of cybernetics" to her food choices. According to her, she began "psyching herself up" to "think in each food situation what choice a normal person—not a food disordered one—would make and act accordingly." In addition to these acts of mindfulness, she intuitively turned to another tool of the program, which redressed her essential isolation. She reconnected with her sister, who shared the family eating disorder, and they committed to speaking long distance to each other daily and telling each other their food plans. The sisters, in effect, acted as "sponsors" for each other, as she had learned in her OA experience.

In this act of reattaching to her sister, she recaptured the strength they once had together during their early years of isolation and inferior social standing. It was a sisterly "us against them," which had given them strength and hope as children. It worked for the months she remained in therapy, when the instability of her precarious lifestyle finally disrupted our work. Despite other serious difficulties, however, she thought to use [the mind of] her sister in staying on her food plan during the time of our work, and that was key. An alter ego twinship with another is necessary during difficult tasks (Kohut, 1984, pp. 200–201). I think that the strength of purpose it generates comes from the sharing of the mental burden.

THINKING AND THE RESTORATION OF THE DIALECTIC OF THE SELF

In addition to the preceding cases of unresolved disordered eating, I have observed the changes in mind and habit of many others in successful recovery. Often, after many failures, they came to think of their condition as similar to alcoholism or drug addiction and sought relief through sustaining the "groupobject" (Segalla, 1996) identification of a 12-step program. The program is often resorted to by people who have had no lasting success of their own through concentrating on a *single* solution, such as medication, fad diets, weight loss, exercise, or even surgery. Such thinking is replaced by an understanding that theirs is a multidetermined disorder in which will power does not last. That recognition is arrived at through different routes but almost always involves reaching a point of genuine despair and an awareness that the thought that one can master control by one's own efforts is a delusion.

Paradoxically, the self-experience of helplessness and defeat that drives one into a 12-step program often provides the strength to break through the autistic barrier of compulsive eating. The "defeat" is of the grandiose idea of self-sufficiency and will power, which simply is not operable for any but a short length of time in those for whom food is an addictive substance and a lifestyle obsession.

The psychodynamic factors of the group experience that I am discussing here are those which affect the capacity for thinking in anything other than an omnipotent paranoid-schizoid mode. In this mode—even in an otherwise neurotic person—one's denial has a delusional quality. Thinking has collapsed into the essentially sensate "thoughts" characteristic of the autistic-contiguous position.

In the group experience, sharing previous delusional mindsets regarding food lifts them out of what previously have been only autistic practices. These "food histories"—a mix of often tragic, outrageous, and comic autistic acts—are now related in a depressive (whole-object) mode of thinking. "The Whiskey in the Milk" kind of experience becomes part of a communal folklore that stimulates hopefulness.

For example, a now abstinent "sponsor" in the highly structured subgroup of the OA program, HOW,[15] described her final act of bingeing and vomiting before coming to the program as occurring on the way home from the hospital after she had just undergone gastric stapling![16] This act was done by an otherwise intelligent woman who thereby placed herself in the gravest physical danger. This and other equally desperate examples of food-addictive behaviors are not uncommon for members to share. The sharing of each other's histories helps to transform previously self-destructive autistic acts into whole-object modes of communication and sources of inspiration. Through the telling, self-destructive, autistic acts become acts of transcendence.

In comparing those who succeed in overcoming their addiction with those who have not, the relationship between self-soothing with food and failures of attachment becomes clearer. By building attachments (through meetings, ceremonial rituals, sponsoring-relationship, service to the group or organization, etc.), one gives the disorder the constant daily care and attention it requires for change. Each of these components calls for mindfulness and connection to another. Like the care of an infant, one's recovery must be continuously kept in mind, because the physical and emotional power of the disorder is so great for some people that it defies logic.

The principles of recovery are the same for all degrees of the disturbance and weight, for they require a sustained presence of mind and connectedness to something outside the self. There is a learned awareness that the connection must be ongoing and not dropped from attention.[17]

Being, Thinking, and Doing

Attachment built up by having and becoming a sponsor is an enduring feature of the OA-HOW program that is also a function of modes of thinking. In the beginning phases of the program, there are daily calls to one's sponsor with one's food plan and the reading of responses to questions on one's emotional and food history. In a persecutory mode of thinking, the daily calls can be experienced as an unwanted intrusion and control over the omnipotent wish for unlimited license unhindered by constraints.

In the "whole-object" mode of thinking (Klein's depressive position), attachment to the good object lends a sense of security against destructive, impulsive eating. This impulsivity often has defeated one's best intentions and perpetuates the addictiveness. Although the states of thinking are often mixed in the beginning, the deepening attachment with those who "suffer through" the early negative feelings helps to overcome persecutory feeling. For most, the daily connection is continued in some form indefinitely, even after the physical addictiveness has subsided. Hence, the telephone establishes a dialectic between the autistic, persecutory, and depressive modes of thought—ending the collapse into only an autistic mode of experience.

Similarly, turning toward the "other" during emotional disregulation, rather than seeking the autistic self-soothing of a food response, is a crucial mental shift necessary for physical and emotional recovery. Disregulation most often occurs from overstimulation as a result of food and troubling affect states, such as resentment, anger, and fears. One learns to keep in mind "putting down the food" (i.e., turning away from autistic self-soothing) as the first response to any disregulation and then doing whatever necessary to reestablish emotional equilibrium. The internalization of this shared learning serves as a "second skin"—if not "first mother" for emotional turmoil.

These are *rituals of mindfulness* that come to replace the sensation-dominated *rituals of autistic eating*. They are dependent on the maintenance of attachment and a shared mindset. They are "remembered" and incorporated as part of one's daily existence. The restoration of self that occurs through a shared mindfulness presents the dialectical collapse of one's thinking. If an automatic collapse into autistic self-soothing with food is rejected, one has to "work the steps" in order to shift out of dangerous and depressive persecutory modes of thinking. Projections have to be taken back in to the self, and unpleasant affect is experienced, tolerated, and worked through. Paradoxically, the process lessens what one has had "thin skin" about previously. Destructive responses are gradually diminished as stimuli are experienced as less toxic.

Psychoanalytic theory since Freud has seen frustration as necessary for mental development (O'Shaughnessy, 1964). In Bion (1962), too, the origin of a *thought* is the hallucination of the *absent* breast. But nonpsychotic thinking, as Bion (1965) showed, arises only through the mentalization of one's chaotic bits of experience through the presence and reverie of another. *Mindfulness*, as I am calling the *act of thinking* that helps one to break through the autistic condition of compulsive eating, can be achieved only through the mental presence of someone or something other than the self. It cannot be achieved in autistic isolation. It requires the other for the maintenance of hope. For it is only through the dialectical interplay of our mind with the mind of another that we develop within ourselves the dialectical interplay between the autistic-continuous, paranoid-schizoid, and depressive modes of experience—that interplay which results in what we call thinking, or mindfulness.

Notes

[1] My focus is on individuals at the bulimic end of eating disorders, whose caloric intake and food amounts have proven excessive for their bodily needs. I am not addressing here the issue of anorectic self-starvation, which has more profound psychotic underpinnings involving severe delusions of body image. The two conditions, however, are not mutually exclusive, and I have observed these different aspects alternating in the same person.

[2] In particular, Tustin's (1986, 1990) work on the autistic aspects of being have significance for a wide spectrum of personality disorders. This chapter is concerned with the "autistic enclave which needs to be reached and brought to light, if real personal growth is to be achieved."

[3] Tustin (1990) spoke particularly of the use of a protective shell (e.g., wearing a hard object such as a big belt buckle) by autistic children who suffer terror. I have thought the same of guns that are carried even by young children who face a daily street life filled with violence. The gun is their hard object to keep a pervasive sense of terror at bay.

[4] One common source of rage in couples is one partner's absorption in an autistic pursuit that "shuts out" the other. The partner who is the "absent object" comes to be experienced as the hated bad object, "which is leaving the baby to starve and die" (O'Shaughnessy, 1964, p. 134).

[5] Her father had been a compensatory figure until her adolescence, when she felt abandoned by him, as she experienced him as "returning" to the mother. It is sometimes difficult for fathers to negotiate their daughters' emerging sexual development, especially when the mother is having envious or anxious difficulties with it herself. Gilligan's (1982) findings may also reflect this in her work on female adolescent development.

[6] Grotstein (1990) and others have grappled with the issue of infantile depressive illness "as to whether it is deficits in primary narcissism or in primary object love" (pp. 380–381). Grotstein's conclusion is to offer his dual-track (dialectical) hypothesis. The mother–child interaction is a "Siamese-twinship" of simultaneous separateness and nonseparateness (p. 381a). I share this view and see no contradictions between the known capacity from birth for the infant to make distinctions (Stern, 1985), and even to feel separate and individuated, and the existence of a sense of unity between mother and infant.

[7] *Lack of awareness and denial* of their caloric overloading in general and on large amounts of refined carbohydrates and fats in particular are typical of the mindset of compulsive eaters. The addiction is not experienced as such. Few people have a consciousness of how much they are *really* eating and how *little* they are moving.

[8] Ms. F's weight and massive volume of breast tissue rendered a mammographic reading impossible. Since her mother had died young of breast cancer, it was

thought that nonprimary-site cancer in her liver was probably metastasized breast cancer. In very rapid order from a diagnosis of gall bladder difficulty as the probable cause of severe back pain (the now cancerous liver), she succumbed to a stroke shortly after entering the hospital for the initial surgery.

9 She had unconsciously carried the effect of this sibling's death on her parents during her predictable "annual anniversary season of loss," when her depressive tendencies would increase. The period would start earlier than that of her parents' death, and we were not surprised when she learned that the time span included the anniversary of the death of this brother prior to her birth. After she learned of the existence of the brother, the uncanny interest she had in her "colonial genealogy" ceased. She may have found the lost relative for whom she had unconsciously been looking.

10 A major distinction between alcohol and food as addictive substances is that, if one is to be successful in controlling compulsive eating, food intake must still be dealt with on a daily basis. Paradoxically, a food-disordered person must both eat *and* mentally abstain from using food as an abused substance. This tricky split accounts for the "cunning and baffling" aspect of food disorder and makes it one of the most difficult addictions to overcome and easily denied.

11 Freud (1920) took Barbara Low's term for the death instinct to describe the longing to return to nonbeing. One's effort is over.

12 Known as the "Big Book" in AA. It arose from the mind of the same man who invented securities analysis for Wall Street investors, Bill Wilson, cofounder of Alcoholics Anonymous.

13 Most often the addiction is to fat and carbohydrates in refined forms, as well as individual specific foods that cannot be eaten in normal quantities. A thoughtful food plan usually omits or limits these foods.

14 An attachment rejection typical of someone with this disorder was expressed by Ms. D (chapter four) when she "did not like the nutritionist," thereby defeating her internist's and her own attempts to restructure her eating. The rejection was gratuitous and symptomatic of the mindless rebelliousness one has to overcome in order to recover from an addiction. At a later time—as in the history of many compulsive eaters who reverse their disorder—Ms. D was less resistant to following a plan made appealing through the joint effort of family members to whom she was attached.

15 HOW stands for honesty, openness, and willingness. It is actually a phrase from *Alcoholics Anonymous*, on which the program is based.

16 A procedure resorted to in morbid obesity that does not rely on changing eating habits but, rather, restricts the intestinal absorption while maintaining the fantasy that one can eat all one wishes and not get fat. Deaths from this procedure have been noted.

17 The necessity for the connection is the intrinsic difficulty in distinguishing between food as an *abused substance* and food as *nourishment*. In alcohol or drug abuse recovery, "abstinence" or "sobriety" is more easily defined, although not necessarily more easily managed. Food is unique in that it can be consumed in either an "abstinent" (controlled) or "nonabstinent" (binge) state. One has to be on the alert for nonabstinent thinking, which usually requires maintaining an attachment to others who share an abstinent mindset.

Chapter Six

Hidden Spaces

Psychotic Residues in a Neurotic Structure

Therapeutic impasses and disruptive moments in treatment always have to be examined from the countertransference viewpoint.
— PETER GIOVACCHINI, *Psychoanalytic Practice*[1]

Like the preceding chapter, in which the consideration of autistic residues was not limited to conditions of autism per se, this chapter on psychotic residues is about people who are not ordinarily thought of as psychotic. In a neurotic personality, *psychotic residues* exist as archaic pieces of disorganizing anxiety or rage which have never been acknowledged, named, and integrated.[2] They remain embedded in a character structure that keeps them at bay. Unresolved, they linger on, affecting the life narrative and contributing at various times to a collapse of the self.

Bion's (1957) differentiation of psychotic from nonpsychotic thinking is instrumental in understanding that both these mental states coexist and play themselves out over time in the same personality. It enables us to avoid automatically equating psychotic with delusional or limiting psychotic to those who seemingly function well but have a *psychotic core* underneath (Eigen, 1986). Everyone is capable of having psychotic thoughts, psychotic anxiety, and psychotic rage in an otherwise nonpsychotic personality. In some persons, there is a longing for these residues of the self to be transformed and transcended.

PSYCHOTIC ANXIETY

The need to bring one's psychotic anxiety to the right analytic environment has been vividly illustrated by Little (1990). She described her internalization of the disorganizing psychotic anxiety that had plagued her

97

mother throughout her life, despite her other successes. Little finally brought herself to Winnicott after two previous analyses that had not reached it.[3]

Despite this acutely damaged part of her she had also functioned well enough to complete her medical studies, become an analyst, and take an active role in the intellectual life of the analytic community. The psychotic and nonpsychotic parts of her self coexisted. Winnicott understood her psychotic rage, could tolerate it, and was able to help contain it and work toward its integration with her nonpsychotic parts. It was a long and tempestuous task.

She began her analysis with him by a deliberate dramatic act of smashing his vase. Winnicott's response was first to remove himself from the room (in order to contain *his* hate) and then later to sweep up the pieces and replace the vase. His actions conveyed his comprehension of both *her* hate and *his* capacity to contain it. Unlike her previous analytic experiences, she could proceed knowing that her rage (and her anxiety) had not destroyed the other. This knowledge is a crucial feature of analytic containment. She had found her analytic home.

The chief characteristic of a "psychotic residue" is that *it will not quit* of itself unless treated, despite other aspects of the personality developing along more normal lines. The meaning of what is psychotic in a nonpsychotic person is conveyed in the first example. The collapse of the self owing to psychotic residues is clinically illustrated in the more extensive example of Ms. J. The latter also involves an unusual dramatization of a psychotic transference in a well-functioning neurotic woman. Both cases exemplify the search for the transforming object.

Psychotic Residues in a Neurotic Structure: The Case of Mr. I

Mr. I came to therapy with a proscribed agenda and a twinship selfobject need (Kohut, 1984) to help him carry out a difficult professional project. His task was to negotiate his way through a high-pressured prestigious institution to produce an extensive work of intellectual merit. He brought a background of knowledge to the task—which was the basis for his current invitation to produce this work—but felt insecure because his academic credentials had been not typical of those who had been similarly engaged by the institution. He sought treatment during this stressful period.

The structure of his personality was basically sound. In addition to his professional achievements, he had enjoyed a happy marriage for a number of years, was on congenial terms with his family, had long-standing friendships, could play as well as work, and related in a friendly way in our hours together. All these genuine assets also provided the character armor (Reich, 1949) that allowed him to function well and undisturbed through much of life. Unlike Little's tumultuous beginning of her work with Winnicott, the course of Mr. I's work began and continued evenly, with his psychotic anxiety emerging only at its very end.

The Course of the Therapy

Several increasing levels of completion of his task posed little difficulty for him. He was not "blocked" and his overall vitality spoke of an absence of neurotic conflict in many areas of his life. His lack of complete confidence, which had prompted him to seek help, was not unreasonable given the difficulty of his task. He had considerable interpersonal skill and was able to work out problems that called for mature aggression. For example, he struggled through his fear of the only staff member who was critical of him, who fed his anxiety that he was not qualified for the task. He took her on as much as necessary ("duked it out") and was successful in holding his own against her. He eventually earned her grudging respect. We later uncovered the competitive transferential aspects to his older sister in this configuration. However, she had been his only actual detractor among the many high-level people he answered to, and he was well regarded by the others who were overseeing the project.

He proved quite capable of getting through the intellectual and interpersonal demands of the task, despite his anxiety about being good enough to be "up there with the big boys." Eventually, he approached completion, and the success of his project was assured. By this time, he had an excellent offer of a position in another city, owing to his visibility and success with this project. He had come far and all looked well. Then our soon-to-end work took a surprising turn.

He now faced the last part of his task, a minor ritual of presenting a summary of his findings to a lay audience. It was only a formality, and his project had already been fully approved. This final task should prove much easier than the rigorous presentations he had had to make all along the way to his knowledgeable board members, who could have found him out of his depth. He also had considerable experience in public speaking. Essentially, all he had to do was "show up" and present his findings, which were interesting and uncontroversial.

However, he started to fill our hours with thoughts of dread of his upcoming talk, and after several sessions of his coming back to it I noticed my *silent* incredulous reaction of, "You're bringing this up *again*?" His trepidation, in the light of all he had accomplished, did not make sense to me. Theodore Reik (1947) pointed out the analytic usefulness of *surprise*, so I paid attention to that which seemed "senseless" to me. It usually signifies that I am experiencing a projective communication because I am not yet empathically in tune and knowledgeable, and the patient has to prod me further (see chapter eight).

To my mind, Mr. I had already successfully dived into a very deep pool and had surfaced triumphantly with his prize catch. Now he faced—with unrelenting anxiety—what was tantamount to the crossing of a puddle. I then realized that he was experiencing an intense performance anxiety that had a "stage fright" quality to it. Gone was the successful man who could purposively stride into the task at hand. A masterful Charlton Heston had become a nervous Woody Allen!

Within this same brisk and efficient personality was the little boy who went alone, ill prepared to perform in the school talent show. He particularly recalled being humiliated at one such performance and "was sure" his sister played better than he did. (We were able to link this recollection to his problem with the detracting older woman colleague whom he had successfully prevailed against.) The earlier event was both traumatic in itself and as a memory also signified a greater anxiety.

The anxious reliving of the inadequate performance further evoked a persistent idea about his father that had deeply affected his development. Neither of his parents had attended the event, which left him barely able to contain his feelings by himself. His anxiety was natural given the circumstances and never fully metabolized. It could still be kindled in those moments when his characteristic counterphobic pluck and fortitude wore thin. Most importantly, it was fueled by a dread-filled thought that lingered on.

Like the patient in chapter one who seized on my "So-o-o-o" to address a pathological part of her internal world, Mr. I took what was on hand—his upcoming talk and its attendant performance anxiety, as well as our impending termination—to confront a lurking demon. Not only was his anxiety due to stage fright, but the stage fright itself reflected a damaged piece of him that did not allow the anxiety to quit. Having found sanctuary in the containment of our work, like Little (1990) he seized his chance to give coherence to this damaged part of himself.

It was further revealed that his much-admired father was often not present at other crucial developmental events. The ultimate desertion came at his father's early death, just as Mr. I was finishing college. It left him with an unintegrated morbid thought that haunted him for years. It was his belief that his father, a man of strong intellectual interests would really have preferred not to have had children and would have traded them for greater success in the world. It may have been his father's absences at the times he was truly needed by his son that fed the thought that the father had the wish to be "not-father" to him. The internalization and reification of "no-father" greatly affected his own decision not to have children, and to concentrate on his professional life.

In the course of our work, he was able to revisit this regret about his choice to remain childless in a nonetheless strong marriage. Both partners devoted themselves instead to their ideals of work and to each other, which worked well for them. His "performance anxiety" was a signifier of the residual terror of the unprotected little boy who walked alone across the empty stage, and whose father was not there to wish him well. What should have been an "easy piece" to play instead evoked his terror that his father may have longed for his nonexistence.

The brisk vigor Mr. I usually displayed for the world was the defensive armor of a second skin. While he did not continuously "leak out," like a typical psychotic patient, this protective shield could fall off, exposing his thin psychic skin. He both longed for his father and took pride in the "not-needing" of him. These conflicting needs deeply disturbed him. At times like the upcoming talk, his father was the *absent object* (O'Shaughnessy, 1964), leaving him unable to be the "man." His shame about his little boy neediness remained, and his residue of psychotic anxiety contained vestiges of a fear of his loss of valor.

Rather than experience the demands of his employer as unwanted controls that restricted him, he had met his assignments with zest because doing so provided him with the support necessary to do the task. It afforded him selfobject containment, as did our work. When faced with having to go it alone—as he would have to do once again on a public stage and in the shadow of our soon-to-end connection—ordinary anxiousness became phobic panic. Despite all his genuine successes, in the timelessness of the trick of memory, he would be walking out on that stage to play his little piece, haunted by the fear that he was probably unwanted and certainly not good enough.

Glimpsing a Psychotic Transference: The Case of Ms. J

> *If the patient cannot distinguish . . . two environments, then a psychotic transference develops.*
> —PETER GIOVACCHINI, *Psychoanalytic Practice*

Finding the right analytic home to transform one's psychotic residues took an unusual turn in this case. Ms. J managed to convey this aspect of herself less literally than had Margaret Little breaking Winnicott's vase, but no less dramatically. She did it through the medium of a psychotic transference to a colleague.[4]

During our initial consultation, Ms. J suddenly expressed a thought about working with a male therapist. Since the referral source was the patient's former therapist, who knew me well, I was surprised that gender was introduced at this late juncture and was certain it had arisen in the context of our meeting. I was aware that the initial analytic session often reflects the patient's leading anxiety about how the analyst might fail her (Ogden, 1989, pp. 169–194), but I made no further interpretations at that time. I chose instead to take her words at face value and offered her the names of two male colleagues.

My ready acquiescence to referring her was based on an assessment of her history of "man trouble." I went along with her idea that she *literally* might need to work this out with a man. I later thought that the approach of summer might have been a countertransference factor in encouraging her to go off and explore. It turned out that she, indeed, needed to go off with a man—and carry out her summer project. She returned at summer's end, bringing with her a picture of her experience.

Because her desire for a male therapist seemed so literal, and I was not certain of its meaning, I deliberately chose as potential transference figures two colleagues who were different in background, intellectual style, personality, and mental makeup. However, both were experienced and excellent therapists whom I shall refer to as Dr. A and Dr. B.

The Nontransference to Dr. A
Dr. A was a skillful clinician who previously had taken over the case of a young man, after years of my working with him, because the patient needed to complete his psychosexual development with a male figure. Dr. A was ideal for this man because the patient would be able to experience him as both tender and masculine. That patient—who found in Dr. A a "strong but sensitive" paternal object (instead of a bullying, weak and insensitive one)—was finally able to achieve a long-desired goal of marrying. I speculated that Ms. J also might need to complete such a developmental task.

Dr. A was unlike Ms. J's father and the man to whom she had been married. She consulted with him only once, after which he called to tell me she would not be working with him and had gone on to see Dr. B. Dr. A's recollection of her was of an intelligent, interesting woman. He noted that she seemed anxious and despairing as she discussed her stalemated situation with her current boyfriend. Although Dr. A was usually adept at establishing an empathic alliance, he felt that there was an "absence of transference." She later told me that she had not found Dr. A "warm." Her remark was a code for his not being a "hot enough" transferential object (see chapter one regarding analytic objects of identification).

The Psychotic Transference with Dr. B

Dr. B called to say that Ms. J had begun work with him. I assumed that the similarity of their intellectual and cultural backgrounds had been useful in this case and that these partial identifications had acted as an entryway for working through deeper issues. They did, but they also had the effect of eliciting the same problem with Dr. B as she had with the previous important men in her life.

In her few sessions with him, the ghost of her father had immediately asserted itself. In its positive aspect—Dr. B's background presence, from which she took strength—she immediately resolved the long-standing masochistic attachment to a man whose intentions were "not honorable." At the same time, however, she began to experience Dr. B as a very disturbing presence.[5] All the while she seemed to him to be "hesitant" and "tepid" about committing to the work, but unbeknown to him she was experiencing the following: "There was a 30-foot wall of water coming at me, threatening to completely engulf me. There was no way around this wall—it had no edges. I felt trapped and terrified."

She did not tell him. Her apparent "lack of commitment" to their work served to protect her from being further caught in the undertow of a dangerously familiar (engulfing) object. Dr. B was so similar to the other men in her life that being with him activated a powerful signal anxiety that precluded her being able to distinguish between Dr. B as an intelligent, strong, and caring therapist and Dr. B as another arrogant and dangerous male.

He was, indeed, an "object of identification," but he also evoked the bad object with whom she felt trapped with "no way around it." She did not become part of the work, and she took flight instead. She returned to work with me and brought these vital data with her.

The Return

Her experience represented a necessary counterpoint to my primary identification with her nonpathological strengths. Its imagery unmistakably conveyed her psychotic terror and rage as clearly as Little's (1990) had communicated hers to Winnicott. I could have a better grasp of the psychotic residues affecting her woman to man relationships. After she had made good use of her time with Dr. B to resolve an attachment to a bad object—and with the clarity that came with her transferential experience—she had renewed her hope that I would be able to help her resolve her difficulties.

Her returning and relating her psychotic transference with Dr. B also did service as a cautionary tale, which helped us, in turn, to avoid creating a transference psychosis—derailing the work and causing her to flee.[6]

I was now alert to this part of her in whatever way it might express itself in our work.

Psychotic Residues in the Present Transference

She had made me aware of her vulnerability to engulfment through this vivid visual imagery. Therefore, I did not oppose her when she chose to come only once a week, although I would have preferred to meet more often. I neither interpreted this as her "resistance" nor urged her to take on more sessions than she could handle. Although I gave her a good deal of latitude and avoided exacerbating her terror of engulfment, she was still unconsciously searching for a way to bring this part of her directly into our work in a way that would not sink it. When the opportunity I offered arrived, she took it. This time she did not hide her feelings, and we could optimally use them.

A crisis arose through the matter of finding the right hour to fit her schedule. Having brought herself back to treatment unexpectedly, I was short on hours and could give her only temporary ones at first. This temporary situation did not appear to create an immediate problem, which I had expected it might. As soon as I could offer her a regular hour, however, she accepted it but with great reluctance as it was not a comfortable one for her vis-à-vis her work. Nonetheless, she took the hour feeling that she had no alternative and immediately showed signs of distress.

At first, I experienced her oscillations around the hour as confusing. It was usual for others to find it a prime time, and she had complete freedom to set her own hours at work. If the time did not suit her, however, she was also free to continue a bit longer with the temporary scheduling, although I understood the latter was intrinsically unsatisfying. It put in motion her feelings of being trapped. Her distress became palpable, but the quality of it did not make complete sense to me. This was a pivotal time when I could have activated a transference crisis in an area of the patient's sensitivity.

Because I was now alert to the possibility that she was communicating the part of herself that could be "made crazy," I was able to avoid reacting to her as merely demanding, or by thinking of her as "unreasonable" (Giovacchini, 1985, p. 11). Instead, I took her distress as a communication I did not yet fully understand, and it became the analytic issue. One day, at the end of a productive session, she once again expressed a hopelessness that I would ever get just the right permanent hour for her and, in a black, agitated funk, said, "Perhaps I should give it to the end of the year and then go to someone who could give me the right hour."

I was startled, but I reflected a moment and responded, "Look, don't get in too much despair about how you feel about not having the right hour. You know, we only have a little to go on, working once a week now.

Your feeling awful about my not getting it right for you is one of the few ways you can show me how confusing and terrible it is for you to have the thought that the only way you can have your needs met is by *giving in* to someone else. It's not a signal that you'll have to leave this to get what you need—or that you will never get it from the other. It's a sign that something important is getting worked on."

She stood up, thought a bit, and, with a little smile breaking through her thundercloud, said, "Oh, okay—that makes sense!"

Her anguish lifted, to our mutual relief. A power struggle ending in disaster might have emerged had I insisted on getting her to accept my reality without truly understanding hers. I understood the essential, life-and-death "Whose reality is it?" issue underneath the problem of the right hour. The problem seemed now to naturally resolve itself.

The Course of the Work
I learned that she had a sensitivity to entitlement or arrogance, especially if she experienced it in figures of authority. When it was stimulated with men—as it had been with her father and her husband and with Dr. B—it was "crazy-making" for her, especially in situations where she was also needy (as with Dr. B), or erotically connected, as in her relationship to her husband. These relationships were colored by the archaic oedipal attachment she had with her father and had never worked through. The original strong libidinal connection she had had with him as a child turned sour as she grew to experience him as pathologically needy and dependent on her mother and his children. This Kafakaesque view of the man–woman relationship carried over into her own marriage. The stronger the libidinal need she had of her object, the greater the threat it presented to her.

In our work, my own position of power, which had me in control of the time, plus *my need* for her to be comfortable with the situation as it stood presented a similar configuration, albeit in a less eroticized form. Her agitation was similar to that she had experienced with Dr. B, but her expressing herself and my understanding of it enabled me to contain it. I did not lapse into arrogance myself by responding to her as if she were "unreasonable." Insofar as my intervention was "supportive," it was because it enabled her to better integrate her feelings by making sense of them. It did not so much "gratify" her, or even "support the defenses" as it helped her name her psychotic-making dilemma and lessen its hold.[7]

Discussion
In analyzing the foregoing, I think the following narrative was at work. As a woman in a biological hurry, Ms. J had seized the transferential opportunities she had with Drs. A and B and me. She unconsciously made a

rapid assessment during our first session that, although I comprehended the nature of her intellect and creative drive, it would "take too long" to get at this disturbed man–woman part of her with me. I would neither stimulate it nor understand it. She left me with an unthought purpose.

She went next to Dr. A but rapidly skipped over him, "knowing" that there would not be an intense enough mental connectedness. This lack would preclude the process of identification necessary for projections to take place (Tausk, 1919). Ms. J then went to the heart of the matter with Dr. B, with whom she could better identify. He provided her with "just right" transferential dynamic and projective opportunity. During this period of exploration, however, I appear to have remained the "background presence of primary identification" (Grotstein, 1990, p. 402). She returned with a hope that the "visual aid" of her transference to Dr. B would help the work. Neither planned nor conscious, each of us was capable of a strong response to visualization.

Adhesive Identifications

The result of her experience with Dr. B enabled me to understand more quickly her most disturbing internal object-relationship, which accounted for the derailing of her emotional development. Perhaps the most interesting question that we could ask is: why did the potential for a psychotic transference to Dr. B exist in Ms. J's mental makeup?

Her reaction to Dr. B is best understood as coming from the adhesive identification she had with her father (Meltzer, 1975). Early on, Ms. J was pulled into her father's limited orbit of reality, which became increasingly inadequate for her. It precluded her having the free choice in love and work that partial identifications allow. In defining herself through an adhesive identification, there is "the defensive adherence to the object in the service of allaying the anxiety of disintegration. Imitation and mimicry, for instance, are utilized in an effort to make use of the *surface of the object* as if it were one's own" (Ogden, 1989, p. 71, italics added). In the service of remaining adhesively attached to her father—despite her now virulent dislike of him—she married a man whose background and profession her father could comprehend. Inevitably, she was pulled toward experiencing her marital relationship as identical to her Kafakaesque view of the parental one, despite the fact that there were actual differences.

Although, unlike her mother, she pursued a professional life outside the home, the adhesive identifications persisted. She directed her formidable intellect to enter her husband's profession and her father's choice for her. That she could succeed at this job though it was of little actual interest speaks to the caliber of her intelligence as well as the power of the mimicry. She also felt *impelled* to take care of her husband, who she felt *expected* her to do so—just as her father had expected her mother to care for him.

Her marriage to this man was both a result and extension of this adhesive identification with her father. The choice of both the husband and the profession was wrong for what she ideally needed. She could not say—as did Tanazaki (1933)—that what she constructed was no less than what she wanted. At the time, it was far less.

She eventually successfully pursued the field of interest that was professionally right for her. She found the strength to do this through a partial identification with her mother's strong cultural interests, even as she disidentified with her mother's role as a homemaker. In doing so, she carried out her mother's unrealized ambitions. She used the identification with her father's professionalism—if not his profession—as the entryway to establish her own professional life and carry out that part of her mother's ideal.

In choosing a partner, it was harder to extricate herself from the libidinal enmeshment with her father on which her earlier psychic life had depended. The forces at work there were stronger, more complex, more confusing, and more ambiguous for her. She expressed the essential dilemma in the metaphor of the psychotic transference to Dr. B, who—in his "need" to have her commit to the therapy—called up the old dynamic whose subtext was, "I once again have need for the strength of a man. But I will be overwhelmed by the sheer force of his presence and be pulled under by *his* needs which are doomed to overwhelm mine."

Her father had rescued her from a disastrous maternal collapse in early childhood. However, he himself was a needy, depressive, passively dependent man who operated within a narrow sphere of psychological safety, relying on his wife for everything but the actual carrying out of his professional life. Ms. J saw her mother as drowned in the neediness of her father, taking for herself only the time she could filch, outmaneuvering others by remaining indefinite. The rage accompanying Ms. J's terror in the psychotic transference to Dr. B provided the necessary push to either get out or go under. As Mitchell (1993) writes, "Ogden points the way in which the pure loving and hating of the paranoid-schizoid position can serve as the wellsprings of passion, breaking apart the measured balance of ambivalence and integration when they have become stale and constraining" (p. 258).

Thus, when Ms. J first put me aside, refused Dr. A, broke with her boyfriend, and fled Dr. B, she signified the breaking up of an archaic dependency that had been damaging for her and no longer served her well. She was ready to move on from the psychic space in which feelings of love were always accompanied by a possibility of engulfment and the threat of annihilation of self.

The Maternal Selfobject Failure

The other relevant question to ask in a search for an understanding of the psychotic transference is: how did Mr. J's father become so important a figure to her that the identification with him was adhesive? In turning to him and clinging to him as a young child, she was turning away from an increasingly problematic maternal figure.

Ms. J had come to experience a desperate need for a compensatory figure to fill in for the elusive mother. A dithery woman by nature, her mother became even less present for Ms. J following the birth of additional siblings and the increased demands on her. Her mother relied on evasiveness and indefiniteness to help maintain her own autistic space in the management of her dependent husband and several children. Although she took care of her family, she would negatively assert herself by never committing to a time, a place, or a plan. She seemed instead to run on whim. This was the only way she escaped her confinement, and Ms. J was temperamentally unsuited to that style of control, preferring things to be more certain and to her strong-willed liking. More important in her own development, her mother's indefiniteness conveyed to her that she was very ambivalent about her role and fought against feeling imprisoned in her family life.

Ms. J's visual image of the anxiety the mother generated in her holds a clue to understanding the overattachment she later made to her father. Ms. J said her mother was "like a two-dimensional canvas that had no surface texture—you couldn't get a 'purchase' on it; it was flat. You couldn't get a sense from her of something definite. Just when you thought she was 'there'—she wasn't!"

She had turned to her father as a more solid presence who relished the dependency of his children, which he compulsively fostered. His once welcome attention to her had its price. He took pleasure in Ms. J's intellect but appropriated it. He carried a not-so-secret ideal that she follow the professional model of his family. He believed that he was bestowing a badge of honor on her, but it became a stranglehold. In the classical sense, she had an oedipal victory but it was a Pyrrhic one.

The Paternal Selfobject Failure

However more present her father was in comparison with her mother, he was there only by default and good only as a background presence of identification for her childhood years. The limitations of his unimaginative stolidness began to wear after then. He did not seem to want her to grow up or beyond his sphere of influence. Ms. J experienced a severe lack in his comprehension of who she was as she entered young womanhood.

Benjamin's (1995) observation that women have a great need for the father to grant them an independent sphere of initiative is especially relevant in Ms. J's case. The task of the father is to convey this separateness and, at the same time, accept and properly contain the natural libidinal attachment that so powerfully unites them. Paternal failure to negotiate either the erotic attachment or the daughter's independent sphere of initiative may have serious pathological repercussions. Ms. J's father did not err on the side of erotic seduction; but, after rescuing her from her absent mother, he offered her only his collapsed self, which precluded his encouraging individuation and separation from him.

He failed to release her to her own strivings, and that failure acted like a seduction and abandonment. Like Mr. X (chapter three), she lacked Kafka's ruthlessness in pursuing her own passions. She fell back on adhesive identifications that were inadequate. To break from the earliest object of love is still as hard as it was in Freud's time. Our earliest libidinal objects still linger in our background. Breaking from Fairbairn's (1954, pp. 105–125) "exciting and rejecting object" can still create havoc, and we still are prone to feel both exquisite love and exquisite hate toward our meaningful objects. Changing any part of this is in the nature of a heroic task and most often cannot be done without therapeutic intervention.

In trying to break the yoke of marital bondage, Ms. J later chose men whose interests now more suitably mirrored hers. In their own need to remain independent, the men cherished that aspect of her, as well as her capacity for loyalty and attachment. She was a perfect companion and, in that sense, an ideal woman for them. The difficulty came only when her longings to create her own family met up with their needs not to do so. It was in that frustrating place that the drama with Dr. B was enacted.

THE NATURE OF "DELUSION" IN NEUROSIS

Ogden's (1989) observation on transference is useful here: "Transference in a paranoid-schizoid mode has been termed '*delusional*' (Little, 1958) or '*psychotic*' (Searles, 1963) transference. The analyst is not experienced as *similar to* the original childhood object, he *is* the original object" (p. 21). Because Ms. J was not psychotic in the usual sense, her transference experience in a psychotic mode illustrates some further issues. The first is that each experience of the patient, delusional or not, is a form of *communication*—as was so dramatically illustrated in her case—and comes from the capacity for imaginative thinking.[8] Another issue is that to fully understand Ms. J's feelings of engulfment with Dr. B, it must be understood that—although she was *not* psychotic—in her experience of unendurable engulfment with Dr. B, he was not so much only transferentially *like* her father, he *was* her father—at least for that moment.

One learns *not* to make "as if" statements to *delusional* patients such as, "It is *as if* I am your mother." Or, "You feel *like* a robot" (Ogden, 1989, p. 22). For the delusionally psychotic patient, the analyst *is* the mother—and that he is a different gender from the mother is a mere inconvenience. A patient could very well correctly respond the his latter comparison *to* a robot: "I don't *feel* like a robot—I *am* a robot." I have found it correct to assume that the same self-state of identification operates even for nondelusional patient.

Even with neurotic patients the feeling state of the disturbed part is not an "as if" state, but rather a state of "I am." The anguish Ms. J felt in her marriage was not because she had been driven to choose a man who was "like" her father. He *was,* for her, her father, and she became as anguished, distraught, stifled, and diminished as a wife as she had been as a daughter. She had not finished her business of an adhesive attachment to her father and was compelled to continue it with her husband. In Ogden's (1989) paradigm, the fact that her husband was not *actually* her father (and in some ways was unlike her father) was a mere inconvenience—just as Dr. B was neither father nor husband but was, at the same time, both of them for her. It is only in that way that the true nature of the anguish becomes unmistakably understood.

In a neurotic person, when the psychotic residue is activated, there is a collapse of the self, and

> in a paranoid/schizoid mode, there is virtually no space between symbol and symbolized; the two are emotionally equivalent. This mode of symbolization termed *symbolic equation* (Segal, 1957), generates a two-dimensional form of experience in which everything is what it is. There is almost no interpreting subject mediating between the percept (whether external or internal) and one's thoughts and feelings about that which one is perceiving. . . . In this mode, thoughts and feelings are not experienced as personal creations but as fact, things-in-themselves, that simply exist. Perception and interpretation are experienced as one and the same. The patient is trapped in the manifest since surface and depth are indistinguishable [pp. 20-21].

It is interesting in this context to observe that the imagery employed by Ms. J was of an impenetrable wall of water (her father) and a "two-dimensional canvas" (her mother). In these images there is a flattened surface that lacks a dimension of depth. They reflect the despair of a woman who is capable of emotional depth and imagination but is living a life without it. It is this lack of depth and texture to her reality she was struggling with that I found myself responding to in our work.

For example, after some time, when she had broken through her isolated lifestyle to engage in the rich panoply of activities that her now correct, self-chosen profession afforded her, I would respond to her report of these activities with, "Oh, just like real people do" or "That's real too"—without being certain at the time what I was saying or why I was conveying it in this oddly simple-minded way. They were activities that reflected her emerging independent initiative, and I might have heard the remaining "psychotic thought" of her adhesive identification—that there was no true reality outside of the narrow one of her father's mind. She had to struggle against this prohibition. She was taking the first steps of a psychologically reborn child, and I was creating the language of her new self. As in so many expressions of self, I had pulled up something from my past. My responses were those of a Wittgensteinian (1953) "word-game" (*Sprachtspiel*) through which the child learns to identify and differentiate what is self and what is the nature and meaning of things that are outside the self.[9] I was naming for her that which belonged to her real self.

I was naming her new reality in the face of her lingering doubts of its substance. I was not so much approving her activities as recognizing that it was difficult for her to feel real within her own expression of self, as it increasingly took on forms that the parental imagos could not relate to. These were psychotically confusing issues of attachment and dependency that had tortured her thinking and development.

Notes

[1] See Giovacchini (1985) for a discussion of the psychotic aspects of "The Unreasonable Patient" from a helpful *dual perspective of* both the patient's disorder *and* the empathic problems of the analyst.

[2] This chapter concerns the psychotic residues I have encountered most frequently: anxiety and rage. Other psychotic residues of the self can be unrelenting in their imperviousness to change and their destructiveness to self or other but are not discussed here.

[3] Guntrip (1975) also writes of his search to have his damaged part understood and contained in his analyses with Fairbairn and Winnicott. In the end, it was his self-analysis that brought him peace.

[4] I am indebted to Ms. J and my colleagues for helping me to present this material. I have given as few actual identifying details as possible in order to preserve confidentiality, while conveying the essential meaning of the phenomenon.

[5] Although, in my subjectivity, I did not experience Dr. B as arrogant (nor did I experience Dr. A as not warm), I could understand how she did so. It would be a

serious technical error to override the germ of truth in her perceptions and what in these figures it stimulated. To do so would be to treat her perceptions merely as unfounded hostile projections, which is an analytic position of arrogance. Also encoded in her perception of arrogance or lack of warmth is her fear of her own.

[6] Grotstein (1981) and Giovacchini (1985) have helped to make this useful distinction, which is essentially about how much distance there is from the experience itself. A collapse into a transference psychosis, even with nondelusional patients, is a very difficult, sometimes impossible pitfall for the analyst/therapist to negotiate.

[7] "Supportive," like "gratifying," may have a pejorative connotation in analytic work. However, meeting a need (especially the need to be known) is not merely gratifying but essential. Thus, all interpretations that are subjectively correct for the patient are "supportive."

[8] The communicative and imaginative aspects of a delusion are further discussed in chapter eight, in connection with Tausk's (1919) classic paper, "The Influencing Machine."

[9] The philosopher Ludwig Wittgenstein conceived of learning in terms of "wordgames"—that is, that a child learns that the sphere being tossed is a "ball" by associating, each time, to "Throw me the *ball*" or "Catch the *ball*." Language is an internalization of games of naming.

Chapter Seven

From "Hysteroid Dysphoria" to "Posttraumatic Stress Disorder"

A Case for Psychoanalysis in the Era of Neurobiology

I have come to believe that there are mind memories and body memories. Mind memories are documentary, grounded in who, what, when, where. Body memories are a reliving of sensations and have a tendency to blot out the documentary factors.
—SUZANNAH LESSARD, *The Architect of Desire*[1]

Increasing attempts to treat states of mood through biochemical means since the 1950s—and the current emphasis on affective disorders—enable us to consider Freud's (1923) dictum, "the first ego is the bodily ego" (p. 26) as newly relevant for our own time. Interest in the somatic aspects of affect and mood from varying points of view is relevant to this chapter—from psychoanalysis (Krystal, 1988; Grotstein, 1995), psychology (Tomkins, 1962–63), and psychopharmacology and neurobiology (Leibowitz and Klein, 1979; van der Kolk, 1994).

The current dialectic between neurobiology and psychoanalysis is reflected in this mix. Since my primary concern is increasing the effectiveness of analytic therapy, these observations, taken as a whole, are important contributions. They enable us to give fuller meaning to the complexity of the interaction of mind and body in such states of disorder as depression and anxiety as they affect the collapse of the self. Each discipline adds a different piece to the puzzle which can be gathered into a coherent whole.

Hysteroid dysphoria, coined in the late 1950s by psychopharmacologist Donald Klein (1968), was his category of atypical depression belonging to a general class of *nasty disorders of mood*. While use of the term hysteroid dysphoria never came into widespread vogue, and much of the associated psychiatric literature seems to doubt its utility as a special

113

category, it marked the beginning of the push to find a biochemical, rather than a psychoanalytic, solution to disregulated states. It continues to stimulate thinking (see Grotstein, 1995; Kramer, 1993), and it proved useful in the case presented here both for what it can and what it cannot describe.

Similarly, my reference to posttraumatic stress disorder (PTSD) concerns the effects of traumatic events that are "remembered" (van der Kolk, 1994) by the body. Kramer (1993) observed that

> PTSD, originally applied to people who had suffered recent trauma (like shell shock . . .), but is now used also in reference to adults who suffered stresses at crucial developmental phases of childhood. The emergence of PTSD is, under a new name, and with *more attention to biological damage*, the rebirth of the traumatic theory of neurosis and personality disorder, a century after Freud first proposed it [p. 372, italics added].

I share this view and illustrate in this chapter that "trauma" includes the experience of such violent emotions as an infant's terror than was uncontained by another and remained unmetabolized in the bodily self. It also includes the trauma of growing up in an atmosphere of severe neglect or constantly demeaning criticism. In a sense, for some persons, life is lived—or relived—in a state of incompletely metabolized posttraumatic shock. The therapeutic task is to make living with these feeling states bearable until they recede as a function of new experience, new learning, and new attachments—and to really understand how medication works or does not work for a given person.

Each era has had its preferred diagnostic metaphor, usually reflecting a single perspective. Since the overt collapse in this case was after the birth of a baby, it was first thought that Ms. G was undergoing a "postpartum depression," the diagnosis with which she was referred to me. What began as "postpartum depression" was later reified by all concerned as "The Depression," and unsuccessful treatments, both psychoanalytic and biochemical, were geared to those diagnoses.

The diagnoses were catchalls that eluded the subtlety and complexity of her self-experience and initially made treatment from either psychoanalytic or biochemical means ineffective. If it had been in the 1950s—given the touch of drama and panic in her personality—Ms. G might well have been diagnosed as suffering from the newly coined hysteroid dysphoria. It is quite possible that she would not have been more successfully treated biochemically as a hysteroid dysphoric had she been a patient in that earlier time. It is doubtful that the intent of that diagnosis—*to medicate out* a nasty state of mood—would have sufficed any more than do those in the present era.

In keeping with the changing times, over the years she was successively diagnosed as having dissociative disorder, attention deficit disorder, and, finally posttraumatic stress disorder.[2] She was treated with conventional antidepressant and antianxiety medications popular at the time, again with incomplete success.[3] The medication itself became a source of uncertainty, frustration, and anxiety. Each diagnosis was intended to be explanatory—and had some element of truth—but they all functioned to limit thinking and misguide treatment. They were the proverbial tail wagging the dog.

What finally emerged in the course of our work was that, hidden beneath her mask of depression, lurked an elusive kind of anxiety that haunted her and could make her mood-state and finding appropriate medication a torment. It was a psychotic anxiety that took time to clearly understand, having been masked by flare-ups of affective and mood disorders. They were the symptoms of something more pervasive in her structure. It was only after we grasped her psychotic anxiety that it began to mitigate and medication became useful.

Ms. G's case is one for our time as it raises issues of the nature of treatment—analytic and biochemical—and the implications of diagnosis. It is especially helpful in teaching us more about the relationship of soma to psyche. Therefore, I have framed this case around two issues: first is the issue of the *psychoanalytic theory,* which is most pertinent to Ms. G's case. The second issue—coming in our neurobiological era—is the philosophical one of the *mind–body split* and the question of how it can be resolved in our current clinical atmosphere.

THE CASE OF MS. G

Ms. G sought intensive analytic therapy following a diagnosis of postpartum depression some years ago. With a rapid flurry of calls—from the consulting colleague, the patient's therapist, and from the patient herself, who was en route from another city to meet with me along with her husband and child—her case had a zany flavor to it. Hers was a collapse of the self involving the intercomplexity of mind and body that activated a good many people.

She was accompanied to the hour by her immediate family in a dramatic preliminary consultation. She spoke movingly of her "depression" and—almost as an aside—her great fear of being left alone. Her husband spoke soothingly to her. When their baby cried, one thought it was "gas," and the other said it was a response to the excitement and tension in the room. They were both right! The baby, like her mother, Ms. G, had an easily disregulated system. They were all to return to their home city and finalize their decision to relocate.

They did so some months later, and, on the day they arrived, Ms. G telephoned from the train station and cheerfully announced that she "was heading for inpatient psychiatric treatment at one of the local hospitals, but that [she'd] be in touch!" She soon was.

Using the ward pay phone as her office, she organized arrangements for household help, for her mother to come down to care for her baby, for my contacts with her psychiatric resident, and for whatever else was necessary for living the good life! I remarked to her that she seemed to function better in a depressed state than most people did when they are feeling well. A nervous young resident was relieved and happy to discharge her to my care.

It was only years later that I understood that in the preliminary consultation she had unconsciously assured herself that I would welcome a new analytic child and that she would have a good home.[4] Although she had not been psychiatrically hospitalized before or since, she had "stopped by the hospital" to bring herself home as the reborn baby. This time, however, she was determined not to "suffer the catastrophe of premature psychological birth" (Tustin, 1981a, p. 183)—"colicky" or not!

The course of our work together indicated that Ms. G and I shared an ideal from the very beginning—her wish to be properly cared for, and mine to care for her properly. It was the first of our *mutually constructed* model scenes that would come to represent our work together (Lachmann and Lichtenberg, 1992).[5] The search to determine "what was wrong" was the metaphor for our joint project.

In fathoming her case, I recalled her previous therapist's injunction, "She will make you forget your other patients." While this did not happen, I believe the former therapist's caution reflected the patient's communicative projection (see chapter eight) to have a deep and consistent interest paid her in order to get well. She was not to be "dropped from mind," and she remained successful in having me think about her—and what was wrong with her—for many years. In a sense, taking on the puzzle and challenge of her case met the "analyst's selfobject need" (Bacal and Thomson, 1996) as well as her own.

The Clinical Search

After we settled into steadily working together several times each week with some limited help from medication, the first thing to draw my attention was her highly complex lifestyle, which always seemed to involve intense preoccupation with a great many people. This persistent hoard of objects in her thoughts and life was unique in my experience. On the alert for explanatory ideas, I then came across a description by Grotstein

(1986): "a new category known as hysteroid dysphoria: an entity known for its particular hypersensitivity to *object loss* and its compensatory use of objects in an entangled, addicted manner" (p. 7, italics added). This description struck me as exactly capturing her intense mental preoccupation with people and her pattern of incessant and complicated connections with an unusual number of them. Keeping her in mind, I researched hysteroid dysphoria, which still has relevance to the issues raised today about diagnosis, treatment, and the redefined role of psychoanalysis.

The Metaphor of Hysteroid Dysphoria

Hysteroid dysphoria as a diagnostic category arose from Donald Klein's (1968) essential dissatisfaction with Freud's theory of anxiety as caused by intrapsychic conflict. Thus, panic could not effectively be relieved by "talking about it" in psychoanalysis. Klein would instead have said that someone like Ms. G was "simply suffering from extremes of reactivity due to an unstable control mechanism which could be explained either as an inbuilt or acquired defect, or as an interaction of both" (Leibowitz and Klein, 1979, p. 561).

While I would have been in general agreement about the nature of the suffering, I would not agree with his conclusions regarding functional autonomy, which followed. His conclusion implied that, if symptoms become unmoored from their origins, there is no longer any reason to imagine that truth (i.e., understanding) will have the power to heal (Kramer, 1993, p. 76). This I have not found to be so.[6] My own data suggest that the identifying and naming of her psychotic anxiety carried its own truth and had the effect of eventually considerably extinguishing it. Even if she had been an "easy to medicate" patient, I doubt that medication alone would have extinguished the anxiety as effectively as the analytic working through. Her panicky state of being masked her deeper anxiety.

However, Klein's thinking led to his creative attempts to solve the problem—particularly that of panic—biochemically. In an unexpected way, his thinking proved fruitful for my understanding of Ms. G and deepened my understanding of the "bodily self" and the role of analytic therapy in profound disorders of mood. It also brought to the fore the problems inherent in the biologizing of the mind.

Hysteroid dysphoria is still a useful metaphor even if it is no longer used as a diagnosis for our time. Klein was describing certain hypersensitive patients with atypical depressive symptoms, that is, excessive eating and sleeping rather than loss of appetite and sleeplessness. His patients seemed very vulnerable to object loss and had extreme difficulty with mood regulation. From the vantage point of the 1990s, it is clear that hysteroid dyphoria describes people who are experiencing what I consider major *disregularity of self*. Like Grotstein, I was intrigued by Klein's reference to "vulnerability to object loss" and now know that Ms. G's addictive object entanglements served as a "psychic second skin" to keep intact a leaking self. Medication was also sought as a second skin, but that did not provide it as well as the objects with whom she surrounded herself.

In a finding that seemed odd to researchers at the time, panicky patients were responding well to antidepressants. For in the 1950s—and to some extent in the present time—anxiety and depression were considered to be two distinct disorders. Furthermore, in one of the early studies that is especially relevant here, hospitalized patients who were successfully medicated for their panic attacks were still almost as frequently coming up to the nurses' station. The investigation showed that, although they no longer had the attacks, they had anxiety that the attacks would return! For that, they needed human contact (Kramer, 1993, pp. 81–82).

Although Klein thought of hysteroid dysphoria as a *chronic nonpsychotic* disturbance, in its refusal to quit, my patient's anxiety was similar to Little's (1993) report of her own lifelong disorganizing (psychotic) anxiety (see chapter six). This kind of psychotic anxiety exists alongside the healthy, nonpsychotic parts of the self and, as with Little, can be found in otherwise highly functioning people.

It was the "nonquitting" aspect of the anxiety underneath Ms. G's depression that eventually gave me the analyzable diagnostic clue to her psychodynamics. As noted in chapter six, *psychotic thoughts reflect residues of terror that can be present even without a disorder of mood and without the person being psychotic*. However, to treat a patient biochemically only for mood disorder without attention to underlying terror is to unmoor those residues further from their origin and make the feeling-state more experience distant and psychotic.

Grotstein (1986) found hysteroid dysphoria to be useful for psychodynamic thinking, especially in understanding the terror characteristic of psychogenic autism (see Tustin, 1986). Kramer (1993), in a scholarly treatment of Donald Klein's work, has thought through the puzzle of the implications of regulating mood disorder biochemically, an undertaking that led to his understanding of the "Prozac revolution." He noted what seemed to be Prozac's effectiveness in overcoming a *sensitivity to rejection*. The difference in the two angles of vision of Grotstein and Kramer complement each other.

It turned out that my patient could not be successfully medicated on Prozac. This lack of success may have been because she was prone to agitation—which Prozac sometimes exacerbates—or perhaps because she falls into that category now officially known as difficult to medicate. Being "difficult to medicate" may also indicate that we are dealing with underlying "traits" of being and not just "states" of mood (Grotstein, 1995, p. 7). I find a significant difference between rejection-sensitivity and the profound terror of object loss, which you can see in Ms. G's comment: "My husband doesn't understand. He doesn't have to be gone for a few days for me to feel this way—he just has to walk into the next room!"

It was clear that she was suffering from the experience of terror, not rejection. Technically, both are dysphoric states of a disregulated self; *but a morbid fear of object loss with an underlying terror of death and abandonment is not simply a mood state,* which would be altered by Prozac! It calls for more extensive "rewiring" than can reasonably be altered through biochemistry—and needs a working-through of psychotic anxiety with another human being.

It was only after I began to understand the meaning of her lifelong residue of psychotic anxiety—what her parents and teachers would critically and dismissively refer to as her "senseless worrying"—that the diagnostic picture cleared to our mutual satisfaction and led to more effective work. Understanding her psychotic terror led to a further consideration of the neurophysiological and genetic aspects of her condition. It evoked her state of being and did not lead to an automatic assumption that her condition could be "medicated out." As with Mr. I (chapter six), the persistence of worry that others think needless may point to a residue of psychotic anxiety that is most effectively extinguished through a psychodynamic working-through.

"Orphans of the Real"

Grotstein (1995) had a further important insight regarding patients whose intense *affective vulnerability* may be a function of insufficiencies in the *stimulus barrier* normally present at birth or the failure of build-up of the stimulus barrier that normally comes from the interconnectedness of infant–parent bonding and attachment.

Without this stimulus barrier, he saw these patients as unprotected "Orphans of the (Lacan's) 'Real.'" Buffeted about by their hypersensitivity and hyperirritability they can experience the *ordinary* as a *terrifying reality*. Their defective stimulus barrier leaves them vulnerable to the psychotic states of terror, as Tustin's (1986) observations of children with autistic-like features showed. Ms. G's reaction to her husband's leaving the room can be understood in this context.

For someone in this state, there is no event so ordinary that it cannot be experienced as a "black hole" of psychic abandonment and elemental depression. The naming and extinguishing of Ms. G's psychotic residues effectively built up the stimulus barrier necessary for withstanding affective vulnerability. *The selfobject containment* achieved through the analytic bonding was crucial to treatment and recovery.

Analytic Bonding and Attachment

The "subjective third" (Ogden, 1994) that Ms. G and I together constructed in the transference–countertransference was related to addressing the underlying primary failure of maternal attachment, which I had come to understand as central to her difficulties. It had profoundly affected her way of being in the world and rekindled her depressive and anxious states of mood. On looking back, I also found that the metaphors and theories I resonated to in my wish to understand her were those constructs which gave name to a vulnerable infant.

Although I consciously experienced her as strong and determined (which I kept in mind), I also knew that she had a hypersensitivity that was psychic in nature and somatic in expression. In resonating to that nonverbally, I remained calm, patient, amused, interested—and attached. These communications were atmospheric rather than in the usual form of interpretation, but they made the point. Two examples of maternal disconnection—her mother's and her own—were especially revealing:

We returned many times to the following story as a model scene. It occurred early on in our work when her mother—who had gained the ability to relate better to her as an adult in large part to her own emotional recovery—came to help out when Ms. G was hospitalized. She was far more functional than during Ms. G's childhood.

Even so, her mother was clocked at lasting four hours alone with Ms. G's "fussy baby" (who resembled Ms. G in this regard), before she engaged a professional nursemaid. On learning of this I responded "What took her so long?"

History was repeating itself, and this anecdote became part of the analytic narrative that Ms. G and I were forging. In the creation of our "subjective third," we jointly acknowledged she could not have been properly contained by this well-meaning but dysfunctional mother in her early years. She was, and always had been, "too much" for her mother.

At another point, Ms. G urged me to interview her mother during a visit. She felt it would be very worthwhile for our work, which turned out to be correct in a way that surprised us both. When her mother spoke of Ms. G's younger sibling, born when she was 18 months old, her mother suddenly said: "I never could connect to _____ [sister]!" Ms. G then coaxingly said to her mother, "Oh, Mother, not even a little?" "No," her mother said, "not at all." "But, Mother," Ms. G went on, "don't you think you could, now that_____ [sister] is grown?" Her mother paused and replied matter-of-factly, "No—no, I don't think so!"

Ms. G and I each registered our individual astonishment—which we covertly conveyed by catching the other's eye and giving a slight shrug of the shoulders. As shocking as this revelation was, it was a relief to hear what was known but until then had been unspoken. I referred to this refreshingly frank revelation many times later in the work—not only because I enjoyed its "W.C. Fields"[9] quality but because its truth gave her freedom. We used it also as a way of understanding that, like "Topsy," she would have to "grow herself" into being a mother, since it was not likely that she had had enough of one to internalize prior to adulthood.

The remarkable reparative self-awareness of which her mother was now capable helped reduce the anxiety and guilt Ms. G had about her limited capacity to respond appropriately to her own baby.[10] Encoded in the lack of connection to the sibling that her mother was reporting was the acknowledgment that it had wreaked further havoc with her connection to Ms. G.

The birth of a sibling when Ms. G was 18 months was indeed catastrophic for her. She had a long-standing "faulty memory" that she was sent to day care at 18 months, a placement that would have been extremely rare for that time, place, and her social class. It turns out that, in actuality, she was four years old when she was sent to a fashionable preschool. However, when she was 18 months old, *both she and her mother were disregulated* and *disaffected* by her sibling's birth, as the mother's comment implies.[11]

Whatever tenuous place she occupied in her mother's mind was now completely lost. I suspect that, with her father gone most of time during her first year, her mother was already disregulated prior to the birth of the sibling and alternated between clinging to Ms. G and feeling helpless in the face of the child's "fussiness." The situation was uncannily replayed when Ms. G's own, similarly "high-strung" child reached 18 months. Ms. G announced one day in session that she had passed a house with a "Day Care" sign in front and went in to check it out on impulse, saying that it might be a good thing for her daughter. There was not yet another child, nor did she have the press of professional demands that might make this an a priori necessity—and she had a full-time nursemaid. Her behavior struck me as "out of place."

Not yet having the correct information that it was the birth of a sibling and *not* having been sent to day care that took place at 18 months as she believed, I, startled, responded to her casually dropped statement, "What are you trying to do—clone your mother?"

It was not one of my more elegant interpretations, but it told her what part of herself needed to hear. She had been "dropped" as the baby at 18 months, although she had *not* actually been sent to day care. What she heard in my remark was an acknowledgment that something catastrophic had happened to her at that time that should not have happened. She was using my voice to "check out" such a possibility. She was haunted by an internal landscape that lacked a mother-who-could-care for her child. My unequivocal response was a battle with her identification with her mother's defective "I" (Racker, 1957), which was repeating itself with her own child.

There was an even more dramatic enactment between us regarding the strengthening of her desire to mother. Ms. G had been raised almost entirely by caretakers whom her mother was able to substitute for herself, especially after the birth of Ms. G's siblings, but who eventually left. She had begun to repeat this pattern in her own mothering, but also had an ideal—which she eventually reached—of being able to be the "mother."

From the beginning of our work, she had become obsessively attached to the full-time nursemaid who now lived with them, who was more necessary as a background presence for Ms. G's well-being than she was a caretaker for the child. Here dependency, however, did make her vulnerable to the potential loss of this elderly figure, as well as creating gaps in her own capacity for attaching to her child. I was alert to this when—in one of the few times during our long work together that she telephoned me in an emergency—she wanted to know "whether it was necessary to return home from her out-of-town trip that evening, because of an explosion in the kitchen she had learned about when she called home. The nursemaid (who had caused the accident with some flammable liquid) and her child "were only just shook up, but not hurt, and it was late anyway, and they could come home tomorrow . . . and what do you think?" I immediately replied, "If you move fast, you could catch the last plane home!"

My voice was the missing maternal link with the correct "instinct" to protect and comfort its young, which she was also searching for within herself. I voiced only what she already knew and needed to hear.

The Problems of Diagnosis and Diagnostic Categories

If the original diagnosis of postpartum depression had been correct, or meaningful, in Ms. G's case, it would have reflected a predominantly (although not always entirely) biologically based disruption of mood stemming from the loss of the placental hormone shortly after giving birth (C. Aisenstein, 1997, personal communication). In her case it was an incorrect diagnosis and a misleading oversimplification. Her case was far more complex than that.

The disregulation of mood that was set off during the earlier period had strong psychodynamic features that went beyond whatever was coming from hormonal sources. In contrast, there was no postpartum depression per se following the birth of her second child, which took place during the strong containment of our work. By the time of her second delivery, we had determined what had gone wrong before, and she took pains to avoid that scenario.

With the connectedness of our therapeutic work, she remained more in charge of the birth: letting the doctor know her mind before the delivery and avoiding the protracted period of frightening, isolated labor that had doomed the first birth experience. She also stayed more anchored to her professional identity than she had during the first pregnancy, when she had completely given up her place of security (and second skin) in the professional world.

In contrast to the birth of her first child, she experienced this second one as a great success and had a sense of satisfaction and well-being in the postpartum period. Not unrelated to the greater security of the experience all around, this baby—in contrast to Ms. G's first-born and her own infancy—was easier to care for and remained so. She became a sunny delight for her mother.

"Depression" and Psychotic Residues

My next biochemistry lesson came a good while after this birth, when Ms. G announced that she was again getting "depressed." Her announcement came at a time when she was now the mother of two young children, working out complicated sadomasochistic aspects of her relationship with family and colleagues, and overrelying on alcohol to relax. All this was taking its toll. She resumed taking Imipramine, but it was again only of limited usefulness. During a Bion-like moment of reverie one day, I began to muse on her plaint that she "still wasn't feeling well and that the antidepressant wasn't working on the depression." I found myself expressing my unthought known (Bollas, 1987): "Perhaps it is because you are not depressed!" I wasn't completely certain of what I meant by that at the time.

My remark led me to think that regarding this patient merely as depressed, or even in an agitated depression, had already led to a reification of what was really a complex mind–body disorder. The panic and anxiety her former therapists and family as well as herself thought of as a "nuisance" to be medicated out was in reality an indicator of a very old anxiety that could *not* be medicated out. I was finally able to name her "psychotic anxiety"—the anxiety that wouldn't quit. It resonated with her and was useful. Paradoxically, she began to get a handle on her anxiety by becoming less frightened of it through our work.

Attachment as A Stimulus Barrier Against Terror

The function of our attachment turned out to be a significant factor in mitigating her terror of abandonment. In contrast to these terrors, which she experienced with almost all of her objects as an "orphan of the real," she was strikingly unanxious about our separations. Even during times of her panicky feelings, she would say, "Today I wish I didn't have to leave, but I know I'll feel all right once I am outside." She very seldom called between sessions. When I later asked her why she thought all this were so, she replied, "Oh, I always knew you were there for me."

I believe that she correctly determined that I would remain "with her" from the very first interview. The steadiness of my background presence was a key factor in both reducing her terror and building a shield against its impact. Through the bond of our attachment, her stimulus barrier was built up, and she gained the ability to "suffer through" her periods of affective vulnerability.

Hysteroid "Unbelievability" and Selfobject Containment

In addition to the early disconnect from her maternal object, which failed to compensate for whatever genetic defects in her stimulus barrier contributed to her hypersensitivity, her experience of childhood also failed to be corrective and further contributed to her tendency toward disregulation. Both parents warded off, rather than helped her with, her affective states throughout her development. Her father kept his distance through virulent criticism of her, which was traumatic. Her judgment was continuously questioned and she was dismissed as a "worrier."

I have found the factor of not being "believed"—and thereby becoming "unbelievable"—not uncommon in the history of patients with hysteroid characteristics (Kainer and Koretzky, 1988). The rejection of one's self-state as not worthy of belief is taken back into the self and reprojected out as histrionic unbelievability. For example, Ms. G would say to me at a session following a bad day, "I wish you could have seen me yesterday; I may not be able to make you understand how terribly I felt." Although I understood quite well how she felt, she expected that her realm of the "*Real*" existed far beyond my realm of the "*Imaginary*" (Lacan, 1977).

With an already thinned stimulus barrier at birth, the lack of parental empathic attunement and constant criticism was a form of neglect and abuse that persisted throughout her development and further traumatized her. Her "worrying" as a child and her panic as an adult were not incidents unmoored from their origins; they were responses to situations that *were a repetition* of her deeply stressed, uncontained, and unbearable early postnatal states. Given her constitution, she was an emotionally battered child. As an adult—and in the containment of the work—she fought back those who would "batter" her yet again.

Containment and Theories of Self

My use of the idea of *containment as a selfobject need* was stimulated by the post-Kleinian work of Bion and further informed by a self-psychological perspective. My view is similar to the bridging of object relations theory and self psychology begun by Bacal and Newman (1990). But it also comes from my own sense of the experience-near meaning of early selfobject containment. While Bion's (1970) "spatial metaphors" of "container" and "contained" have seemed experience distant to self psychology (see Lichtenberg, 1962, p. 66) and therefore not ideal, the idea of the selfobject need for containment seems to me to directly describe Ms. G's experience and to be useful for self psychology.

Kohut did not conceptualize containment per se, and my adding *containment* to his basic selfobject needs of idealization, mirroring, and twinship has enabled me to extend crucial selfobject needs back to the moment of birth. It is there that the object's *affective mirroring* and *affective attunement* (Basch, 1985), must begin. In later development, I find containment implied in Kohut's (1984) description of the selfobject need for "idealization" of the figure who can be experienced as "strong and calm" and thus be an instrument of the containment of our fears. This containment was markedly absent from Ms. G's later development.

Although the bridging of schools presents problems of both mixed metaphors and creative wills, *selfobject containment* seems to me to come from a natural flow between self- and object relations theory. For example, the intersubjective view (Stolorow, Brandchaft, and Atwood, 1987) directly considers the function of the caregiver's "containment of strong affect":

> It is the caregiver's responsiveness that gradually makes possible the modulation, gradation, and *containment of strong affect*, a selfobject function alluded to in the concept of the parent as a "stimulus barrier" or "protective shield" against psychic trauma (Krystal, 1978), in Winnicott's (1965) notion of the "holding environment" and in Bion's (1977) evocative metaphor of the container and the contained [p. 71, italics added].[12]

Looking at the case of Ms. G in relation to selfobject needs stimulated by the emotional experience of one's affects, I agree with Basch (1995) that "when the negative affects of fear, distress, anger, shame, contempt, and disgust overwhelm the brain's ability to order stimuli and result in anxiety or depressive withdrawal, the person calls for and is in need of selfobject experience" (p. 412). I would add that, for someone like Ms. G, there is both a *normal selfobject need* for containment of affects from the moment of birth for all and an *urgent need* for someone. These are people who may be especially vulnerable through constitution, environment, or a combination of both (Grotstein, 1995).

In the language of motivational self-theory, the system most relevant to this case is *the need for psychic regulation of physiological require-ments* (Lichtenberg et al., 1992). I would add that a prime requirement is the regulation of tension, which expresses itself psycho-physiologically as a disordered mood state or negative affect. Stolorow et al. (1987) note: "Selfobject functions pertain fundamentally to the affective dimension of self-experience, and that the need for selfobject ties pertains to the need for specific, requisite responsiveness to varying affect states throughout development" (p. 67).

Particularly for issues of tension held in the bodily self, *the selfobject need for containment using the freely available mind and presence of the analyst as object* is crucial. I noticed that I remained very steady in my relations with Ms. G—often when others around her were reacting with anxiety and agitation. I was able to maintain this steadiness by the amused and fond feelings she stimulated in me. It was necessary to our particular work that this be so.

Intersubjective theory reflects the psychic reality that it is unlikely that we can conceptually separate self from other. There is evidence now that we can no longer conceptually separate mind from body. For ex-ample, Thalen and Smith (1994) even link such neurological functions as locomotion and cognitive skills to the interactive effects of environment. Starting with Fairbairn, the basic unitary quality of self and other has been increasingly articulated, especially in Kohutian, motivational, and intersubjective theory. We seek, are shaped by, mutually influence, and define ourselves through that which is other to the self.[13]

The Final Crisis: The Beginning Is in the End

In her first therapy, which had taken place in the previous decade and prior to our own work, Ms. G captured its frantic air in her recollection: "We were working on recalling my childhood and I could only think about whether I could make it home from the office. I was just getting worse." The thinking driving the treatment at that time was that her symptoms were indicative of sexual abuse, a theory that was coming into popularity at the time. She dutifully tried to recall such abuse, but to no avail and she became increasingly agitated. Even this well-intentioned fixed idea limited effective treatment.

Her underlying psychotic anxiety could not be identified and brought into the work within this context. Rather, her psychotic anxiety was being experienced by everyone around her—through a communicative projective identification—and played out in their frantic efforts on her behalf. In this heightened climate, no medication worked either. This fluster paradoxically created a reenactment of the difficulty that was part of her life narrative: "I am suffering and *no one* can help me." The birth of her first baby rekindled her own birth, and she later identified with the maternal collapse she had experienced in her own mother.

After some years and a particularly stressful series of life events—including the long absence of her husband during the time a crisis arose regarding one of her children—she became deeply disregulated and distraught. She had taken over the care of her children without her historic reliance on a live-in mother substitute. By this time, she also had reduced her work with me to once a week as part of her determination to be more self-reliant.

Her efforts to run the household, to "mother," to tend to her professional life, to cope with her husband's absences and experiencing of him as critical, emotionally detached, and unavailable, coupled with some loss of the therapeutic containment owing to the reduced therapy hours and her being completely alcohol free, brought her over the edge. She felt that her medication—the Imipramine—was "not working."

In his work on the neurobiology of posttraumatic stress disorder, van der Kolk (1994) has recognized the biological havoc it creates, which remains locked in the body. But even this essentially descriptive diagnosis for her did not preclude a treatment crisis. In her struggle to "get well" this time, she sought the help of another medicating psychiatrist whom I knew to be both a gifted analytic clinician and astute in pharmacology. The analyst began treating her for the now popular PTSD, with attendant "panic and depression, both dysthymic and major unipolar." Attempts to awaken memories of sexual abuse—and introducing the new eye-brain retraining—fell flat.

Instead, she became drowsy, and subsequent attempts to augment and micromedicate her various complaints led to havoc. The drug mix—Effexor and Zoloft for depression, Klonopin for anxiety, and Dexatrin to overcome her ensuing sleepiness—greatly concerned her because of its side effects, particularly her "forgetfulness." I commented to my beleaguered psychiatric colleague that "Ms. G could override any medication yet invented" given the right conditions and her *seemingly* compliant style!

These drugs created the kind of storm that hearkened back to the frantic flurry of her early postpartum depression days, when she could not be successfully medicated. Attention deficit disorder and dissociative disorder, which were also getting attention just then, were additionally diagnosed. I think now that the cognitive difficulties she had during storms like this reflected the panicky feelings she was prone to when stressed.

The dissociative disorder diagnosis was the most interesting psychodynamically. In psychoanalytic thinking, I knew that she split-off, or disavowed—that is, *dissociated* herself from—her own negative feelings for fear of offending the helping figure. She had always been able to get those close to her (through projective identification) to express what she could not directly. As in the distressed days of her "postpartum depression," she was again highly successful in having her distress felt by others. Although reactivity is certainly in my countertransference repertoire, I once again found myself remaining calm. This time the storm proved fruitful.

The mix of drugs had badly scared her, but she did not experience this fright directly. Rather, she succeeded in getting her husband, then *his* therapist, and finally *her* family to voice alarm. She also succeeded in getting my colleague to back off. I think the search for the magic elixir had always been somewhat half-hearted for her, as she knew that her path lay elsewhere. However, she used this crisis in her own inimitable way, to align herself with her husband. This is what she had wanted all along—and they regrouped as a couple. She once again had his full attention, and she was ready to move on. Her husband and the marital relationship was her next project!

This last bout of dysphoria "kindled" the freeing thought that I too, like her medication, was not strong enough to "contain" her. She expressed concern that I would not know if she were getting sick (that I had lost my omniscience). Her de-idealization paved the way for her even to consider terminating our long period of work and our relationship without terror. The loosening of her belief in my omnipotence was the beginning of a necessary, benign, and nonpremature "twoness" (Tustin, 1981a). This loosening would have been unthinkable in previous years, even in the years that were without crisis, for I had become a given of her existence and a necessary background presence. The idea that she could function without my being there, just as she could take over being the mother of the house without the nursemaid, arose from her capacity for a hearty and natural "twoness" coming from a now more fully individuated self. The era of hysteroid attachments was over.

The certainty of my existence and my selfobject containment of whatever feeling state arose within her enabled her to begin her separation from me in a peaceful way. After the treatment crisis, she did some exploration herself and consulted with a visiting research psychopharmacologist. After seeing him, she reported back that he had diagnosed her condition in the following way: "He said I had a little bit of *this* and a little bit of *that!*"

We both agreed that it was the best diagnosis she had ever had! It seemed so *exactly* right to each of us that the fact he was to return to another country in a few months was now a minor regret rather than a major catastrophe! She had come a long way, and she heard what she needed to hear. Perhaps she had always had "a little bit of this and a little bit of that," but it was certainly most true of her now. Her search for the definitive diagnosis—for what was wrong—was ended. Her condition no longer terrified her. She could now live with who she was, affect and all.

THE MIND AND THE BRAIN

In addition to the issue of the psychoanalytic theories that are most explanatory in such a case as Ms. G's, the issue raised by the medication problem is really the philosophical "mind versus brain" dichotomy that is at the heart of the efforts to biologize the mind. In dealing with the complexity of the human psyche, are we ever correct in totally substituting brain for mind? My question here is—imprecisely using the image of "wiring"—what can we expect to effect through a "rewiring" of the brain through chemistry, as Donald Klein (1968) hoped, and what gets "rewired" through therapy (see Kandel, Schwartz, and Jessell, 1995)? What may already be "wired" because of genetic factors?

Identification and Genetic Predisposition

Perhaps the most important issue to be addressed in the mind–brain question comes from the great weight I give psychoanalytically to the role of *identification* in both the formation and the collapse of the self. A question that could be raised in this vein concerns the role of genetic predisposition in psychological difficulties. I would like to raise the further question of the role of genetics in identifications.

For example, one of Ms. G's recurrent anxious projections was of a destitute old age in which no one would care for her. It was Freud (1917) who first pointed out the importance of the mechanism of *identification* in "hysteria" (p. 249) and the striking feature in melancholia (depression) of the dread of poverty (p. 252). Although the language is old, the ideas are still current.

In Ms. G's case, her history is tantalizing because of its possible *genetic component* as well as the psychodynamic determinant of *identifications*. For example, a beloved grandmother also had a psychiatric hospitalization after childbirth. In later life, following the death of her husband, this grandmother required round-the-clock care owing to a terror of being left alone. This grandmother had an important place in Ms. G's internal object world. Did Ms. G resemble her in genetic or constitutional makeup, or was she perhaps just simply *overly identified* with her? Or do we choose as our internal objects those with whom we somehow already unconsciously identify because of our genetic makeup? *Is there a genetic component to identifications?* I raise this question in the hope that further light can be shed on it.

POSTSCRIPT

In a posttermination interview several years later, I was greeted by a calm and composed Ms. G[14] who was adequately maintained on a very low dosage of Zoloft[15] and whose rich and full life was in manageable order. She had continued in couples work and reported that they had put on "quite a show" for their psychiatrist at their last session, before her husband left to go abroad for his work. When I looked at her inquiringly, she read my unspoken question and airily replied, "Oh, I was so mad at him before he left, I was *glad* to see him go!" She could make so brief a statement only after so long a journey.

I have used hysteroid dysphoria and PTSD as metaphors for describing the complexity of the mind–body psychodynamics of a patient. My observations prompt me to agree with Kramer's (1993) prediction that "Neurosis of the twenty-first century will be a disorder that encompasses the effects of heredity and trauma—risk and stress" (p. 289).

I would add that, in the future, neurosis will *still* reflect the struggle for individuality (the dialectic of self and other), the struggle of a *conflict of desires*, and the dialectical self-struggle between pathological identifications and transcendent longings that has been the subtext of this book. Our therapeutic role will be to perceive *all* the components of the self— mind and body—and help the patient make out of them a coherent whole.

The role of the bodily self will increasingly play a role in the treatment of the next generation of patients. The hyperirritable and hypersensitive baby of a disregulated mother—biochemically, emotionally, or both—makes it difficult for an already compromised maternal figure to provide the necessary soothing and containment desperately needed by a baby who is difficult to comfort. Although we are now more sophisticated than to label all such babies "colicky,"[16] easily disregulated infants— "fussy babies"—may become the ones variously diagnosed with depression, attention deficit disorder, dissociative disorder, substance abuse, and posttraumatic stress disorder.

My hope is that they will no longer be the "difficult to medicate" patients because all these disorders will be seen as forms of a disregulated self requiring the containment of a therapeutic presence to enable medication, where necessary, to be effective. The body does keep score and makes containment and the metabolizing of the psychic pain of the bodily self with another—and with others—a crucial part of treatment.

Notes

[1] "The most remarkable quality of *The Architect of Desire* is the way its narrative slowly coaxes to the surface *memories so terrifying that they lack all meaning to the author*" (Lehmann-Haupt, 1996, italics added).

[2] In a 1995 West Coast conference on "Medicating the Difficult Patient," she would have fit at least five of the six categories, including panic disorder, dissociative disorder, posttraumatic stress disorder, attention deficit disorder, and depression. She is not schizophrenic, the sixth category they mentioned.

[3] Earlier trials of the noreleptic Imipramine and later attempts at the then newly developed SSRI Prozac were not particularly successful with her. While difficulties in medicating the borderline personality (Eist, 1985, personal communication) are not uncommon, it proved better not to explain the difficulty away by this further categorization of her. Medication is most helpful when the patient feels adequately contained.

[4] I am indebted to James Barron, Ph.D. for this insight and discussion.

[5] Lichtenberg's (1989) idea of model scenes also refers to *the patient's* experience of his or her history, as well as pivotal moments in the narrative constructed by the analytic couple in the work done together. They become part of the mutually shared history of the work. McDougall (1995) relates a similar idea of recounting moments with a patient where they together entered a realm characterized by a colleague as "an hypnotic state" they mutually constructed.

[6] As S. Kainer (1994, personal communication) has observed in his work with patients with schizophrenia at Chestnut Lodge, "as symptoms become detached from their moorings, the resulting effect is psychotic." The greater the "unknowing" of its source, the greater the chance for it to make one feel "crazy." This observation should be kept in mind when considering the effects of spontaneous "kindling" on mood disregulations.

[7] I understand that brain research indicates a specific site for *worrying*. There is some speculation that they may refer to it as the "Woody Allen" region.

[8] In pediatric psychiatry, "fussy baby" clinics now exist for babies whose parents have not been able to soothe them and are in danger of disconnecting from them. The intent is to help the parents to be able to connect to the infant whose well-being depends on maintaining the connection. The term "fussy baby" has replaced the catchall "colicky" baby, whose parents were often unhelpfully told that "it will pass."

[9] It is W. C. Fields to whom the classic line, "Any man who hates dogs and children can't be all bad!" has been attributed. My own countertransference may

come from a capacity for irreverence, already noted in chapter two, which exists side-by-side with an equal capacity for reverence.

[10] Nonetheless, there later was heroic reparative work in regard to the mother's care of Ms. G's sibling, disabled as an adult. The mother has also been highly reliable in regard to Ms. G, who once said, "I have two different mothers: the one she is now, and the one I had then."

[11] That "disorganization" plagued her throughout life as it was projected outward into the clutter and misplacement of material objects and her trying to manage too many relationships with equal intensity.

[12] The constructs "container" and "contained" are in Bion (1962b, 1970).

[13] Perhaps the parallel to Winnicott's (1950) dictum, "There is no such thing as an infant" (i.e., without a mother) is in the intersubjective theory that there is no such thing as a self without an other.

[14] I am indebted to Ms. G for her interest in having her experience "made useful" for others. Those experiences, and our work together, were invaluable sources of learning.

[15] Possibly, given her current strengthened structure and the present homeopathic climate, she might well be the kind of person for whom the herbal remedy saint-john's-wort in popular use in Germany would be suggested. It seems to be a possibly useful "tonic" for those who have "a little bit of this and a little bit of that!"

[16] Especially now that many infants are feeling the effects of the substances abused during the pregnancy of their mothers.

PART III

The Therapeutic Restoration
of the Self

The chapters of the final section are devoted to clinical metapsychology and the construction of a theory about what takes place in the clinical encounter and its therapeutic effect. There is a return to the role of the pursuit of the ideal self and the ideal object, this time in relation to the therapeutic transformation of the pathological parts of the self. The role of imagination and empathy—a further look at the creative aspects of projective identification—is discussed. The idea of the catastrophe of the premature birth of the self, epitomizing the need for the selfobject function of containment, is raised.

Chapter Eight

The Role of Projective Identification in Imaginative Empathy

Projective identification . . . [is] the instrument for all phantasies . . . it is responsible for the creation of the objects which comprise the inner world. Imagination is the metaphor for projective identification.
      —JAMES GROTSTEIN, *Splitting and Projective Identification*

A piece of good analytic work is an artistic creation fashioned by patient and analyst in collaboration.
      —HANS LOEWALD, "Psychoanalysis as an Art and the Fantasy Character of the Psychoanalytic Situation"

THE BACKGROUND FIGURES OF IDENTIFICATION

The dialectic of psychoanalysis has seldom generated greater heat than Klein's concept of projective identification. Rooted in observations of the delusional (Tausk, 1919), and offspring of the death instinct (Klein, 1946), the negative origins of projective identification have cast a long shadow. Klein made death instinct phenomena a core issue of her theoretic concerns, particularly around the destructiveness of greed, envy, and sadism. In a sense, her theories complemented Freud's emphasis of the libidinal and gave increased attention to the destructive. She interpreted Freud's (1920) new duality of Eros and Thanatos as the struggle between good and evil and made this struggle the cornerstone of her work.[1] In this chapter, I interpret that struggle in the light of post-Kleinian and post-Kohutian theoretical advances.

While Klein is best known for her focus on the functions of the death instinct, she is less known for her recognition of the human capacity for integration as well as splitting, for gratitude as well as envy (Klein, 1957), and for her idea that projective and introjective processes also involve

135

the good parts of the self and object, as well as the bad, in the formation of the personality (Klein, 1946). The introjective and projective processes she described were mechanisms for the conveyance of constructive as well as destructive forces. Her theories reflected her belief in one's capacity to experience the world in both a fragmented state (the paranoid-schizoid position) and in the integration and greater wholeness of the depressive position.[2]

Klein (1958) spoke of the necessity for integrating the splits in the self through a reconciliation with the death instinct:[3]

> I attribute to the ego from the beginning of life a need and capacity not only to split but also to integrate itself. Integration, which gradually leads to a climax in the depressive [i.e., whole object] position, depends on the preponderance of the life instinct and implies in some measure the *acceptance by the ego of the working of the death instinct* [p. 245, italics added].

However, Klein's emphasis on projective identification as an evacuative function of the death instinct left a legacy of technical difficulties in the clinical setting. Insofar as projective identification is seen only as the "prototype of an aggressive object relation" (Klein, 1946, p. 8), or as a predominantly psychotic form of communication (Rosenfeld, 1971), I believe that its usefulness has been unnecessarily limited and its potential for clinical misuse made greater. I view projective identification as a special form of intersubjective empathic communication found in nonpsychotic, ordinary, as well as artistic discourse, and rooted in the human capacity for identification of one with another.[4]

Klein's view allows for the acceptance and integration of the death instinct, and the possibility of calming the patient through its acknowledgment, provided the interpretation correctly expresses the state of mind of the patient (V. Hendrickson, 1997, personal communication). However, unempathic interpretations of projective identification as a primarily destructive piece of the death instinct phenomenon, especially when such interpretations have resulted in a negative therapeutic effect for which the patient is blamed, have correctly disturbed self psychologists (see Brandchaft, 1983; Stolorow et al., 1987; Lichtenberg, 1992). Such interpretations are especially unfruitful when they are ego dystonic or when the function they serve in the patient's survival is ignored.

Kleinians have tended to focus on the experience of being the object of the projective identification, whereas Kohutians have focused on the subjective experience of the patient—although this generalization is not without its exceptions. Regardless of professed school of thought, insofar as the analyst experiences himself or herself as the *target* of the projective identification and therefore cannot use the experience to further understand the patient's communication, there may be hostile retribution of analyst toward patient.

Self psychology has engaged in an important dialectic and corrective regarding projective identification, but in the process has discarded it. There has also been a negation and loss of the concept of identification itself (Lichtenberg et al., 1992, p. 66), which I have found to be crucial to the clinical understanding of the patient's life narrative and the formation of the self (see chapters two and three on the role of identification in the formation of the ideal and of the sadomasochistic self). I want to bridge the gap between Kleinian and Kohutian thought so as not to lose these powerful constructs to clinical misuse or nonuse.

I believe that the self's acceptance and integration of "death-instinct"-like phenomena (i.e., our sadism, envy, and psychotic residues) take us beyond the depressive position into a longed-for position of transcendence (Kainer, 1993b; see also Grotstein and Rinsley, 1994). The *imaginative aspects of projective identification* act as a vehicle for the transformation of destructiveness and are employed in the service of expanding the self. In this chapter, the development of the ideas about projective identification spans an arc preceding Klein's thinking of it as "an aggressive object relation" to my present consideration of it as an imaginative and transformational phenomenon.

I have come to my present view of projective identification through the work of Bion (1959), Money-Kyrle (1956), Malin and Grotstein (1966), Rosenfeld (1971), Grotstein (1985b), and Bacal and Newman (1990), among others who have distinguished between its evacuative and its communicative aspects (i.e., its pathological and nonpathological functions). I also call upon Grinberg (1962), Racker (1968), Searles (1973), Meltzer (1984), and Ogden (1989, 1994) for their use of its creative role in countertransference. All these authors have helped to loosen the concept from its primary roots as a hostile defense against innate destructiveness.

THE IMAGINATIVE ASPECTS OF PROJECTIVE IDENTIFICATION: FORESHADOWING BY TAUSK AND KLEIN

An object is found by the intellect and chosen by the libido.
—VICTOR TAUSK, "On the Origin of the
'Influencing Machine' in Schizophrenia"

Among Freud's followers, Victor Tausk and Melanie Klein were both greatly stimulated by his ideas concerning projection and identification, but their responses reflected different periods in Freudian thought: Tausk's (1919) essay originated in the heyday of the great interest in the sexual origins of pathology and predates Freud's (1920) introduction of the death instinct.

Later, Melanie Klein (1946) became the primary follower of Freud to incorporate the death instinct and make it an integral part of her theory. Both Tausk and Klein were highly original thinkers, although Tausk's early death left his "influencing machine" paper his last contribution. Tausk's (1919) classic paper, "On the Origin of the 'Influencing Machine' in Schizophrenia," and Klein's (1955) essay, "On Identification," are especially relevant to the discussion.

Tausk and the "Influencing Machine"

It is generally acknowledged that the "concept of 'identity' itself was first introduced into the psychoanalytic literature by Tausk" (Roazen, 1971, p. 188). Tausk's discovery of the relationship of identification to projection was the forerunner of Klein's actual naming of the phenomenon and her expansion of it to a fully developed theory of the mind.[5] In observing the thought processes of his delusional patients, Tausk noted the relationship between, first, the patients' *identification* with an object and their subsequent *projection* of blame onto that object as a source of their ills. These were deteriorating patients who were searching about for causal explanations of changes in their bodily sensations, which were incomprehensible to them. Some patients felt themselves tormented by persons known to them, and some felt themselves to be victim of an "influencing machine."

As an example of the former, Tausk (1919) wrote about Miss Emma A, a psychotic woman who complained that her eyes had "twisted" from their proper place in her head, which she attributed to the "twistings" by her deceitful and evil lover. Once, she experienced a "sudden thrust" while in church, "as if she were being moved from her place," just as her lover "moved himself from one place to another" by disguising himself (pp. 525–526). Tausk wrote:

> This patient did not merely feel herself persecuted and influenced; hers was a case of being influenced by *identification with the persecutor*. If we take into consideration the view held by Freud and myself that *in object-choice the mechanism of identification precedes the cathexis proper by projection*, we may regard the case . . . as representing the stage in the development of the delusion of reference preceding the projection . . . . The identification is obviously an attempt to project the feelings of the inner change on to the outer world [p. 525, italics added].

Other patients ascribed what was happening to them—such as the loss of sexual vitality—to being manipulated by the "influencing machine," as if it were a person. The influencing machine could produce "feelings of inner change accompanied by awareness of an external originator as a result of identification" (p. 525). The delusional mind, with its shrinking ego and dissolving ego boundaries, still sought an explanation for feelings of self-estrangement. The patients, experiencing disturbing inner changes, explained them away as resulting from external mechanical manipulation. For example, a patient who had lost genital sensation said that the machine had lost its genitalia. As their mental disease progressed, these patients described the machine as also deteriorating. As with the evil lover, there was an introjective process of identification in that what was ascribed to the machine was then also experienced by the self.

The foregoing suggests to me that, even in a pathological state, there is a search for an object of identification, which comes from a powerful need for a shared identity—a "sameness" (Kohut, 1984)—albeit in this case it is of a nonhuman and persecutory kind. In addition, the belief in a mechanical influence has both a logical and a metaphoric quality to it. The belief reflects a projection (onto the machine, with which one has come to identify) of the nonhuman (mechanical) quality of the feelings that cannot be tolerated. The machine is also a metaphor for how a person who lacks sexual vitality gradually comes to feel: mechanical, robotic, and nonhuman. These catastrophic feelings are disavowed by being attributed to (projected onto) the external machine, but they are clearly also an attempt to make sense of one's experience as well. The defensive function of evacuation exists together with a struggle to understand the incomprehensible.

Although Delusional, the Mind Is Still Imaginative

Although the example comes from observations of the mind in delusion, we can also see the imaginative process at work in that same mind: "We are here concerned with the discovery, *or rather the invention*, of a hostile object; but for the intellectual process it is unimportant whether the objects observed are hostile or friendly, and the psychoanalyst, at least, will certainly have no objection to the equating of love and hate in this instance" (p. 525, italics added).

Through Tausk's attention to the mental inventiveness of the patient, we can glimpse the imaginative as well as the pathological part of the mind which seeks to express itself.[6] I am struck by how, even in a delusional state, there is a need symbolically to express what can only be a devastating sense of loss of bodily sensation, and a need to attribute causation that connects the self to someone (or something) else. The fantasy construction of an "influencing machine" has an integrative aspect to it that exists side-by-side with its pathology. The will toward integration in the analytic situation is also present, despite the presence of pathology.

Grotstein (1985) noted that, "Tausk's paper . . . shows him to have been alert to the enormous importance of the relationship between projection and identification, and to have sensed the importance of projective identification in the formation of normal and pathological structures within the ego" (p. 147). Tausk's work shows us that, no matter how fragile one's connection to reality, the wish to connect to something outside the self is so powerful that it engages the imaginative processes. Where there is no person for the purpose, we will even produce an imaginary machine with which to identify.

MELANIE KLEIN'S "ON IDENTIFICATION": THE INTERPENETRATION OF SELF AND OTHER

The literary analysis Klein (1955) undertook in "On Identification" further illustrated her ideas on projective identification, first introduced in 1946. Through her interpretation of the protagonist Fabian in the French novel *If I Were You* by Julian Green,[7] Klein (1955) allows us to glimpse something of the imaginative process underlying her meaning of an identification that occurs through projection. As it is evoked in the pure art of Green's novel—stripped of the mechanistic metaphors that have disturbed her critics—one can grasp the meaning of what I call the *interpenetration of self and other.*

Klein may have identified with *If I Were You* because of its uncanny similarity to her basic ideas. The fantasies of the dying Fabian involve his serially hurtling himself into the personae of those he has envied and taking on their identity, through a secret pact with the Devil. The projective aspects of Fabian's identification were impelled by envy, greed, and longing. Indeed, the subtext of *If I Were You* is, "Then I could have what I am certain you have that I lack." Covetousness propelled Fabian's flights into taking on the identity of various characters. In addition to being enviously motivated, however, Fabian also had reparative longings for love and wholeness which also moved him.

Fabian's identifications not only were projective but were introjective, as his projection into the other resulted in the introjection of its persona back into himself. Identities became merged, unlike Rank's (1939) double or Kohut's (1984) alter ego, where the other is experienced as separate, although part of a strongly shared identification. As Fabian takes on the persona of the other, however, he still experiences himself as Fabian, but in an increasingly diminished form.[8]

In his own reading of the novel, Grotstein (1985b) was struck by this diminishment: "It is important to remember that in projective identification there is a self left behind or disavowed, much as in *If I Were You* where Fabian's deserted self lies alone for three days in a coma" (p. 131).

Loss of Self and the Creation of a New Self

The loss of the self through projective identification illustrates another tenet of Klein's thesis: that excessive projection identification is a pathognomic indicator. While this is probably true—as Tausk (1919) illustrated in reporting on the increasing projections of his patients in a deteriorating state—it has tainted all projective identifications with the aura of pathological fragmentation of the diminished self. However, I am more in agreement with Ogden (1994):

> Although Klein (1955) focused almost entirely on the experience of psychological depletion involved in projective identification, it is now widely understood that projective identification also involves *the creation of something potentially larger and more generative than either of the participants (in isolation from one another) is capable of generating* [p. 102, italics added].

Here I think Ogden has captured the creative and generative aspects of projective identification, unmoored from the death instinct. I believe these aspects are a function of the human imaginative and transformational capacities. The projective identification serves as the basis of a mutually creative experience between two people.

The creative and generative aspects of projective identification are particularly relevant when they involve neurotic patients. Although the sense of self may be temporarily lost during the interpenetration of selves, not only is the self not ultimately diminished, as it might be in a psychotically evacuative process, it is enhanced. The recipient/analyst is the other player, who is undiminished by this temporary submergence of self. Neither loses, and the gain is shared. The patient gains by a better integration of split-off parts of the self, and the analyst gains by experiencing the generative creativity that he or she helps to construct.

Thus, it is in its communicative rather than its splitting and evacuative aspects, and in its imaginative rather than its psychotic aspects, that I am here exploring projective identification. In neurosis, it can be used nonevacuatively to unconsciously communicate the pathological part of the self in the search for wholeness and integration. It is an externalized dramatic reenactment—undertaken with the "assistance" of the analyst— of a constricting part of the self that the patient wishes to have understood.

Integrating the Self in Art and Therapy

In the evocative powers of its drama, projective identification is also an important factor in the connecting experience of art. Klein (1958) noted that "Though the rejected aspects of the self and of internalized objects contribute to instability, they are also at the source *of inspiration in artistic productions and in various intellectual activities*" (p. 245, italics added).

I would add that, while the artist may find inspiration in working out the troubling aspects of the self and internal objects, the artwork itself is not necessarily a direct expression or reification of the pathology. Rather, the artwork reflects the working through of it. The *will-to-form* in the creation of art carries with it the push toward integration and creative transcendence. The transcendence is achieved both through the intensity of the identification with the artwork, which provides a cohesing selfobject experience, and through a return of the artwork back to the collective, reuniting self and other (Kainer, 1984).

A similar longing for integration and wholeness is brought to the analytic situation. The very fact of presenting the pathological part of the self to the analyst invariably implies a longing for its transformation (Bollas, 1987), if not redemption (Kainer, 1993a). Even when I have not been successful in reading the pathological "text" of a patient during the course of the work in enough time to name it and possibly reverse it, I have caught the longing itself (see chapter ten). The projections offered up not only are reifications of destructive urges, but also represent attempts to have them lifted and become part of the creative process. Both parts of the self, the destructive and the redemptive, exist simultaneously and over time.

THE EMPATHIC IMAGINATION OF THE CREATIVE ARTIST

Perhaps the factor of the pathological roots of projective identification has created a barrier to its wider application.[9] There has, however, also been a particular misuse of projective identification: a denial of the analyst's contribution to what is being created, along with a "blaming" of the patient for the state being created by both of them. Brandchaft and Stolorow (1988) have addressed this well-taken point. If this potential for misuse is held in check (by not automatically blaming the patient or ascribing the unfolding clinical events as all due to the patient's instinctual makeup), the phenomenon of identification through projection has great clinical vitality.

In addition, projective identification has great relevance to art. Our response to the artist's projections experienced through the artwork is a clear example of an empathic human exchange at the level of pure imagination. It is the prototype of the form of imaginative empathy found in the clinical situation.

Artists of genius have a remarkable gift for empathically entering "into" the other. For example, it was through his empathic imagination[10] that, as a mature man, Shakespeare not only knew and then could project the heart of an aged King Lear, but could equally imagine and convey the covetous, hard, and pure hearts of the king's three daughters as well. It is the astonishing capacity of his empathic imagination that as a man of 32, he could not only capture the quality of a Romeo, but equally enter into the heart of a 14-year-old girl (R. Ornstein, 1989, personal communication). Through his inspired projection, which is received by us through successful projective identifications, he stirs us into taking Romeo and Juliet into our own imaginations as eternal symbols of young love. He is vastly successful in having us identify with his projection.

Eugene O'Neill and The Great God Brown

My own direct experience of projective identification in art occurred some time ago during a 1960s revival of Eugene O'Neill's (1925) play *The Great God Brown*. It was my first encounter with the evocative powers of a great artist's projective powers. Although the play takes place in modern times, O'Neill had his characters don masks in the manner of an ancient Greek drama. These highly stylized masks were originally used by actors to convey the identity of characters across the vast distance of an outdoor amphitheater. O'Neill riveted my attention through the sheer unexpectedness and originality of using them in a modern, intimately psychological drama.

In an imaginative way, O'Neill used the donning and removal of masks to express the intricacies of hiding and finding the self. Just barely out of my own adolescence, I was greatly drawn to the struggle of the two young men—the dissolute but very talented Dion, and Brown, who envied his friend Dion's genius and had long loved Dion's wife. When Brown, a conventional, hard-working man who was capable of devotion as well as envy, bent down and slowly took up the mask of the dead Dion and then agonizingly placed it over his own face, claiming Dion's persona, it was electric.

Caught in the sheer power of that moment, I somehow *knew* that O'Neill was talking about his own adolescent struggles with convention and art, and that, to some extent, the struggle was also mine. I clearly identified with his projections. That moment forever illustrated for me that the success of a work of art, like the survival of Bion's infant (1965,

p. 62) depends on having the audience identify with, accept, and take in the projections of the artist.[12]

The projective aspects of both art and therapy are similar, with the artist projecting parts of the imaginative self outward, and the therapist bending *toward* the enactment of the patient, receiving it (while being part of it), in the space usually occupied by the audience. The natural completion of the cycle in art occurs when there is an audience, sufficiently stirred, who identifies with and becomes the willing container for the artist's projections. In our analytic work, there is an imaginative empathic process necessary for bending ourselves to receive the projections of the most inchoate, split-off parts of the patient. The analytic drama may take on a Pirandello-like flavor, where the usual space between actor and audience is compressed and audience is made into actors. Similarly, the analyst becomes an integral part of the dramatic action of the therapy.

Ogden (1994) takes the analyst's role even further: "It does not suffice to simply say that in projective identification one finds oneself playing a role in someone else's unconscious fantasy (Bion, 1959). More fully stated, one finds oneself unconsciously both playing a role in and serving as author of someone else's unconscious fantasy" (p. 103). This view of projective identification emphasizes not only the intersubjective nature of projective identification but, in part, the catalytic role of the analyst. My own sense is that the mental makeup of the analyst can be used creatively by the patient in varying degrees in the analytic drama.

Differentiating Imaginative Empathy from "Vicarious Introspection"

The phenomenon I am describing differs from the empathy we know as Kohut's concept of "vicarious introspection." Kohut (1984) described a process in which the analyst makes an "attempt to experience the inner life of another while simultaneously retaining the stance of an *objective observer*" (p. 175, italics added).

In the empathic process I describe here, *objectivity is temporarily lost*, and we are no longer in the realm of ordinary empathy. The imaginative and creative aspects of projective phenomena can be extended to the analytic situation. The therapist's experience of a projective identification as imaginative empathy is illustrated in the next section through a case vignette of a neurotic patient whose "will to integrate" a central pathological dynamic was so strong that she resorted to a powerful projective and introjective engagement with me when I failed to understand her through ordinary empathy. She unconsciously seized upon my empathic failure as a way to connect on a deeper level. Through this illustration, I hope to counter some of the criticism of projective identification that has come from post-Kohutian theorists.

THE DIALECTIC OF PROJECTIVE IDENTIFICATION

Whereas Klein (1946) acknowledged the duality of the *death instinct* (in the paranoid-schizoid position) and *reparative longings* (of the depressive position), her primary legacy regarding projective identification remains in her description of it as an evacuative death instinct phenomenon. With this conceptual underpinning, remembering that the patient also has reparative and redemptive longings may be difficult in the heat of clinical practice, when the patient manifests such aspects of the self as enviousness, greed, and sadism. They may be experienced by the therapist only as an attack from a hostile object. The therapist may be drawn to respond unempathically to these phenomena if there is a belief that they represent an intrinsic "evil" in the patient and may, in turn, return the attack (Kainer, 1994, pp. 54–56).

Self psychology has as its basic tenets the "acceptance of the patient with whatever symptomatology" and "the ability of the analyst to make the patient's self experience the center of attention" (Hertz, 1989, pp. 33–51). Self psychology is antithetical to projective identification on two major grounds, the first being the shift away from the patient's *self-experience* by relegating feeling states to unconscious derivatives of the death instinct. This "death-instinct discharge" view not only negates the intersubjective aspects of the phenomenon, it does not allow for the possibility that the experience of the therapist may also reflect the self-experience of the patient (Hendrickson, 1995).

The second antithetical push has been against the mechanistic quality evoked by the term projective identification and in particular the spatial metaphor of "viewing parents and therapists as containers processing affects projected into them" (Lichtenberg, 1992, p. 65).[12] However, while I find it important to move the theory of projective identification beyond the death instinct, I still wish to retain Bion's imagery of the container because of its direct relevance to the *selfobject need for containment*, which at heart is the need for communication. (This discussion is taken up further in chapter nine.)

Self Psychology's Corrective

Self psychology has provided a necessary dialectic response to the tendency for projective phenomena, and especially projective identification, to be defensively used by analysts to explain away negative therapeutic reactions (Stolorow et al., 1987). Adherence to the death instinct may lend itself to the analytic view that the "patient's difficulties arise from vicissitudes of aggressive-drive processing" (p. 112). Further, "we have found . . . that the analyst's insistence that negative reactions in analysis are to be explained by the patient's innate aggression or envy, or by his projections of aggressively distorted internal objects, can be demeaning to the patient, to the unfolding selfobject transference, and to the analysis (Brandchaft, 1983)" (p. 114).

That quote captures the essence of what I believe is needed to make projective identification a viable clinical instrument for non-Kleinians, and a better one for Kleinians. The belief that what is being witnessed is only the patient's drive state and the refusal of the analyst to acknowledge that the present moment reflects something also actually taking place in the room—which includes the "present actuality of the analyst's mental state" (Loewald, 1975)—can lead to a prolonged negative therapeutic interaction, as the patient twists about to resist the analyst's hostile counterprojections. Paradoxically, the shift from a one-person psychology to a two-person psychology must be clearly in evidence in the analyst's experience and interpretation of the event in order to give the event a meaning that is relevant to the patient. *While the analyst may be both actor in, or even catalyst of, the drama, the chief analytic role is that of narrator of the patient's psychic life.*

It would then follow that the processing of a projective identification must come not as a "revealed truth" of the analyst handed down to the patient, but as a shared truth between analyst and patient. This truth is codetermined by their collaboration on the meaning of the mutually experienced interpenetration of self and other. The following clinical vignette, which includes the independently written notes of the patient and myself, obtained after the work was completed, served as the point of observation of these ideas.

Ms. C and the Initial Encounter

My notes on the initial contacts read:

RK: My first recollection was of a telephone inquiry from her shortly before my summer vacation, about the possibility of starting therapy. She said she was having pressures at school, and I asked her if she could hold on until September, since I wouldn't be available if she needed immediate and sustained help. She assured me she could, and I told her I would try to see her for an initial consultation before I went on vacation. I was able to arrange one and found her to be a plucky and determined young woman who already had some prior therapy. She was experiencing difficulties in graduate school but again reported no urgency at that time. It seemed an unexceptional meeting, and we agreed to begin work in September.

However, her own notes of that call and consultation are far more dramatic:

Ms. C: I felt that I had been "holding on" for a long time. I knew much of my resources had been used up. I had encouragement [from the referring colleague], who hinted about self-esteem issues. I still found it difficult to make the first call to Rochelle to ask for help and begin therapy again. I called once. The call was not returned. I called again. No appointment was available. When making that first appointment, R asked me if I could hold on until September as she would be on vacation until then. I said yes and felt nothing pressing. R asked me if I wanted to see another therapist as she would be unavailable for a month. I said no—it had taken me a long time to decide on R, and I did not want to see a "stranger." I wondered if I was acceptable and felt the beginning of a will battle—sure I would be turned away.

My tepid notes are in clear contrast to the strong transferential reaction she already was having while my head seemed to be in the Off position. The dynamic that would eventually be the focus of our work had already been called into play. Although I was not conscious of it, I was already enacting it with her. Her notes go on:

Ms. C: R called with an opening for an appointment at the end of July. The day before the appointment I had an anxiety attack, the second in my life. Saw R the next day. It was fairly uneventful. I felt that R did not understand my worries. I thought I expected too much from R. Felt reassured and that perhaps I was exaggerating my difficulties to myself.

In addition to the clear countertransference of my resistance to engaging with her before what I understood to be the mutually agreed upon time (which turned out to be only an act of acquiescence on her part rather than real agreement), my not hearing or understanding her was also central to her dynamic, which we had both unconsciously begun to reenact. In retrospect, it seems likely that the anxiety attack the day before the first consultation was related to it, although she linked it to difficulties at school. She dutifully repressed the extent of her neediness in response to my unspoken message, which she heard as an archaic parental message: "I'm tired, I have no time, I'm writing a paper, I'm on vacation, I'm going out of town—you go away too!" I was clearly not yet on the case and not tuned in to her on a conscious level. Unconsciously, I was very tuned into averting the projection. She continues her notes:

Ms. C: I wondered why I was beginning therapy as the meeting was so mild, although I remember many tears. I also remember worrying about what R would think of me as a professional. She told me that people in the profession are the worst, and I wasn't sure what she meant.

This projection into her (paralleling hers into me) in the form of this careless comment, was addressed to the exaggerated self-diagnoses I had heard over the years, not excluding autism and borderline personality organization. While it was meant to lighten her anxiety about any "judgment" of her and her adequacy, the remark was also my unconscious attempt to trivialize her inner state, which I was not ready to hear. Although I experienced it as a frivolous remark, it was also a technical error and an empathic miss that further served to stimulate her intense self-demeaning tendencies, of which I was as yet unaware.

Ms. C: Felt embarrassed, inadequate, self-degrading, looking for warmth.

These were not addressed. In hindsight, it seems astonishing that, in mutual, self-protective denial, we both also experience the hour as basically unremarkable. I had already wounded her several times in just one telephone call and one meeting! She, in turn, disavowed the hurt to keep alive her hope of me as the good object, which a more borderline personality would find extremely difficult to do. Thus, she was able to report:

Ms. C: leaving the hour "feeling happier, having been held, accepted."

She further recollected that August was a particularly painful month:

Ms. C: Many demands made on me. I felt overwhelmed, under prepared, and anxious. I called R at the end of August and got an appointment for September. Resources were becoming depleted, and panic completely overtook me. I walked around the house in an anxious stupor.

I remained unaware of her distress when she called me during August while I was still on vacation and just about to go out of town.

Ms. C: I finally called R. I felt I couldn't make it alone. I felt a cold reception. R was annoyed but concerned. She said she wasn't available this month and asked if there was someone else I could see. I said yes. She called back and gave me a name anyway.

She organized a support system for herself, including some interim therapy. The therapist she saw likened her state to her swimming in a river of alligators with "her loved ones watching but not helping her." Because of my psychic unavailability, the reference is undoubtedly to me. I was also reenacting a maternal ambivalence with her when she pressed her need and I was too preoccupied to hear her, that is also a crucial part of her history which we were reenacting.

Consciously, I was *aware of none of this*. Until the time of the September appointment, contact had been limited to the initial telephone call, the "unexceptional" interview, and the telephone call in late August. I'm sure I felt that the work had not begun. Her notes on the following dramatic session after the summer coincide directly with my own recollections.

Ms. C: I walked in and fell apart. I cried immediately. I apologized for disturbing R. I apologized for crying. I apologized for feeling so miserable. I cried, cried, cried. Tears are everywhere. I wouldn't ask for a tissue. Tears, tears, tears.

As the hour went on I felt like a cross between a child beater and someone dropped into the wrong scenario. I had no idea what was going on, but her reproaches seemed unmistakable. Her incessant crying, combined with her apologies, were particularly distressing. I tried to get her to tell me what was wrong. We tried to process her disappointment at the emergency call to me. She was surprised that I wouldn't see her and was *sure* that I was seeing other clients. I respond with a series of unhelpful comments and reflections, which only made matters worse and which she experienced as:

Ms. C: An attack by a barrage of spears. I wanted mercy and felt attacked instead. I cried but I did not leave. R wonders if we could work together. I felt the door open, almost pushed out. I thought it was all hopeless yet stayed anyway. Was it willfulness? I felt like an ocean wave was washing over me, could get no air, only punishment from a great force. I wanted caring and got a knocking about. I didn't understand why. *I couldn't believe this was happening with a therapist* [italics added].

Her excellent notes perfectly capture the essential awfulness of the encounter. I too felt caught up in a useless undertow of confused and troubling emotion. I did not understand it at all and could not sort it out. I felt a rare uncertainty that perhaps I could not work with her. I knew that I was inflicting pain and felt that this should not go on between two human beings. It was at the height of the moment when the whole thing seemed senseless to me that a realization broke through. Although she doesn't report in her notes that I acted oddly at that critical moment, I was seized with manic relief as I blurted out, "Oh, we're just engaged in a sadomasochistic interaction!"

Her more appropriately sober notes read:

Ms. C: Suddenly, R realized sadomasochistic dynamic and the sun came out again! I had been through a hurricane, got drenched in tears, and was exhausted. Relieved, although in the aftermath of terror. I left the appointment feeling as above.

The fever had broken. In hindsight, I think that now that I was actually ready to work, I was able to receive the projected images of her murderous internal world, made what I think was a leap of imagination into it, and named it. The understanding that together we had re-created a sadomasochistic interaction somehow freed me from having to continue it, and I was able to lift both of us out of it. The therapy that followed yielded some important background information that helped me to understand why it was important for her to have this dynamic activated within a therapeutic holding environment. I believe that she was unconsciously searching for a transformational relationship that would free her from the pull of her sadomasochistic world view.

Background

Ms. C's childhood had been made a hell by an older, much larger, and possibly psychotic sister who chased and terrorized her daily while their parents worked. Of very modest circumstances, the parents were well meaning but preoccupied with earning a living. They sought help for the disturbed older girl only when she finally threatened her sister with a knife. For a large part of her life, Ms. C experienced herself as silently screaming in a world where no one came to her rescue. Much of the way in which she experienced the world reflected her endangered, abandoned self.

Initially, I was willing to identify only with her plucky courage and her enormous survival capacity. She, however, was determined to work through the damaged part of her, which existed side by side with her courageous self. She was able to sustain enough of an idealization toward me to keep her hope alive until I finally could identify with it and catch on. I did not arrive at the damaged part of her through the more usual empathic mode of vicarious introspection, in which the analyst functions as an objective observer. Owing to the initial misalliance of our intrasubjective worlds, and my empathic failure, she was able to make me comprehed her by engaging me in a rather powerful projective/ introjective process.

Imaginative Empathy

I had to allow myself to become thoroughly immersed with her, swept away, as it were, in the "spiraling interchange" between us. In this mode, "we name experience and invent a new language in metaphor to crystallize that which is not yet either in consciousness or existence. Here we create something together, make a link between disparate parts of experience and synthesize in new ways things already and almost there, but never before in *this* way" (Margulies, 1989, p. 143).

Imaginative empathy is my way of describing the therapist's attunement to pathology that has become embedded in the character structure and worldview of the individual that the patient wished to transcend (Kainer, 1993a). This pathology can function as the chief organizing principle of both experiencing and relating to the world and its objects. Imaginative empathy is the therapist's receiving the projective identification in imagination and, through the experiencing of it, freeing it from the pathological core from which it stems.

Together we gave name to the sadomasochistic aspects of our interchange. The naming helped integrate the sadistic and masochistic parts of her, resulting in her greater stability and relief from its sway. Through our mutual creation, it also gave me an important clue to the major difficulty that she sensed I could help her with. She had used my mental makeup to identify an important aspect of her own.

The Unexpected

The rewriting of her internal sadomasochistic text became the work of the therapy and took on the flavor of a zany comic novel. Whenever she slipped into a masochistic posture and felt hopelessly defeated—perhaps by the impossibility of getting a becoming haircut or getting to the analytic hour in the snow—I used my wits to challenge her assumptions while managing not to attack her. Once, when it had snowed and she was fearful that she couldn't get her car moving, I left with her after the hour and helped shovel her out. Although it was a natural gesture under the circumstances, she experienced it as not "what she expected" from a therapist.

The "unexpected" became my therapeutic ally and served a function to that in creating the "new" in art—it shakes up the old order. This encounter and others like it were unconscious moves to challenge her sadomasochistic worldview in one way or another. For up until then, everything had been narrated through the eyes of a terrified young child who would even feel abused by life's ordinary traffic and snow, or who would unconsciously and naively construct situations that invited abuse. Some time after our work ended and I called to invite her participation in preparing a paper on our work together, she remarked as I was sketching the paper for her, "You know, I don't do that any more." The "that" was vague, but we both knew what she meant.

IN THE REALM OF ENACTMENT

Differing Intrasubjective Worlds

The foregoing analytic encounter may be understood in several ways and at several levels. From a self-psychological perspective, the central question would be, "What part is being played at the moment by the state of the ambience between analyst and patient?" (Lichtenberg et al., 1992, p. 66). If that is the question, then it is clear that the subjective views of the patient and the therapist were diametrically opposed at the moment of the tumultuous postvacation meeting. To the analyst, what was a certainty that *the work was only then to begin*, was to the patient an equal certainty that *the work had been unbearably postponed*. The vastly different intrasubjective expectation of each undoubtedly set the stage for the collision. Intersubjectively, the unspoken needs of each (paradoxically based on their individual stresses) were unacceptable to the other and fed a mutual unconscious rejection.[13]

The Past in the Present

In further examining the powerful projective identification we enacted, the data yield more than a collision of wills owing to differences in the "present moment" of the analyst's and the patient's intrasubjective worlds, which were then intersubjectively played out. The patient came with a past that should not be ignored.[14] She brought to the analytic situation a history of adapting to an overburdened mother who could not properly "care for" (i.e., protect) her youngest child. Now, as the "newest" child/patient of an abandoning mother/therapist, she was already in an archaically familiar place. In an attempt to stay connected, the patient employed her characteristic denial of the true extent of her stress. In so doing, she could once again preserve the goodness of the bad object with whom she created a bond of dependency and in whom she still maintained hope.

She then effectively split off that part of herself which contained the rage and terror and being "unprotected," and we colluded to create the bland, "unexceptional" preliminary interview. By not "saying" (not communicating) that which I could not "hear" (contain) at the time, she was attempting to meet "the therapist's selfobject need" (Bacal and Thomson, 1996) to maintain the ideal of the good caretaker. However, there was a genuine selfobject failure of containment on the part of the therapist toward the patient, which was effectively communicated in the postvacation session. The confused anguish of each became a mutually created and shared phenomenon.

The "Turn-around" Transference

At the level of the empathic transference–countertransference aspects of the postvacation enactment, we have evidence of a "turn-around" archaic transference (H. Eist, 1990, personal communication), in which I directly felt the helplessness of the child who is attacked and for an unknown reason. Abandonment was in the air between us. In the deepening interpenetration of selves, we were certainly both swept away as in a "dramatic play . . . a fantasy creation woven from memories and imaginative elaborations of present actuality" (Loewald, 1975, p. 354). She made me feel her helplessness through her own considerable projective dramatic powers as surely as Eugene O'Neill had made me feel the poignancy of his own adolescent struggle in *The Great God Brown*.

The Scream of the Self

However, beyond the first two levels—the difference in the subjective worlds of patient and analyst, and the transference–countertransference present in the turn-around transference—we come yet to a third level in which a consideration of the creative and imaginative aspects of projective identification yielded a great deal of information. This enactment was not only about disappointment, or even helpless rage against a neglectful mother, but about her internal world, in which she could be "murdered" at any moment. This was the characteristic way in which she viewed the world; it was a relic of past damage. Her rage was disavowed and suppressed, but it was nonetheless acted out in her sadomasochistic reaction to life's vicissitudes. She needed me to hear, through my "feeling" of it, the scream she could not produce herself (Ogden, 1994, p.

192). Like Tausk's (1919, p. 525) Miss Emma A, I felt "thrust about" by an evil force I could not understand but with which I identified.

Although this kind of interaction has its "psychotic-making" aspects, it is useful not to limit our thinking of projective identification as a form of communication found only in psychotics (Rosenfeld, 1971). It can be seen here as well in a neurotic patient. Furthermore, it is not pathognomic in and of itself. I agree with Ogden (1994) that the pathology is not measured by the degree of coercion involved but, rather, is a "reflection of the degree of inability/unwillingness of the participants to release one another from the subjugation . . ." (p. 106). Our mutual good cheer at being quickly lifted out of the morass by my naming of it attested to its being a communication of one *to* another, rather than an evacuation of one *into* another. It was created in the service of connection.

The capacity for the analytic couple to "decenter from the mutual projection that the other was the sole cause of their misery" (Bacal and Newman, 1990) was an accurate prognosticator of the fruitful work to come. As Money-Kyrle (1956, pp. 360–366) observed, the partial introjective identifications allow the analyst's observing ego to use one's very emotional experience of the patient's projections as an analytic instrument.

I wish therefore to retain and constructively utilize the phenomenon of projective identification as another form of communication and understanding based on empathic attunement. It is in this dramatic intersubjective mode of interpenetrating selves that I can fathom that the patient is compelling me toward their dark realm of destructiveness and terror, but I go there willingly. I do not blame the journey on the patient's instinctual aggression, nor do I fail to acknowledge my contribution in enabling it to happen. Rather, like Meltzer (1984), I recognize that "the patient may need the analyst to *contain and detoxify* the unbearable feelings and . . . hand[s] them over to the analyst for this purpose" (italics added).

In the case of Ms. C, by tapping and identifying with the residues of my own sadomasochistic organization (which was somewhat more integrated, and therefore less inchoate, within me), I could then clearly name the dynamic we had mutually created. Doing so greatly helped in the reintegration of this part of her and eventually loosened the major place that her inwardly directed rage against the murderous world had previously held for her. If Tausk's (1919) patients could show us that, even in a psychotic and delusional state, it is human to seek and create identifications, Ms. C shows us the overpowering therapeutic need for communicating parts of the self to the imaginative (i.e., willingly containing) object, who will hold those parts for their therapeutic transformation.

Projective identification is indeed "the metaphor for imagination." It also describes the human need to create a connection with another,[15] and does so in this instance through their mutual imaginations. Beyond the mechanism of projection itself lies the longing that, through a projective identification, an other has been found through whom the unspoken thought will be known and through whom the unthought known (Bollas, 1987) will be spoken. Projective identification is a metaphor for hope.

Notes

[1] Laplanche and Pontalis (1973, p. 101) depict Klein's death instinct as a (Manachaean) struggle of good and evil. In this sense, her focus differs from Freud's emphasis on the biology of the Nirvana principle.

[2] Ogden's (1989) creative expansion of Klein's "positions" to include the "autistic-contiguous" position of the body self and his realization of the dialectical tension and collapse of these positions have been major contributions to clinical theory.

[3] Klein's (1946) considered grappling with the death instinct resembles that of Rank (1939), whose major work on the creative will was also in response to the power of Freud's new idea. For Rank, knowledge of our mortality exists alongside the longing for immortality. Art can serve as a creative transcendence over the fact of our biological finiteness (Kainer, 1984).

[4] This view has similar elements to the earlier work of Grinberg (1962) and Malin and Grotstein (1966).

[5] There is no direct reference to Tausk in Klein's writings. She does not list him in a bibliography (Pieczanski, 1994). His seminal paper, troubled relationship with Freud, and early tragic suicide, were well known in Freudian circles.

[6] Tausk came from a journalistic (as well as a judicial) background. His intense relationship with "contemporary Germany's best-known woman author" (Eissler, 1971, p. 21), Freud's disciple Lou-Andreas Salomé, would speak to his strong attraction to the creative aspects of the mind, as well as to its pathology.

[7] Klein (1955, p. 145n) indicated she had read a 1950 English translation of the popular novel.

[8] Just as Tausk's (1919) patients described the gradual diminishment of the "influencing machine."

[9] A. Pieczanski (1995, personal communication) observes that in general there is a problem with the "derogatory connotation" inherent in the medicalization of pathology.

[10] A term also used by Margulies (1989) for the title of his book, *The Empathic Imagination.*

[11] I differ here with Malin and Grotstein (1966), who would limit the idea of projection to instinctual matters. I would prefer to see projection as a fundamental mechanism of the mind not limited to instinctual matters. The distinction I draw between projection and projective identification (similar to Ogden's and differing from Grotstein's, 1985b, as well as Zinner, 1995, personal communication) is taken up elsewhere in the book.

[12] I am more drawn to Grotstein's (1984a, p. 305) idea of the *container as a form of communication.*

[13] In a sense, there was great similarity in the internal worlds of both patient and therapist in that each contained an internal object relationship of the unavailable other to the needy self (V. Hendrickson, 1995, personal communication).

[14] I am indebted to Sandra Palef (1994) for her discussion of these aspects of the clinical material.

[15] Others, such as Bowlby (1969, 1980) and Beebe and Lachmann (1994), speak of an innate urge to connect.

Chapter Nine

Psychic Catastrophe and the Premature Birth of the Self

Implications for Treatment

Yes, the overwhelming spell that we continue to cast on one another, right down to the end, with the body's surface, which turns out to be . . . about as serious a thing there is in life. The body, from which one cannot strip oneself however one tries, from which one is not to be freed this side of death.
— PHILIP ROTH, *American Pastoral*

The bodily self is both an internal state and an instrument of being in the world. It plays a part in our connection to others from beginning to end. While the need for attunements to bodily self-states is particularly crucial in infancy, attunement to self-states continues to be important in later development. Self-states are reflected in the sense of self, in thinking, and in behavior.

In chapters five and seven, I discussed how pathologies of the bodily self remain active in the self-structure and often contribute to its collapse. In chapter five, the focus was on the tensions held in the bodily self that lead to acts of autistic self-soothing owing to the loss of the attunement of the mother's mind. In the absence of the needed mental connection to the other, autistic acts were depicted as compensatory autosensuous attempts to fill the inner emptiness of a black hole of existence and still the pain of a lifelong, elemental depression (see Ms. F, chapter five). *Thinking* during a sensate state of autistic collapse was characterized as a detached "mindlessness." I will presently explore how restoring the capacity to think (through the restoration of the dialectic of the self) is linked to the presence of self-state attunement.

In chapter seven, the focus was on how the effect of the lack of *regulating selfobject containment* affects the psychotic anxiety of someone like Ms. G, who may have a genetic predisposition for affective vulnerability. Her bodily self reflected traits of hypersensitivity that were not merely transient states that could easily be medicated out, but pointed to the necessity for the selfobject containment of the "flowing over" (Tustin, 1981a, p. 183) of unbearable tensions, until self-management could become a possibility.

In this chapter, I go further into the themes of attunement and containment of the flowing over of self as it affects development beyond infancy. I also further explore the way in which self-state issues are manifested in the clinical situation as well as in ordinary life. To help illustrate these ideas as they operate throughout the developmental spectrum, I shall turn again to the work of Freud and Frances Tustin for its beginnings—and to Philip Roth and Pablo Picasso, to illustrate the connection of the bodily self to the other "right down to the end." I am concerned here with the nature of the interrelatedness of mind and body as it affects the self and other.

THE ORIGINS OF THE BODILY SELF

Freud

The idea that the sense of self is first experienced through the body was suggested in Freud's (1923) thoughts on the development of psychic structure.[1] In the formation of the ego, "*the first ego is the bodily-ego*; it is not merely a surface entity, but is itself the *projection* of a surface" (p. 26, italics added). Freud later added: "The ego is ultimately derived from *bodily sensations*, chiefly from those springing from the surface of the body. *It may thus be regarded as a mental projection of the surface of the body*[2] (p. 26, italics added).

In seeing the ego as derived from sensations springing from the surface of the body, Freud was also indicating how stimuli *outside* the ego— but impinging on it—become part of its structure. Although his libido theory did not grant the *object* its full importance,[3] we know that the sensate self is in continuous oscillation with its objects. The sensate self starts at the very beginning of life. We *take in*—or at the very least must struggle with—whatever or whoever affects us. When Freud's instinctual model dialectically yielded to the later object-relational one, the chief stimulus was now recognized to be the object, that is, the other. The bodily self could now be thought of in its object-relational context, with direct bearing on the relationship of self and other.

Freud's ego—as the mental projection of the bodily surfaces derived from bodily sensations—is the precursor of the later work of Anzieu (1985, 1990), Bick (1968, 1986), Ogden (1989), and Tustin (1990), among others.

Bick's (1968) "psychic skin" and Anzieu's (1985) "skin ego . . . an envelope
which emits and receives signals in interaction with the environment"
(p. 132)—are metaphors for our psychic organs of being-in-the-world,
which bring us in to relationship with our objects. For example, Bick's
idea of a second skin is useful in understanding much of behavior that
protects the self—such as Ms. G's intense mental involvement with a large
number of people who served to keep her elemental terror at bay (chapter
seven). Pursuits that serve a second-skin function may also have their creative and social aspects, as well as defensive ones. These functions are derived from how we experience the body-self, which affects our interactions.
In a sense, it is who we are "in our skin," and what we do because of it.

Tustin

Tustin's clinical observations most completely place the bodily self in its
object-relational context, and the importance of her work has been recognized by a growing number of theoreticians and clinicians (Mitrani and
Mitrani, 1997). Her seminal constructions of the "flowing over" of the
self, "oneness," "twoness," and the "catastrophe of premature psychological birth" (Tustin, 1981a, pp. 181–196) have direct bearing on the
self-state, the sense of self, and the way in which one perceives and relates
to the world.

The following example illustrates the meaning of these constructs in
relation to the self-state of a young child.

Example 1

A colleague related the following event between herself and her two-
and-a-half year-old child. They were at the check-out counter of the su-
permarket as part of a leisurely afternoon outing. Suddenly—and
uncharacteristically for this usually well disposed youngster—the child
emitted a piercing cry and became extremely upset, sobbing loudly. The
checker said dismissively, "Oh, she just wants attention," as a way of
dealing with the disturbing feelings that the distressed little girl was stimu-
lating. However, the mother unhesitatingly picked the child up and held
her closely, while quietly checking the child's forearms on the chance
that she had somehow pinched them in the movement of the conveyer
belt. Seeing no apparent physical damage, she continued to comfort the
child, who was still sobbing. They slowly went out hand in hand, with the
child still upset. The mother stopped on the short walk home and sat
with the child on a low ledge, speaking gently to her and sometimes holding and patting her without words. She did know what was wrong, nor
could the child tell her.

The event was unusual in this child's history, and the mother reported thinking about it later. Reverie yielded the idea that the child— who had always required a good deal of sleep and recently had given up taking two naps a day—just may have been too tired and was thrown off by the physiological time-clock changes she was undergoing. Noting that this behavior had not been seen before (nor since, she later reported), she reflected that perhaps she had witnessed an act of the "terrible twos" in this ordinarily self-possessed child whose system was in shock.

Although uncertain as to the cause, the mother had no doubts about the need to hold and comfort the child. She did not experience the child's "need for attention" as the act of a "spoiled" child, as the clerk's comment implied, but, rather, felt that it indicated something that needed her immediate attention. She responded to the child's elemental howl of pain without qualification. Their "I"s were syntonic.

The child as an adult recalled the scene, for which she had a partial memory. She was not certain if she had actually felt a shock from the conveyer belt, but she did remember having what she termed a "shock to the system." She felt that the incident had had less to do with her being physically tired than with her having a sudden realization that "A bad thing could happen to me."

The mother had intuitively reacted to the child's collapse without even knowing its cause. The child had a catastrophic awareness that the world could be a dangerous place and communicated this knowledge through a "flowing over" to the mother.[4] The mother responded by reviving the soothing and protective gestures that had always been available to her child during infancy. The individual *edges of their emotional selves* met once again, fitting together both physically and mentally.

The mother had the not-quite-correct idea that the child's distress was due to the shift in the child's decreased naps, that is, that she was emerging from her baby stage. That idea was a code for a realization that she would not always be able to protect her "babe-in-arms" from danger. The child knew this too. The mother caught the undertow of the child's fright and identified with the anguish. There was a wordless, mutually shared sense that the world could indeed be a dangerous place. The mother's taking the child into her arms was an instinctive act of *protectiveness* as well as an attempt at soothing.

The "Catastrophe of Premature Psychological Birth"

Tustin (1981a) would say that the mother restored their "oneness" to counterbalance what at that moment was the catastrophe of the child's sudden awareness of her "twoness"—that is, a separateness—that was overwhelming to her. The catastrophe is of a "premature psychological birth." When it occurs postnatally (as with Ms. G in chapter seven) it contributes to disregulation and psychotic terror. I believe, however, that premature psychological birth continues to occur at times beyond infancy—with a catastrophic consequence to the sense of self if the self-state is not properly managed.

In this example, the checker's response was a conventional one to what seemed to her to be a bid for attention that was not to be minded. Her response could have resulted in the mismanagement of an important moment in the child's development of self. In working to restore the child to calm, the mother correctly managed the "flowing over" of the child's emotions, as well as projectively occupying the same mental space to catch the moment of the child's awareness of being thrust into a new world. She was in attendance at a stage of *psychological birth* for the child.

This psychological birth involved a sudden catastrophic sense of vulnerability in which the child cried out for—and elicited—an earlier mode of maternal protectiveness. The mind (emotional attention) of the mother was solely engaged with the child's experience, and the body of the mother went to shield her. The child's need was for the sanctuary of the mother's mind as well as her arms. States of "flowing over" are pivotal moments in the need for attunement, not only in the first stages of postnatal development, but beyond. The continued failure to contain the overflow of emotions in the case of Ms. G (chapter seven) is an example of its catastrophic consequences. The mental and emotional edges of self and other must somehow fit together if the catastrophe of building up unbearable states of tension and a damaged sense of self is to be avoided. Tustin's clinical observations left her with the unmistakable sense of the need restore "oneness" in the delicate balance of maintaining ongoingness in the aftermath of postnatal psychological birth. Nothing could be more important in recovery from disruptions to the ongoingness of being. Since the differentiation of self and other is in place at birth (Stern, 1985), the child's sense of separateness may have been further heightened in this natural developmental period of twoness.

The Dialectic of "Oneness" and "Twoness"

Thus far, I have been concerned with the negative effects of premature twoness, that is, with the catastrophe of premature psychological birth. Oneness and twoness, however, operate within a dialectic of unity and separateness between self and other. The danger comes when oneness with an object is necessary but not forthcoming—or, by contrast, when it is prolonged into an adhesive or fused state when not necessary. Similarly, twoness becomes a source of pathology when it asserts itself prematurely and becomes fixed in the character structure as an isolated or autistic aloneness. Twoness is also a problem if it is not achieved. A quotation from Larsen (1997) expresses my meaning: "[The artist] Mr. Fuss spent his month at the Shaker farm gathering ladders, which he prized as examples of Shaker "twoness": square, strong, upright, eroded by hard use" (p. 32).

Twoness implies a firmness of self and its structure and self-definition. Much that is creative implies a firmly bounded hardness of self, distinct and separate from the other, and a standing alone. The importance of Tustin's work is in understanding, rather, the toll that *premature* twoness takes when the other is, in fact, necessary to development and it comes too soon. The distinction should be made between the catastrophe of premature twoness, and the necessity for an appropriate twoness without which further psychological growth cannot take place, as in Ms. G's case in chapter six.

Tustin's "Hardness" and "Softness"

Intertwined with Tustin's ideas of oneness and twoness are those of *hardness* and *softness,* which are the beginnings of the self-states of comfort and discomfort. Tustin (1981a) described the characteristics of the earliest sensations of the fundamental dyadic encounter—the nursing situation:

> Gradually, "soft" sensations become associated with "taking-in"—with receptivity. "Hard" sensations become associated with "entering" and "thrusting." At some point, these become "male" and "soft," "receptive" becomes "female." When on the basis of a cooperative suckling experience, "hard," "entering" nipple and tongue are experienced as working together with "soft" receptive mouth and breast, then a "marriage" between "male" and "female" elements takes place. Out of this union of "hard" and "soft" sensations, a new way of functioning is born. . . .
>
> In a satisfactory suckling experience sensations of "softness" and "hardness" work together to produce a state of "well-being." Well-being is a psychological as well as a bodily experience. Thus, bodily sensations have been transformed into *psychological* experience through reciprocal and rhythmical activity between mother and infant. The stage is set for percept and concept formation. But this is a mysterious process . . . [p. 186].

Comfort, Discomfort, and the Capacity to Think

I believe that percept and concept formation in thinking is affected by anxiety arising from an internalized sense of a discomfort of fit. The following example of an attempt to teach Tustin's work, from which the above passage was taken, is illustrative.

Prior to the group discussion, seminar members were asked about their individual reactions to the essay.[5] I had hoped to introduce this group of clinicians to Tustin's ideas on the effects on the mind due to early bodily sensations, to prepare them for further work on autistic features in neurotic patients (Tustin, 1986, 1990). Initially, the essay created a sensation of acute discomfort for most of the seminar members.

In my enthusiasm for her originality and the evocativeness of her ideas, I "overlooked" (denied) her equation of "hardness and softness" with "maleness and femaleness." At some level, though, I was dimly aware of the possible cliché and the potential for resentment in the gender consciousness of the present day. I ignored it at my peril. The group—in its infinite capacity to reflect *every* bit and piece of the experience available (Bion, 1957)—*did not* overlook it. For all but one member it evoked a reaction that halted their further thinking about the material.

Where I had an immediate "oneness" with Tustin's ideas, most members had a reaction of a tantrum of "twoness" that was catastrophic. Her nipple imagery and their general unfamiliarity with her language also made it hard for them to take in, let alone digest it. The first member's response set the tone of the group discussion. She opened with, "Why are we reading this?" This signaled the start of a variety of bewildered and negative responses. All but one of the members commented in a similar vein. The majority of the group vigorously claimed *they did not understand* the essay. There was general upheaval.

However, the final respondent, a gifted and intuitive clinician, had another and quite different reaction. She said she had seized on the essay, found it "wonderful," and had already found application for it in her understanding of one of her patients!

In responding to the majority assertion of noncomprehension, I first interpreted that their bewilderment and distaste indicated that they *indeed* "got" the material—through its projective qualities—and they were now communicating their exact understanding of Tustin's idea of the discomfort of a dystonic fit through the arousal of sensations of unpleasant "hardness." They had experienced her message in a "Bionesque," inchoate, "beta" bits fashion, by first rejecting its meaning. It took them but another moment to completely understand Tustin's meaning when I interpreted their reactions in her own "mouth sensation" imagery: "In Tustin's imagery, your reactions indicate that there was a lot of 'spitting out' of unpalatable stuff. It must have felt 'hard' and therefore unpleasant. It didn't fit together correctly. You ejected the material with your mind/tongue as a foreign-tasting substance."

And to the member who had connected instantaneously with the material, I also drew on my experience of her as a creative thinker. I turned to her saying, "And you have a 'mouth-brain'—you sucked in the material, became one with it, and immediately used it to fire and excite your imagination!"

Containment of the "Tantrum of Twoness"

My acceptance of the group's expression of distress seemed to satisfactorily lift the anxiety that had blocked the thinking of those who needed to eject it. Linking the group dynamic to the phenomena of ejection and *taking in* enabled those who had not felt a "oneness" with the material to do so now and begin to consider it. Their distaste for what was the unpalatable, ill-fitting "hardness" of the material had affected their receptivity and thinking. Lacking a sense of "oneness" with it, they had a cognitive "tantrum of twoness."

My moving toward containment of the anxiety of the group was similar to the movements of soothing containment offered by the mother to the distraught child in the first example. In both cases, the "flowing over" emotional state of the other was, without question, accepted as legitimate. It is the basic posture of attunement. The selfobject containment (through an identification with their distress) helped to mitigate the spitting out of the foreign-tasting ideas. Furthermore, the material now "fit together" for them in a comprehensible way.

The seminar members went on to be able to consider and find enrichment from what had at first been unpalatable (and therefore unknowable and unspeakable). They gained a greater access to their thinking. The anonymous evaluation comments at the end of the semester were positive regarding the once rejected readings. "Hard" and distasteful had been integrated with "soft" and satisfying. "Oneness" was restored, and the mismatched edges between self and not-self were evened out. This firmer oneness was not based on symbiotic attachment or adhesive identification, but, rather, on a new concordant identification of the "I" of the self with the "I" of the other (see chapter one).

In the reaction of the seminar members, I was struck by the relevance of Winnicott's (1950) and Bion's (1957) ideas on containment to the creation of mind and its task of thinking. We know that if containment is missing early on, a psychotic state of "unmentalized" experience exists in varying degrees in one's mental makeup that can become somatized (Mitrani, 1996). I think that *self-state containment is absolutely essential for the development of thoughtfulness and thinking beyond infancy and in ordinary life, because flowing over is a fact of existence.* The lack of self-state containment is a crucial factor in the psychopathology of everyday life. This is what we need from the other.

IN THE CLINICAL SETTING

Let us turn to the clinical recognition of patients who have not fared well owing to mismatches of fit between self and other beyond infancy. Among their symptoms are fussiness, aversive behaviors, and anxiety regarding anger and rejection, both their own and others'. Understanding the nature of a self-state of discomfort within one's skin, where one also does not fit with the other is crucial. When these self-state mismatches appear clinically they are not merely a tantrum or an "aggressive object-relation" (Klein, 1946, p. 8). They are pathognomic of a deeply rooted sense of distress.

They are found among patients across the treatment spectrum. They will be manifested in an analysis where regression is expected and in therapies where it is not. They are ongoing as part of the structure of the self and need to be properly understood and appropriately contained. The bodily self in relation to the other, and the uncomfortable bodily self-state, are especially relevant in the following clinical examples.

Example 2

Almost all my patients have their preferred way of arranging themselves on a couch, which is across from my own chair, in such a way as to allow them either to face me or to look away as they choose, as well as recline or sit up. Many recline, but each establishes their own intrapsychic space, and regulates their own preferred interpersonal visual distance.

This particular patient exemplifies an extremely fussy mode of being-in-the-world in the way in which she cannot settle in until "just the right" arrangement of pillows is attained. While most patients take a moment to arrange things to their liking, her movements are striking. Her elaborate preparations are accompanied by tiny, pursed-mouth movements of distaste if one of the pillows should not be arranged *exactly* right. If her favorite soft pillow is temporarily hidden from view, there is a flurry of upset. It is as if she were trying to settle down but finds her place too uncomfortable, too hard. Her "fussiness" is due to anxiety that the maternal receptivity will not be right.

She also has an interpersonal style that is fraught with anxiety. If she should need to change a future appointment, she is immediately agitated. Fearfully interpreting a moment's hesitation on my part as annoyance or anger—and perhaps trying to ward off her own—she tries to short-circuit the anxiety by responding the *instant* she utters the request: "Oh, it's O.K., it's O.K., I understand that you can't do it" before I can even reach my calendar to see what the possibilities are for change!

This is someone whose bodily self-state also included a serious rejection of food. In addition to using food as an autistic object for self soothing (as in the examples in chapter five), she had a period of starving herself and ejecting food in a literal and figurative way. Her eating disorder followed the acute distaste for what was provided for her.

The acute distaste—her "spitting out"—for that which comes from the outside is reminiscent of Freud's (1923) description of the ego's experiencing of all that is within as good and all that is noxious coming from without. Her acute sensitivity to "hardness" as a way of experiencing the world is now manifested in her elaborate pillow arrangements, which must obliterate anything but the perfect fit. Her catastrophic anxiety about any possible lack of immediate "oneness" with her needs, such as a change in appointments, highlights the impairment of fit that has haunted her all her life.

Failures of Fit During Later Development

Although the natural developmental period for regulating the "flowing over" of excitation is infancy, the need for resonance to unbearable feelings to restore the cohesiveness of the self-state of an older child is clear in the first example. It is possible to imagine what a mismatch (empathic failure) between mother and child would have looked like if the mother had not resonated to—or had dismissed—the emotional state of the child at an age when the sense of self qua self is more firmly established. What took place instead was a shared oneness in *which the edges of the individuated self of the mother and child matched*, establishing a sense of trust in the child that she could weather bad things.

The failure to have the edges of self and other come together at later developmental periods—particularly in adolescence—also takes its toll and manifests itself in tension held in the bodily self and on self-esteem, as in the following case.

Example 3: Ms. H
A woman whose basic early fit with the maternal object seemed secure, Ms. H did not manifest acute physical fussiness about softness and hardness as such in the classical, Tustin sense. But she had a great uncertainty about her appropriate "fit" in the world and a pervasive sense of discomfort. There were indications of narcissistic trauma involving her father's poor attunement to her during her young girlhood.[6] As one result, her mature erotic object choices had been of deeply narcissistic men who resembled that aspect of her father and who inevitably greatly disappointed her.

Manifestations of the Bodily Self

In the clinical hour, her uncertainty of being—of her self, her worth, her desirability, her femininity—was also subtly expressed in her unusual "settling in" behavior each session. Very carefully dressed, she would conduct a debate with herself as to whether or not she should sit up or recline. The fact that it was entirely up to her and did not make too much of a difference did not address the meaning of her concern. When this behavior went on for many months, I asked her why she thought this posed such a struggle for her. Why, if she wanted to recline, could she not do so?

She replied that she feared "mussing" her clothes. Disturbing her picture-perfect attire at the cost of giving up a more comfortable posture had many meanings. She had multiples of the same expensive pants suit that was in vogue at the time, and at one point she made a single purchase of 14 of them! Although such extravagance could possibly be justified by the demands of her professional life, and her need to rotate her outfits, it had an odd flavor to it.

I could be certain that this was compulsive behavior when she returned from a professional trip abroad with a very expensive gold watch she had brought there. It was an *exact* duplicate of one she was wearing. While the need for duplicates of clothing might have some utility, clearly an identical second watch could not. Although I did not have the vocabulary at the time, I now understand that this was her "hard object" protecting herself from the feeling that there was no one in her life to give her this loving gift. The suits were her second skin and must not get "wrinkled" or worn out with use and the age she was beginning to feel.

The following clinical moment with Ms. H was revealing. She was the colleague of another patient, and both had demanding professional positions that sometimes required their immediate presence with very little notice. When one such circumstance arose that conflicted with an hour, their solution—made with my consent—was to exchange their hours. However, at the moment in question, I was startled to see her colleague in Ms. H's place without my knowing it was going to happen. Although I said nothing to her, having quickly realized what had occurred, she of course did not miss my look of surprise and of course reported it to the patient.

Ms. H came to her next hour and, noting that I had seemed surprised at the switch, angrily said, "Why should it matter to you who uses the hour, as long your time isn't being wasted?"

Like her purchases, her rationale demanded following a certain logic. She was confused and upset that it had not been a matter of complete indifference to me. Not entirely sure what was at work for her, but hearing something, I quietly responded to her, "Don't you think it would make a difference to me whether or not it was *you* who were here?" At that point this very controlled and often false-self hearty woman, broke into sobs and immediately had the following association: she recalled always anticipating her father's homecoming with great pleasure. She once rounded the corner of the room and came upon him unexpectedly and beamed a pleasure-filled "Hi" to him. Perhaps startled, his response was a dismissive, "Why do you always say 'Hi'?"

The narcissistic injury to this eager young girl who adored her father and his exciting work was palpable. In an unguarded moment, it was a rejection that had the force of a slap. It had the effect of diminishing her sense of self-worth and contributed to her discomfort in the world and in her own skin. Fearful that her presence would be unwelcome at worst, but at best only an occasion for indifference, she carried around the sense of the "surfaces" of her self *not ever* connecting with the 'surface' of the other. Startled at my being startled (and perhaps fearful of my anger)— and in momentary identification with her narcissistic father—she first lashed out with the same sadistic anger he had.

The emotional mismatching with her father, coming at this crucial developmental level, perverted the love she had for him and for his exciting work. Although she grew up to do the work, the ragged edges of their fit took its toll on her love life. Until our work, she had always chosen men who loved themselves more than they loved her. After the "joining" together made possible in our work, she "found" someone who deserved her love. She was able to let go of her layers of extra psychic skin once afforded only by clothes and jewelry.

TUSTIN'S "FIT" WITH ANALYTIC THEORY

In a review of Tustin's work, Spensley (1995) noted that this "brilliant clinician . . . opened up and articulated a level of experience which is recognizable and intelligible to psychotics, to neurotics and to some so-called normals. . . . Yet Tustin has not attempted to accommodate her thinking about autistic states into the body of existing psychoanalytic theory and is not always clear in her books how they do fit in" (p. 54).[7]

With the importance I give to the dialectic of past and present (see chapter two), I believe that Tustin's work brings back and completes some of the forgotten ideas of the earlier days of psychoanalysis. Without her being aware of it, Tustin's "oneness" directly hearkens back to Lou Andreas-Salomé's (1921) construct of "proto-narcissism" and the oceanic feeling of mother–child "at-oneness," which she felt "preceded the ego's struggle with the instincts."[8] Like Andreas-Salomé in her removal of the "at-oneness" of mother and child" from sexual and aggressive instincts, Tustin lifted it out of any embeddedness in drive theory and placed it in an object-seeking, relational matrix in which autistic nonattachment is its pathological opposite.

Thus, Tustin's work connects early psychoanalytic ideas on the bodily ego (Freud), and the unity of self and other (Andreas-Salomé, 1921), with the present infant research on the individuated self. As discussed in chapter five, infant research (Stern, 1985) has established that awareness of the differentiation of self from other exists from birth, (in contrast to Mahler's theory of an initial stage of symbiosis that later gives way to a state of differentiation).

This has provided a somewhat thorny theoretical issue for those trying to describe certain aspects of early infantile states of unity, such as Tustin (1981a) and Grotstein (1995), whose clinical observations have been of those who *were catastrophically affected by the premature rupture* of the emotional unity of the mother–child connection.

Grotstein (1990) solved the theoretical problem of differentiated boundaries by offering the dialectical hypothesis of the "Siamese-twinship" (p. 381) of mother and child. While keeping in mind Stern's research on differentiation, he said that "the infant can be pictured as being both separate and non-separate at the same time. Insofar as the infant is non-separate in one domain of experience, then an object loss is equated with a narcissistic loss" (p. 381).

My own sense is that Stern's (1985) work—and that of others—on the capacity for discriminatory differentiation from the first moments of life suggests *that the potential for experiencing the other's disconnection* exists from birth, and disconnection is a developmental catastrophe. In her work on autistic phenomena, Tustin (1986, 1990) demonstrated just how terrifying and permanently devastating a premature awareness of bodily separateness from the mother can be for an infant who may be constitutionally or psychically vulnerable.

In the first example of the mother's response to the distraught child, the mother instinctively held her close in an attempt to ease the child's distress, in a basic gesture of protection. *Differentiation and awareness of separateness makes attachment and connection all the more important.* The mother who eases the distress of the child can certainly be the differentiated mother, as Grotstein (1990) concluded. Side by side with the early capacity for differentiation is an emotional connectedness that Tustin (1981a) calls the overflowing or ecstasy of "oneness" that is happily established in relation to the mother who is in tune with catching its "overflow."

Maternal reverie has been equated with empathy as "a process that involves feelings and thoughts as deeply interwoven with one another" (Henry, 1983, p. 83). Tustin evocatively described the mother's containment of the ecstasy of the "overflowing of oneness." She thought it preceded projective identification in Klein's sense, but they seem to me to be two ways of "knowing" the other that are based on empathic identification, as in example 2. The mother was responsive to the emotional *overflow* of the child and, at the same time, identified with the child's *projective communication* of danger. She was attuned to both the emotional urgency of the child's communication and its (unspoken) mental content. She identified with both channels of communication.

Her dual responsiveness appears to mirror the complementary aspects of Bion's and Tustin's work. Bion seemed to have the greater attunement to, and identification with, the *mental content* of the psychotic aspects of the mind (in both psychotic and nonpsychotic patients). Tustin understood the emotional aspect of the self-state. It would be of interest to compare further the roles of these components—the affective and the thought process—as they are reflected in the theories of *vicarious introspection* and *projective identification*. Such an exploration may lead to a better understanding of the nature of the dialectic between their representative schools of thought of Bion and Tustin.

THE MISMATCH OF SELF AND OTHER: THE SEARCH FOR UNITY "RIGHT DOWN TO THE END"

Philip Roth and Pablo Picasso

Even when there is a great failure of empathy for the other and one remains the sole center of one's concerns, there still is a desire to fit with the other that is often expressed through the surfaces of the bodily self. Perhaps there are no better examples of the lingering effects of the mismatching of the edges of the surfaces of the self and the other than in the examples of the writer Philip Roth and the artist Pablo Picasso, not only in the personal aspects of their lives but in their art as well. It is in their art that they brilliantly project these struggles, which, to my mind, they solved more successfully than in their personal lives.

Each is well known as a legendary, if not notorious, narcissist, particularly in relationship to a woman as muse and caretaker (Rank, 1932). The intense need of each for a woman to be both (Kainer, 1990) takes precedence over any latent wish he might have for mutuality. For each, his own caretaking of the woman or their children is foreclosed by the ferocious dominance of his needs. His sense of wrong in regard to the other is inoperative when his own needs prevail.

For each of these artists in his personal life *the connection of self and other has been no ordinary event* (see Bloom, 1996; Huffington, 1996). It greatly depended on the devotion of the other to unequivocally meet his artistic, sexual, and narcissistic needs. The edges of his self with the self of the other who becomes important to him do not meet smoothly. There is an intense struggle for domination and control. Just as the edge marking the self and the other are jagged, their connections through their body surfaces become more difficult over time. The difficulties encountered by the aging sexual narcissist are brilliantly projected into their work—Picasso in his tormented "Late" paintings (Tate Gallery, 1988) and Roth (1995) in *Sabbath's Theater*.

Roth

Roth brings us closest to the meaning of the "surface" of the body and its relation to the other, as in the opening quotation. His use of the same "surface" imagery as Freud, whose primary emphasis was libido theory, is not far from the sexual preoccupations of much of Roth's work. For Roth, the sexual connection is what adheres the mismatched *edges* of differentiated selves—of surfaces that do not meet in most ordinary ways of life. However, he is not without humor about it, which is often its saving grace in his work.

For Roth, a desperate search to make a connection to the other through body "surfaces" is also a way of giving the self meaning. Sexuality becomes the metaphor for connection. However, as the problem of the waning of one's physical power in aging increases in those who have heavily relied on sexuality for their sense of aliveness (perhaps as a result of narcissistic deadness), the search for connection through sexual union takes on a desperate savagery, as in *Sabbath's Theater*.

Sabbath's Theater has the figure of the aging puppeteer Mickey Sabbath facing a developmental end-of-life crisis with about as little grace as he did his previous years. He is more pathetic than satanic, but he is both. He is portrayed as not nice, physically unappetizing, barely pleasant, cunning when it comes to sexual manipulation, cynical, a bit crazed, scornful (especially of the conventional), and as perversely sexually occupied in the most unholy of ways. Like his creator, he is intelligent and has a certain self-knowledge, which nonetheless does not prevent him from presenting his unappealing side. The novel seems like a parody of the ending one might have imagined for the sexual protagonist of Roth's (1967) earlier *Portnoy's Complaint*.

About the only women Sabbath will not readily occupy himself with are his wives, especially the present one, whom he scorns as a piously recovering alcoholic. Sabbath sends her off to AA meetings and psychotherapy with characteristic mockery, the better to pursue his sexual interests. Fortunately for him, his most ardent companion for the preceding 13 years has been the bigger-than-life, hardworking, and devoted innkeeper, Drenka, the immigrant wife of an unsuspecting and decent Serbo-Croatian chef. She has the distinction of having found almost *no* man of her acquaintance (and some women) sexually unappealing—with the exception of her husband. Sabbath and Drenka are the perfectly matched licentious couple, different only in that Drenka is depicted as dear and loving as Sabbath is not. That one day she had four different men (each worthy of her sexual attention in his own way) is really not a problem for either of them; it is proof for Sabbath of her vitality. Roth has their mad love for each other expressed as their manic passion for, and devotion to, each other's sexual parts. Cheats, liars, and sexual scoundrels though they may be, he is her "American boyfriend," who keeps her hopeful, and she is his vital force, who keeps him alive.

Sabbath is trying to convince Drenka that it is her passionate wish for him to be monogamous with her (he already is but won't admit it) and her trying to fulfill her brief marital obligations to her husband that is making her continuously nauseated. Her misguided wish for monogamy, he says, is the culprit. Unfortunately, it turns out to be her dying wish, for it is not monogamy but ovarian cancer that is doing her in and quickly ends her earthly life—a beauty still in her 50s. Two hundred and fifty-six letters of mourning and condolence are sent to Drenka's husband, each of them attesting to what a remarkable woman she was. Sabbath notes that he received not one.

Roth says that Sabbath had been badgering Drenka so because "he was fighting for his life" (p. 27). Indeed, after her death, Sabbath continues to visit her grave in his own inimitable onanistic fashion with the same passion he brought to their long liaison. After provoking his wife to throw him out, he revisits old friends and family, acts reprehensibly, and prepares for his own mortal ending in his manic and tawdry way. As prepared as he is for it—as much as he is provoking a confrontation with Drenka's policeman son, who now knows of their depravity—he is not to be murdered. The son is too decent a fellow.

Neither will Sabbath kill himself, although he has been preparing to have his life end for most of the book. In Sabbath's logic and Roth's genius for irreverence, the book concludes: "And he couldn't do it. He could not [expletive] die. How could he leave? How could he go? Everything he hated was here" (p. 451). The book—with its dedications to friends now gone—perhaps reflects the author's serious contemplation of his own aging, illnesses, and mortality, but his vital wit is still strong, and the writing has a dedicated and mature mastery. Roth goes on writing, connecting with others in the way that he does best.

Picasso

Similarly, as depicted in Picasso's brilliant, desperate, and equally savage "Late" paintings" (Tate Gallery, 1988), the connection to the other, once made through powerful sexual energy and complete artistic mastery, can no longer be completely counted on. His art—always his driving force as well as his connection to the past—was a second skin and the psychic envelope through which he communicated to the world that lay outside of him. His art kept him connected to those with whom he identified—masters of the past whose paintings he appropriated for his own genius, particularly after he had outlived those of his own time (Galassi, 1996).

Richardson (Tate Gallery, 1988, pp. 17–48) thought that Picasso's identification with the old masters was a form of Freud's "psychic cannibalism" (p. 17). That is the way in which the power of the other is taken in. I think it also was his instrument of redemption. Capable of learning well into his 90s, his appropriation of van Gogh helped with a much needed galvanizing of his paint surfaces.

> It worked. The surface of the late paintings has a freedom, a plasticity, that was never there before; they are more spontaneous, more expressive and more instinctive, than virtually all his previous work. The imminence of his own end may also have constituted a link with Van Gogh. The more one studies these late paintings, the more one realizes that they are, like Van Gogh's terminal landscapes, a supreme affirmation of life in the teeth of death [p. 34].

Even in the self-willed artist, the need for connection is very great. Like the early German expressionists (see chapter two) who turned back to a more primitive art form when overwhelmed by the present destructiveness, or like Tanazaki (1943–48), who recreates a more ideal era, Picasso turned back to connect so that he could continue on as his powers ebbed. For some, connection through the "surface of the self" in the ordinary way is not, or is no longer, possible. Their art becomes their surface ego and—right down to the end—they reach out for their sources of vitality, unity, expression, and connection. They have merged twoness and oneness.

Notes

[1] That is, Freud's (1923) *structural theory* refers to the tripartite structuring of the mind—the id, ego, and superego. In this formulation, known as the second topography, the ego and the superego were understood as having unconscious as

well as conscious parts. In the first topography, Freud had divided the mind into the unconscious, preconscious, and conscious.

2 "This footnote first appeared in the English translation of 1927, in which it was described as having been authorized by Freud. It does not appear in the German editions" (Freud, 1923, p. 26).

3 The object for Freud (1915), is the *most variable* of an instinct's vicissitudes, in its role as that which serves the aim of instinctual discharge. Object relations theory is the direct dialectical response to that position.

4 Tustin (1981b), citing Hermann (1929), stated that in the earliest aspects of postnatal life, flowing over is a precursor to *projection*. Tustin believed that the "flowing-over-at-oneness" with the maternal object helps maintain the "illusion of primal unity" (p. 183). Tustin's idea suggests to me that, in times of deep stress in early postnatal life and beyond, there is longing for this illusion of "primal unity." Perhaps underneath the cries of "I want," "I need," or even "I hate" my mother lies necessary illusion.

5 It has been useful in groups in which I want to encourage thinking to openly call for whatever anxiety or displeasure may have arisen with the material first. If it remains unspoken but is indeed there, it defeats discussion. It may be a way of disarming the antilibidinal ego (Fairbairn, 1944).

6 My clinical observations suggest that the loss of the father's mind at adolescence seems to pose as great a difficulty for the development of the self-structure as the loss of the mother's mind poses a difficulty for the development of the bodily self in early childhood.

7 Spensley's observation could be seen as Tustin's being less theory driven than her precursors, Klein and Bion. The latter carved out a theorectical framework for pathologies of the mind, while Tustin was primarily clinically concerned with describing how it "feels" to experience those pathologies of mind. She understood a child's state of being, most especially the abject terror of the black hole. There is a gentle, noncombative quality to her writing that one could mistake for naiveté but that nonetheless has great power. She has stimulated a whole generation of theorists, most notably Grotstein, Ogden, Meltzer, and Mitrani, among many others. Her work, so experience near, should be of great interest to theorists of the self.

8 "Frau Lou" (Binion, 1968), in many conversations with Freud, related this protonarcissistic feeling to creativity, love, and ethics. She struck "the recurrent note of that primary, undisturbed, peaceful union which she attributed to early infancy, when the struggle between the instincts and the ego had not yet begun." (Leavy, 1964, p. 17). While Freud was struggling with the problem of narcissism as interfering with transference in the analysis, Lou underscored its link to creative energy. The continuation of the *constructive* elements of narcissism in psychoanalytic thinking can be found in Kohut's work.

Chapter Ten

Lifting the Shadow of the Object

Reworking Pathological Internal Object Relationships and Transforming Selfobject Failures

> *We need a term here such as life force.*[1]
> —D. W. WINNICOTT, "Aggression in Relation
> to Emotional Development"

In the unfolding of the life narrative, the parts of the self that have determined its construction are revealed. Students of the self who are attempting to decode this construction must know that there is a continuous struggle among its pathological, nonpathological, and ideal parts. In the analysis, this dialectic is reenacted and reinterpreted by its two protagonists—the analyst and the patient—in the service of reconstructing the self more in keeping with its ideals.

Except in rare cases, we can assume that the longing for the transcendence of the pathological part is a given of the analytic undertaking. What the patient is trying to convey—to express, to have known—is that part which is crowding out the nonpathological self and blocking the fulfillment of its ideals. There is a desire for an integrated, cohesive self, as well as a concomitant unity with others. This desire is not usually expressed as such at the beginning of the task, for it is almost never known in that way. During its analysis, the pathological self is communicated in the imaginative ways available to the individual patient—emerging in the work through the medium of the analyst's mental makeup and skills.

My view of the self as composed of pathological and nonpathological parts resembles the earlier view of Gedo and Goldberg (1973, p. 129), who saw the self as frequently composed of "separate subsets of self nuclei." One of these subsets "may undergo regression without involving the other in the process. These are the mental dispositions that permit

175

the persistence of a 'psychotic core' within an otherwise nonpsychotic personality, as Winnicott (1952) long ago noted" (Gedo, 1989, p. 425). Gedo argues that this complexity should be taken into account in any consideration of Kohut's self-psychological work. If that has not already been achieved in the remarkable diversity of the post-Kohutian dialectic (see Mitchell, 1995), I will add my voice to that purpose.

My view is also reminiscent of Klein's (1946). She was primarily concerned with the mechanism of the *splitting* of the instincts of love and hate toward the object and the need to *integrate* these splits to find peace within the self (p. 175). Owing to the advances in psychoanalytic theory, I, however, need not be locked into the same theoretic dialectic as she of necessity was with Freud—regarding the death instinct vis-à-vis the instinct of libido—and my emphasis can be different.

Thus, I can concentrate on the struggle for attaining the good. The problem as I see it is not one of integration of the *instinctual*—and has less to do with taking back instinctual projections toward the object—but has to do with achieving a constructive *unity* within the self and with our objects. Like Klein, however, I also find it necessary to own the pathological within the self in order to achieve a unity within the self and harmony with others. The tone of psychoanalysis has been softened by the shift from instinct to self and from object to subject. Coming to know and share the mental space of the other helps in this.

Klein, and Gedo and Goldberg, are usually thought of as representing at least two—and possible more—schools of thought. I have woven a dialectical third in which the essentials of their ideas are subsumed and further reworked into a synthesis. Thus, I see pathological sadomasochistic, autistic, and psychotic residues of the self existing side by side with nonpathological parts, and the hate, rage, and deep fears generated by their unworked-through presence as inhibiting the pursuit of the ideals of the nonpathological self.

I have also observed these pathological residues springing to life within the structure of the self and contributing to its collapse. Achieving a greater unity (coherence, cohesiveness) of self is a given of the therapeutic task but is never completely finished. However, what I think of as the "optimistic" finding and naming of that which is pathological within the self in the analytic process helps its integration. The analyst's optimism is based on an acceptance of *all* the parts of the self, which lessens the need for the pathological (and ideal) parts to be denied, disavowed, suppressed, or repressed. The journey on which the analyst accompanies the patient needs to be open to the acknowledgment of the pathological residues in the analyst's *own* structure so that those parts of the patient can be recognized, accepted, and contained.

I agree with Gedo (1989) that, to understand the patient's subjectivity, more notice has to be taken of "the unfavorable consequences for later adaptation of *early identifications* (p. 419, italics added), which are the inhibitors of the transcendent. I have tried to show the structural importance of identifications—both early and late and both *adhesive* in the service of remaining attached to the pathological object and *partial* in the service of more freely pursuing the ideal and creative self.

LIFTING THE SHADOW OF THE OBJECT

The adhesive nature of pathological attachment and identifications makes the removal of the shadow of the object a difficult yet necessary task if the nonpathological aspects of the self are to emerge from it. The problem in removing oneself from the domination of this shadow is that these early identifications have been clung to out of necessity and further rigidified out of helplessness (both genuine and learned), terror, rage, and pity. They are identifications arising as a function of one's powerful early empathic capacity—an overdetermined and overburdened "oneness"— with the original objects of love.

Like others (e.g., Meltzer, 1975; Gedo, 1989), I have observed the dynamic force of these adhesive identifications in the structure of the self. They persist where there has been an inability to withstand the seductive force of the need for the bad object. This identification with the bad object is adhered to because the natural desire to love it has been violently thwarted but—as Freud (1917) said—cannot be abandoned. Part of the structure of the self is built on pathological identifications which come from both *a failure of creative imagination and nerve to relate in any other way to the bad object than to be it, become it, or repeat our early relationship to it*. The analyst, in turn, helps to foster the imagination and courage for its transformation.

REWORKING PATHOLOGICAL INTERNAL OBJECT RELATIONSHIPS

Seeking analytic assistance implies this longing for transformation. With the analyst's mental presence now added to the equation, the patient's struggle has a chance for the realization of the ideal self. Each therapeutic encounter becomes an opportunity to rework the pathological internal object relationship, in which the analyst may indeed be a *new object* with whom it is possible to have *a new object-relationship* (Loewald, 1960, p. 221). But, more important, the analyst can become a newly found object "leading to a new way of relating to objects as well as of being and relating to oneself" (p. 225). Making the analyst into a newly found object rests on the selfobject dynamics constructed by the analytic couple.

For example, residues of disorganizing psychotic anxiety and rage can be contained through the *selfobject experience* of a calm object. Or the soothing rhythm and reliability of the analytic connection may more constructively replace destructive autosensuous attempts to relieve tension. Too, the therapist may become the object of identification that houses some part of the ideal self being searched for by the patient. At their best, all these transformations become possible insofar as the pathological object relationship is recreated, projected, received, contained, and reworked within the therapeutic alliance.

TRANSFORMING SELFOBJECT FAILURES

Essentially, my view is based on retaining the constructs of both *object* and *selfobject*. The reworking of pathological internal object relationships is conceptually linked to the therapeutic transformation of selfobject failure. That the therapy meets selfobject needs (among others) has less to do with gratification of the patient than it has to do with gaining access to the most disturbed part of the self. The selfobject experience sought is not simply an expression of desire—in the classic psychoanalytic sense—with its implication of inappropriate and harmful gratification. It is about *genuine need*. Here is a distinction similar to that between food as an indulgence and food as a necessity for existence. Only if it represents the fulfillment of need does the analysis act therapeutically and contain the nourishing elements required for the integration and recovery of self.

Within the diversity of thought in contemporary psychologies of the self, the selfobject construct and its relationship to the construct of the object (and object relations) has been the topic of controversy (see, e.g., Rowe, 1994), similar to the controversy *between* object-relational and self-psychological schools regarding projective identification (see chapter eight). In regard to my own position, Rowe correctly said, "Kainer [1990, pp. 154–185] . . . attempted to preserve Kohut's concept of *selfobject* as pertaining to a distinct experience of *functions but added a parallel object relations component* to his conceptualization of the selfobject" (p. 13, italics added). Although Kohut meant selfobject as an *experience of self* through which one attains (or fails to attain) self-cohesion—such as a selfobject transference experience—it is often referred to as if it were a person (i.e., agent or object). This common confusion arises because the *selfobject experience is—or fails to be—attained through the agency of the object*. Rowe further noted that my distinction "refers to the experience of the functions provided by the object and to the experience of the object providing the needed functions. Kainer used the idea of the precursor as mentor to emphasize the *functions* and that of the therapist as muse to express the *object-related* aspects" (p. 13, italics added).[2]

Although I was not fully aware of it at the time, by clarifying the confusion I was trying to grapple with the larger problem of why the confusion exists. The confusion over selfobject is *not* because Kohut failed to be entirely clear. He was quite clear. Rather, it exists as a code for the struggle within self theory resulting from the great (and genuine) need to fashion the analytic process as subject oriented. Thus post-Kohutians have intuitively tried to carry out Kohut's will by conceptually purifying theory of any metaphors that are instinct oriented, object relationally oriented (in its usual sense), structurally or spatially oriented (as not experience near enough to the subject); and they perhaps have even discarded those metaphors which are historically oriented and not of the present affective moment.

We must make the analytic process as experience near to the subject as possible. To my mind, however, the (internal) object cannot be far from the selfobject in any consideration of the patient's dynamics, which in turn reflects its self-experience. In the interpenetration of selves of analytic reenactments, the selfobject function of the analyst as well as the analyst's mirroring and re-creating the internal world of the patient—with its attendant affects and thinking modes—*are all part of decoding the patient's self experience.*

In the following example, the object—both as it reflects the *internal object* and as it functions as the patient's *selfobject experience*—were inexorably entwined:

The Case of Mr. W

Mr. W, a young man with problems in work and love, entered into analytic therapy with me with good effect for several years. There was a strong bond between us based on mutual respect and appreciation of each other and a deeply shared commitment to the process. The selfobject containment he experienced through our painstaking working through of his self-defeating, contemptuous aggressiveness toward male authority figures had greatly mitigated it. His contempt was the "projective identification" of the shame he had for his father (Morrison, 1989, p. 105), whose bombastic demeanor he nonetheless had adhesively mimicked.

His aggression in the workplace stuck mightily, but with the patience and good humor of which we were both capable, it was transcended in the course of time. Mr. W's severe difficulties with his hatred of male authority had considerably diminished in his professional life so that his genuine abilities and talents were operable without his pathology's winning the upper hand. His conflicts with love, however, were far from being resolved.

Nonetheless, one day following another romantic setback Mr. W announced that this would be his last year of therapy. For reasons I could not grasp at the time, his decision unsettled me (although I usually do not have difficulty with this kind of self-determination). I tried to analyze what I believed to be his "disappointments" at our joint failure at not yet solving the "love problem" as the explanatory factor in his raising termination at this juncture. There seemed more work to do, and although the ending was not imminent, it was in sight. For the first time, we were not of similar mind and became uneasy with each other. I later understood that his declaration had derailed the work for me, which Bacal and Thomson (1996) would describe as a result of the failure to have the *therapist's selfobject needs met*. It was that—and more.

My derailment came from losing the sense of creative freedom necessary for me to work in a fluid way but that his stricture had foreclosed. Not surprisingly, the loss of creative freedom was an issue for him as well; he had been "derailed" in his attachment to his mother very early in life. During the months he made ready to leave, aspects of the relationship he had had with his mother were enacted by us, especially my difficulty in wholeheartedly accepting his will. Although I could not completely decipher it at the time, my selfobject failure (as he experienced it) was an integral part of his most pathological object relationship.

Thinking that I might be countertransferentially prone to developmental "happy love endings," which would drive my need to have him do this part of the work to completion, I carefully worked to grant him his individual initiative. I suspected, however, that I wanted him to confront his demons of love with the success we had with those of his hate. No matter how careful I was, he, of course, experienced my failure to be fully concordant with his wishes to go it alone. Mr. W later gave me the crucial information that he felt *he was taking care of me* during the time he declared his intentions to leave. His feeling reflected the complexity of the hate, love, and pity he felt for his mother, which was the basis for his ambivalance about all the women in his life.

The subtlety of the interplay between us, reflecting my own mental makeup as well as his, did not allow me to catch this nuance while we were working, and his leaving was necessary for it to become clear. Only after the termination did I fully grasp the nature of the "shadow of the object" that was being enacted. We later uncovered in a posttermination interview, that we had reconstructed an old scenario he had had with his depressed mother, who inappropriately fought his wishes to separate at every developmental turn. Although this was not the literal truth in my case, for all present purposes, *I had become that mother*.

With a psychotic persistence she had particularly denigrated his first great adolescent love. In the latest episode of losing his beloved, he again felt that denigration. The facts were not identical, but the feelings were. Not only did her wounding of him during adolescence (and profoundly so by literally being absent during a crucial early period) finally drive him to cut off from her emotionally, it determined a pattern of always creating a certain distance with all further objects of love. Sadomasochistically, he could not maintain his love for the women who loved him and desired *only* those women he could not have. Although he was capable of tenderness and passion, the shadow of his maternal object—and his relationship to her—made reciprocal love always out of reach. His profound ambivalence became palpable in the work itself.

My empathic "failure" was created by each of us separately and both of us together.[3] It brought into sharper focus a profoundly disturbed part of his internal object world and the damaged object relationship within it. It now became palpable in the work and was eventually put to use. As in my experience with *The Makioka Sisters* (chapter two), one does not always get the underlying meaning of the text until after a total immersion in the reading of it!

SOME CONCLUSIONS REGARDING THE FORMATION, COLLAPSE, AND THERAPEUTIC RESTORATION OF THE SELF

The Structure of the Self

It is in understanding the subtle complexities of such self-experience that I have been drawn to the idea of the self as having a *structure*, Not only does the construct help me to understand structural *collapse* of the self, it conveys the nature of what is ongoing in the patient. This structure is made up of pathological and nonpathological parts that are in a dialectic with each other. The structure of the self houses not only the precipitates of the objects but the relationship to these objects that has impinged on and shaped the structure. Structure allows us to understand a patient's identifications that have had a profound effect on the life narrative. The *self* relates not only to a set of affective states but also to a highly complex and dialectical organization of its pathological, nonpathological, and ideal aspects, aspects that were realized through identifications and selfobject experiences.

Post-Kohutian and post-Kleinian thought, when integrated, have much to offer analytic clinicians in comprehending the self-structure of their patients. To make these schools of thought better serve one another, I have distinguished between *selfobject failure* and the *bad object* and noted their relationship to each other. I have shown how failures in self-regulation and problems with affective states of being are related to pathological identifications with bad objects (chapter five). I have also discussed how failures in self-regulation with neurotic patients can be manifested in autistic and psychotic modes of experience. I have also discussed the relationship between empathic attunement and the selfobject containment of projective identifications.

I have connected the ideas of the schools in two ways. First, I bring a self-psychological perspective to *projective identification,* extending the arc of Melanie Klein's idea from its origin as *an aggressive object relation* to my use of it as a form of *imaginative empathy* (chapter eight). In this way, psychologists of the self can be better attuned to the deeper pathologies that may exist as residues in a neurotic self-structure. Similarly, imaginative empathy as a form of communication allows Kleinian analysts to uncover deeper pathologies without excessive reliance on the death instinct as an explanatory principle.

I further linked self psychology to object relations by extending Kohut's *selfobject* function of mirroring, idealization, and twinship, to include an even earlier function: *the selfobject function of containment* (chapter seven). I now believe containment, particularly that of the excitation and tension of the body self, to be the first and primary parental selfobject task. Selfobject failure to contain disturbing elements of the bodily self yields catastrophic consequences, both in infancy and beyond. In this belief, I have linked the seminal work of Kohut, Bion, and Tustin to better comprehend and treat psychic suffering. *Essentially, this view integrates Kohut's perspective on selfobject need to Bion's theory of thinking and mind as they relate to the development of the self.*

Further Clinical Theory

Regardless of the school of thought from which we borrow our images and metaphors, both analyst and patient must have an availability of life force that outweighs the destructive. The success of any therapeutic undertaking is based on two features of the analytic couple. The first is the decoding skills of the analyst, which are founded on self-knowledge. The other—on which reworking the pathological internal object relationships rests—not only is a function of the reversal of the patient's experience of selfobject failure (through the therapist's ability as agent), but it also rests on the patient's *ability to "suffer" the pain of psychic tensions enough to grapple with it* (Joseph, 1981, p. 99). For example, unbearable psychic tensions, felt somatically and responded to with addictive substances, bear witness to the state of feeling pain but being unable to suffer it and grapple with it. The ability of the therapist to help provide a mental space to contain the pain can greatly increase the patient's capacity to do so but cannot ultimately determine it. That rests on the capacity of each for endurance and hope.

Thoughts on Past and Present

Knowledge of the past and of origins has also been important in this work because of the added richness of understanding that it brings. The history of the profound ideas that constitute the *entire culture of psychoanalysis* spans individual schools and individual eras. For example, my idea of the sharing of mental space—and the longing to be in the mind of the other—can be seen as related to the work of Andreas-Salomé (1921) and the era of the creative ferment of early psychoanalysis. She spoke of the need for the illusion of unity that is fundamental to human nature.

Our quest for empathy is a *longing to be known*, perhaps to achieve or restore the worthwhile "illusion" of unity. I believe it encompasses the longing for caretaking, sensual gratification, and whatever motivation and needs are understood to exist within the self. The narcissistic wish to be known in all one's parts also carries with it the longing for transcending identifications that limit us. By being known, we hope to know and ultimately realize the ideal and nonpathological parts of ourselves. In that way, narcissism is the unconscious creative source of our yearning for self-transcendence and self-creation.

Lou Andreas-Salomé's early ideas on the creative aspects of narcissism are near to those which have very much concerned me here. Thus, she

> made clear how psychoanalysis seemed to her to illuminate creative experience, her own and that of others. She saw, as Freud and all analysts since him have seen, the source of creativity in the unconscious streams hidden and yet also revealed by the ego, but only in a few individuals manifested in art . . . she tried to show how in the unconscious the creative source persists and finds its manifestations not only in art but in *the two other spheres of especial interest to her as a woman and a thinker, namely object-love and ethical behavior"* [in Leavy, 1962, p. 1, italics added].

She was one of the few genuine precursors to Kohut's achievement of understanding narcissism (the self) in its positive, creative, and universal aspects. I wish to clearly acknowledge her in recognition of her kindred spirit, for, in our kindred spirits, even literary spirits, we come to know ourselves and discover that which we hope to realize.

We cannot afford to discard our precursors, for they are the clay from which we fashion the new—be it a new idea or a new self. Discarding important parts of the past from which we have emerged creates an impoverished state both for the self and for theory. It forecloses grappling with the larger body of rich ideas and advancing clinical mastery thereby. Knowledge and integration of both past and present provide the power and texture of the analytic undertaking, creating what is truly new.

Notes

[1] That term can be found in the early analytic writings of Otto Rank (1936). The life force represents the creative will to overcome the fear of life, which, in turn, rests on the acceptance of the obligation of our physical mortality. It was not the death *instinct* that Rank thought was crucial to neurotic inhibition, but the *fear of death*, which expresses itself as the fear of life.

[2] "The percursor as mentor relates to the experiences of past figures in one's life that have provided sustaining selfobject functions, and the therapist as muse is considered to be the actual object, the therapist, who enables the patient to find inspiration by being a 'facilitating object for the realization and expression of the patient's selfobject strivings' " (Rowe, 1994, p. 13).

[3] Similarly, Odgen (1994) refers to this phenomenon as the creation of the *analytic third*—a creation "distinctive to psychoanalysis." As the subjects of analysis, the analyst and analysand create one another. "More accurately, analyst and analysand come into being in the process of the creation of the analytic subject. The analytic third, although created jointly by (what is becoming) the analyst and analysand, is not experienced identically . . . since each remains a separate subject in the dialectical tension with the other" (pp. 4–5).

References

Alcoholics Anonymous World Services (1976). *Alcoholics Anonymous,* 3rd ed. New York: Author.

Andreas-Salomé, L. (1921). The dual orientation of narcissism (trans. S. Leavy). *Psychoanalytic Quarterly,* 30:1–30, 1962.

Anzieu, D. (1985). *The Skin Ego* (trans. C. Turner). New Haven, CT: Yale University Press, 1989.

Bacal, H. & Newman, K. (1990). *Theories of Object Relations: Bridges to Self Psychology.* New York: Columbia University Press.

———— & Thomson, P. (1996). The psychoanalyst's selfobject needs and the effect of their frustration on the treatment: A new view of countertransference. In *Basic Ideas Reconsidered: Progress in Self Psychology, Vol. 12,* ed. A. Goldberg. Hillsdale, NJ: The Analytic Press, pp. 17–35.

Barron, J., ed. (1993). *Self-Analysis.* Hillsdale, NJ: The Analytic Press.

Barron, S. (1991). *Degenerate Art: The Fate of the Avant-Garde in Nazi Germany.* Los Angeles: Los Angeles Museum of Art/Harry N. Abrams.

Basch, M. (1985). Interpretation: Toward a developmental model. In *Progress in Self Psychology, Vol. 1,* ed. A. Goldberg. New York: Guilford Press, pp. 33–42.

———— (1995). It ain't over till it's over. *Psychoanalytic Dialogues,* 5:411–414.

Beebe, B. & Lachmann, F. (1994). Representation and internalization in infancy: Three principles of salience. *Psychoanalytic Psychology,* 11:127–165.

Benjamin, J. (1995). *Like Subjects, Love Objects: Essays on Recognition and Sexual Difference.* New Haven, CT: Yale University Press

Bick, E. (1968). The experience of the skin in early object relations. *International Journal of Psycho-Analysis,* 49:484–486.

———— (1986). Further considerations on the function of the skin in early object relations. *British Journal of Psychotherapy,* 2:292–301.

Binion, R. (1968). *Frau Lou.* Princeton, NJ: Princeton University Press.

Bion, W. (1957). The differentiation of the psychotic from the non-psychotic part of the personality. In *Second Thoughts.* Northvale, NJ: Aronson, 1993, pp. 43–64.

———— (1959). Attacks on linking. In *Second Thoughts.* Northvale, NJ: Aronson, 1993, pp. 93–109.

———— (1962a). A theory of thinking. In *Second Thoughts.* Northvale, NJ: Aronson, 1993, pp. 110–119.

185

——— (1962b). Learning from experience. In *Seven Servants*. Northvale, NJ: Aronson, 1993, pp. 1–111.

——— (1965). Transformations. In *Seven Servants*. Northvale, NJ: Aronson, 1977, pp. 1–171.

——— (1967). *Second Thoughts*. Northvale, NJ: Aronson, 3rd. ed., 1993.

——— (1970). Attention and interpretation. In *Seven Servants*. Northvale, NJ: Aronson, 1977, pp. 1–129.

Bloom, C. (1996). *Leaving the Doll's House*. Boston: Little, Brown.

Blos, P. (1969). *On Adolescence*. New York: Free Press.

Bollas, C. (1987). *The Shadow of the Object*. New York: Columbia University Press.

Bowlby, J. (1969). *Attachment and Loss: Vol. 1. Attachment*. New York: Basic Books.

——— (1980). *Attachment and Loss: Vol. 3. Loss*. New York: Basic Books.

Brandchaft, B. (1983). The negativism of the negative therapeutic reaction and the psychology of the self. In: *The Future of Psychoanalysis,* ed. A. Goldberg. New York: International Universities Press, pp. 327–359.

——— & Stolorow, R. (1988). On projective identification. A reply. *Los Angeles Psychoanalytic Bulletin.* Summer.

Brigham, S. (1997). Weighty matters. *Newsletter*, Institute for Contemporay Psychotherapy, January, pp. 7–9.

Britton, R. (1992). Keeping things in mind. In *Clinical Lectures on Klein and Bion, Vol. 14,* ed. R. Anderson. London: Tavistock/Routledge, pp. 102–113.

Buatta, M. (1981). Foreword to *Found Objects* by J. Ruggiero. New York: Clarkson N. Potter.

Duchamp, M. (1973). *Salt Seller: The Writings of Marcel Duchamp (Marchand Du Sal),* ed. M. Sanouillet & E. Peterson. New York: Oxford University Press.

Edelman, H. (1994). *Motherless Daughters*. New York: Addison-Wesley.

Eigen, M. (1986). *The Psychotic Core*. Northvale, NJ: Aronson.

Eissler, K. (1971). *Talent and Genius*. New York: Grove Press.

Fairbairn, R. (1940). Schizoid factors in the personality. In: *Psychoanalytic Studies of the Personality.* London: Tavistock, 1952, pp. 3–27.

——— (1954). Observations on the nature of hysterical states. *British Journal of Medical Psychology,* 27:105–125.

Freud, A. (1937). *The Ego and the Mechanisms of Defense*. New York: International Universities Press, 1966.

Freud, S. (1914). On narcissism: An introduction. *Standard Edition,* 14:67–102. London: Hogarth Press, 1957.

——— (1915). Instincts and their vicissitudes. *Standard Edition,* 14:11–140. London: Hogarth Press, 1957.

——— (1917). Mourning and melancholia. *Standard Edition,* 14:239–258. London: Hogarth Press, 1957.

——— (1920). Beyond the pleasure principle. *Standard Edition,* 8:3–64. London: Hogarth Press, 1955.

——— (1923). The ego and the id. *Standard Edition,* 19:3–59. London: Hogarth Press, 1961.

—— (1924). The economic problem of masochism. *Standard Edition*, 19:157–172. London: Hogarth Press, 1961.

—— (1928). Dostoevsky and parricide. *Standard Edition*, 21:177–196. London: Hogarth Press, 1961.

Galassi, S. (1996). *Picasso's Variations on the Masters*. New York: Harry N. Abrams.

Gear, M., Hill, M. & Liendo, E. (1981). *Working Through Narcissism: Treating Its Sadomasochistic Structure*. New York: Aronson.

Gedo, J. (1989). Self psychology: A post-Kohutian view. In *Self Psychology: Comparisons and Contrasts*, ed. D. Detrick & S. Detrick. Hillsdale, NJ: The Analytic Press, pp. 415–428.

—— & Goldberg, A. (1973). *Models of the Mind*. Chicago: University of Chicago Press.

Gilligan, C. (1982). *In a Different Voice: Psychological Theory and Women's Development*. Cambridge, MA: Harvard University Press.

Giovacchini, P. (1985). *Psychoanalytic Practice*. New York: Adelphi Society for Psychoanalysis and Psychotherapy.

Glueck, G. (1996). Sculpture with video and a lot of activity. *The New York Times*, July 19, p. C28.

Grinberg, L. (1962). On a specific aspect of countertransference due to the patient's projective identification. *International Journal of Psycho-Analysis*, 1:259–266.

Grotstein, J. (1982). The analysis of a borderline patient. In *Technical Factors in the Treatment of the Severely Disturbed Patient*, ed. P. Giovacchini & L. B. Boyer. Northvale, NJ: Aronson, pp. 261–288.

—— (1984). A proposed revision of the psychoanalytic concept of the death instinct. In: *The Yearbook of Psychoanalysis and Psychotherapy*, ed. R. J. Langs.

—— (1985). *Splitting and Projective Identification*. New York: Aronson.

—— (1986). Foreword to *Autistic Barriers in Neurotic Patients* by F. Tustin. New Haven, CT: Yale University Press.

—— (1990). Nothingness, meaninglessness, chaos and "the black hole" II. *Contemporary Psychoanalysis*, 26:377–407.

—— (1995). Orphans of the "real" I. Some modern and post-modern perspectives on the neurobiological and psychosocial dimensions of psychosis and primitive mental disorder. Presented at conference on the Psychodynamic Approaches to the Treatment of Psychotic Disorders, the Menninger Clinic, Topeka, KS, January.

Grotstein, J. & Rinsley, D., eds. (1994). *Fairbairn and the Origins of Object Relations*. New York: Guilford Press.

Guntrip, H. (1975). My experience of analysis with Fairbairn and Winnicott (How complete a result does psycho-analytic therapy achieve?). In *Essential Papers On Object Relations*, ed. P. Buckley. New York: New York University Press, 1986, pp. 447–468.

Harris, M. (1995). *The Loss That Is Forever*. New York: Dutton.

Hartmann, H., Kris, E. & Loewenstein. R. (1946). Comments on the formation of psychic structure. *The Psychoanalytic Study of the Child*, 2:11–38. New York: International Universities Press.

Haver, W. (1996). *The Body of This Death: Historicity and Sociality in the Time of AIDS.* Palo Alto, CA: Stanford University Press.

Hayman, R. (1982). *Kafka.* New York: Oxford University Press

Henry, G. (1983). Difficulties in thinking and learning. In *Psychotherapy With Severely Deprived Children,* ed. M. Boston & R. Szur. London: Karnac Books, 1990, pp. 82–88.

Hermann, I. (1929). Das Ich und das Denken. *Imago,* 15:89–110, 325–348.

Hertz, C. (1989). A self psychological analysis of *Analysis of Transference* by M. Gill & I. Z. Hoffman. *Contemporary Psychotherapy Review,* 5:33–51.

Huffington, A. (1996). *Picasso, Creator and Destroyer.* New York: Avon Books.

Ito, K. (1991). *Visions of Desire: Tanizaki's Fictional Worlds.* Stanford, CA: Stanford University Press.

Jacobson, E. (1964). *The Self and the Object World.* New York: International Universities Press.

Joseph, B. (1981). Towards the experiencing of psychic pain. In *Dare I Disturb the Universe?* ed. J. Grotstein. London: Maresfield Library, pp. 94–102.

Kafka, F. (1915). *Metamorphosis.* New York: Schocken Books, 1968.

——— (1919). Letter to his father. In *Dearest Father.* New York: Schocken Books, 1954, pp. 138–196.

Kainer, R. (1977). Beyond masochism: The relationship of narcissistic injury to will. *Journal of the Otto Rank Association,* 12:21–28.

——— (1984). Art and the canvas of the self: Otto Rank and creative transcendence. *American Imago,* 41:359–372.

——— (1988a). Overcoming the sado-masochistic features in the awe of the other. Presented at meeting of Division 39 (Psychoanalysis), American Psychological Association, San Francisco, February.

——— (1990). The precursor as mentor, the therapist as muse: Creativity and selfobject phenomena. In *The Realities of Transference: Progress in Self Psychology, Vol. 6,* ed. A. Goldberg. Hillsdale, NJ: The Analytic Press, pp. 175–188.

——— (1991). Brooklyn on my mind: Identifying with the object. *Analytic Reflections,* Vol. 1, pp. 14–19.

——— (1993a). The transcendent moment and the analytic hour. In *Exploring Sacred Landscapes,* ed. M. L. Randour. New York: Columbia University Press, pp. 154–171.

——— (1993b). Sadomasochism: Erotogenic, object-related and self-psychological aspects. Presented at meeting of Division 39 (Psychoanalysis), American Psychological Association, New York City, April.

——— (1994). Defining evil in a post-Kleinian world. *Analytic Reflections,* 4:45–57.

——— (1996). On falling in love with a work of art. Presented at meeting of Division 39 (Psychoanalysis), American Psychological Association, New York City, April.

——— & Koretzky, M.(1988). Unbelievability and hysteric character: Containing the projections. Presented at the meeting of Division 39 (Psychoanalysis), American Psychological Association, Atlanta, GA, August.

Kandel, E., Schwartz, J. & Jessell, T., eds. (1995). *Essentials of Neural Science and Behavior,* Norwalk, CT: Appleton & Long.

Karl, F. (1991). *Franz Kafka: Representative Man.* New York: Ticknor & Fields.

Kato, S. (1979). *A History of Japanese Literature, Vol. 3.* London: Macmillan Press, 1990.

Keene, D. (1994). *On Familiar Terms: A Journey Across Cultures.* New York: Kodansha International.

Klein, D. (1968), Psychiatric diagnosis and a typology of clinical drug effects. *Psychopharmacologia,* 13:359–386.

Klein, M. (1946). Notes on some schizoid mechanisms. In: *Envy and Gratitude & Other Works 1946–1963.* New York: Dell, 1975, pp. 1–24.

——— (1952). Some theoretical conclusions regarding the emotional life of the infant. In *Envy and Gratitude & Other Works 1946–1963.* New York: Dell, 1975, pp. 61–93.

——— (1955). On identification. In *Envy and Gratitude & Other Works, 1946–1963.* New York: Dell, 1975, pp. 141–175.

——— (1957). Envy and gratitude. In *Envy and Gratitude & Other Works 1946–1963.* New York: Dell, 1975, pp. 176–235.

——— (1958). On the development of mental functioning. In *Envy and Gratitude & Other Works 1946–1963.* New York: Dell, 1975, pp. 236–246.

Klein, S. (1980). Autistic phenomena in neurotic patients. In *Do I Dare Disturb the Universe?* ed. J. Grotstein. London: Maresfield Library, pp. 103–113.

Kohut, H. (1971). *The Analysis of the Self.* New York: International Universities Press.

——— (1972). Thoughts on narcissism and narcissistic rage. *The Psychoanalytic Study of the Child,* 27:360–400. New York: International Universities Press.

——— (1977). *The Restoration of the Self.* New York: International Universities Press.

——— (1979). The two analyses of Mr. Z. *International Journal of Psycho-Analysis,* 60:3–27.

——— (1984). *How Does Analysis Cure?* ed. A. Goldberg & P. Stepansky. Chicago: University of Chicago Press.

Kramer, P. (1993). *Listening to Prozac.* New York: Viking.

Krystal, H. (1988). *Integration and Self-Healing: Affect, Trauma, Alexithymia.* Hillsdale, NJ: The Analytic Press.

Kuspit, D. (1993). *The New Subjectivism: Art in the 1980's.* New York: Da Capo Press.

——— (1996). *Finding the Ideal Self Through Discovery of the Ideal Object.* Presented at meeting of Division 39 (Psychoanalysis), American Psychological Association, New York City, April.

Lacan, J. (1977), *Ecrits,* trans. A. Sheridan. New York: Norton.

Lachmann, F. (1991). Three self psychologies or one? In *The Evolution of Self Psychology: Progress in Self Psychology, Vol. 7,* ed. A. Goldberg, pp. 167–174. Hillsdale, NJ: The Analytic Press.

——— & Beebe, B. (1989). Oneness fantasies revisited. *Psychoanalytic Psychology,* 6:137–149.

———— & Lichtenberg, J. (1992). Model scenes: Implications for psychoanalytic treatment. *Journal of the American Psychoanalytic Association,* 40:117–138.

Langer, E. (1989). *Mindfulness.* New York: Addison-Wesley.

Laplanche, J. & Pontalis, J.-B. (1973). *The Language of Psychoanalysis.* New York: Norton.

Larsen, K. (1997). A month in Shaker Country. *The New York Times,* August 10, pp. C32–34.

Leavy, S. (1962). Introduction to translation of L. Andreas-Salomé's "The Dual Orientation of Narcissism." *Psychoanalytic Quarterly,* 30:1–30.

Lehmann-Haupt, C. (1996). Review of *The Architect of Desire: Beauty and Danger in the Stanford White Family,* by S. Lessard. *The New York Times,* Oct. 28.

Leibowitz, M. & Klein, D. (1979). Hysteroid dysphoria. *Psychiatric Clinics of North America,* 2:555–575.

Lessard, S. (1996) *The Architect of Desire: Beauty and Danger in the Stanford White Family.* New York: Doubleday.

Lichtenberg, J. (1989). *Psychoanalysis and Motivation.* Hillsdale, NJ: The Analytic Press.

———— Lachmann, F. & Fosshage, J. (1992). *Self and Motivational Systems: Toward a Theory of Psychoanalytic Technique.* Hillsdale, NJ: The Analytic Press.

Little, M. I. (1990). *Psychotic Anxieties and Containment: A Personal Record of an Analysis with Winnicott.* Northvale, NJ: Aronson.

Loewald, H. (1960). On the therapeutic action of psychoanalysis. In *Papers on Psychoanalysis.* New Haven, CT: Yale University Press, 1980, pp. 221–256.

———— (1975). Psychoanalysis as an art and the fantasy character of the psychoanalytic situation. In *Papers on Psychoanalysis.* New Haven, CT: Yale University Press, 1980, pp. 352–371.

Mahfouz, N. (1956). *Palace Walk.* New York: Anchor Books.

Mahler, M. (1968). *On Human Symbiosis and the Vicissitudes of Individuation, Vol. 1. Infantile Psychosis.* New York: International Universities Press.

Malin, A. & Grotstein, J. (1966). Projective identification in the therapeutic process. *International Journal of Psycho-Analysis,* 47:26–31.

Margulies, A. (1989). *The Empathic Imagination.* New York: Norton.

McCarthy, P. (1989). Introduction. In *Childhood Years: A Memoir,* by J. Tanazaki (1955–56). Tokyo: Kodansha International.

McDougall, J. (1989), *Theaters of the Body.* New York: Norton.

———— (1995). *What Ever Became of Hysteria?* Address to the Washington School of Psychiatry. Washington, DC, May.

Meltzer, D. (1975). Adhesive identification. *Contemporary Psychoanalysis,* 11:289–310.

———— (1984). *What Is an Emotional Experience?* Presented at the 7th Annual Self Psychology Conference. Toronto, Canada, October.

———— Bremner, J., Hoxter, S., Weddell, H. & Wittenberg, I. (1975). *Explorations in Autism.* Perthshire, Scotland: Clunie Press.

Menaker, E. (1979). *Masochism and the Emergent Ego.* New York: Human Sciences Press.

Mishima, Y. (1958). *Confessions of a Mask,* trans. M. Weatherby. New York: New Directions.

—— (1965). *The Sailor Who Fell from Grace with the Sea,* trans. J. Nathan. New York: Knopf.

Mitchell, S. (1988). *Relational Concepts in Psychoanalysis.* Cambridge, MA: Harvard University Press.

—— (1993). *Hope and Dread in Psychoanalysis.* New York: Basic Books.

—— (1995). Self psychology after Kohut: A polylogue. In *Psychoanalytic Dialogues,* 5:351–434.

Mitrani, J. (1996). *A Framework for the Imaginary.* Northvale, NJ: Aronson.

Mitrani, T. & Mitrani, J. (1997). *Encounters with Autistic States: A Memorial Tribute to Frances Tustin.* Northvale, NJ: Aronson.

Money-Kyrle, R. (1956). Normal counter-transference and some of its deviations. *International Journal of Psycho-Analysis,* 37:360–366.

Morrison, A. (1989), *Shame: The Underside of Narcissism.* Hillsdale, NJ: The Analytic Press.

Nin, A. (1959). *A Spy in the House of Love.* Chicago: Swallow Press.

Ogden, T. (1986). *The Matrix of the Mind.* Northvale, NJ: Aronson.

—— (1989). *The Primitive Edge of Experience.* Northvale, NJ: Aronson.

—— (1992a). The dialectically constituted/decentered subject of psycyo-analysis. I. The Freudian subject. *International Journal of Psycho-Analysis,* 73:417–26.

—— (1992b). The dialectically constituted/decentered subject of psychoanalysis. II. The contributions of Klein and Winnicott. *International Journal of Psycho-Analysis,* 73:613-26.

—— (1994). *The Subjects of Analysis.* Northvale, NJ: Aronson.

O'Neill, E. (1925). *The Great God Brown.* In *Nine Plays by Eugene O'Neill.* New York: Modern Library, 1941.

O'Shaughnessy, E. (1964). The absent object. *Journal of Child Psychotherapy,* 1:134–143.

Pawel, E. (1984). *The Nightmare of Reason: A Life of Franz Kafka.* New York: Farrar, Straus & Giroux.

Racker, H. (1957). The meaning and uses of countertransference. In *Classics in Psychoanalytic Technique.* New York: Aronson, 1981.

—— (1968). *Transference and Counter-Transference.* New York: International Universities Press.

Rank, O. (1932). *Art and Artist.* New York: Agathon Press, 1968.

—— (1936). *Will Therapy and Truth and Reality.* New York: Knopf, 1950.

—— (1939). The double as immortal self. In *Beyond Psychology.* New York: Dover, 1958, pp. 62–101.

Reich, W. (1949). *Character Analysis.* New York: Orgone Institute Press.

Reik, T. (1947). The surprised psychoanalyst. In *Listening with the Third Ear.* New York: Farrar, Straus & Giroux, 1983.

Roazen, P. (1971). *Brother Animal.* New York: Vintage Books.

Rosenfeld, D. (1990). *The Psychotic.* London: Karnac Books.

Rosenfeld, H. (1971). Contribution to the psychopathology of psychotic states: The importance of projective identification in the ego structure and the object relations of the psychotic patient. In *Melanie Klein Today, Vol. l,* ed. E. Spillius. London: Routledge, pp. 117–137.

——— (1981). On the psychopathology and treatment of psychotic patients. In *Do I Dare Disturb the Universe?* ed. J. Grotstein. London: Karnac Books, pp. 167–180.

Roth, P. (1967). *Portnoy's Complaint.* New York: Vintage, 1994.

——— (1995). *Sabbath's Theater.* Boston: Houghton Mifflin.

——— (1997). *American Pastoral.* Boston: Houghton Mifflin.

Rowe, C. (1994). Reformulations of the concept of selfobject: A misalliance of self psychology with object relations theory. In *A Decade of Progress: Progress in Self Psychology, Vol. 10,* ed. A. Goldberg. Hillsdale, NJ: The Analytic Press, pp. 9–20.

Schafer, R. (1968). *Aspects of Internalization.* New York: International Universities Press, 1990.

——— (1981). Narrative actions in psychoanalysis. *1980 Heinz Werner Lecture Series, Vol. 14.* Worcester, MA: Clark University Press.

——— (1984). The pursuit of failure and the idealization of unhappiness. *American Psychologist,* 39:398–405.

Searles, H. (1973). Concerning therapeutic symbiosis. In *Classics in Psychoanalytic Technique,* ed. R. Langs. New York: Aronson, 1981, pp. 419–428.

Segalla, R. (1996). The unbearable embeddedness of being: Self psychology, intersubjectivity and large group experiences. *Group,* 4:257–271.

Socarides, D. & Stolorow, R. (1984–85). Affects and selfobjects. *The Annual of Psychoanalysis,* 12/13:105–119. Madison, CT: International Universities Press.

Spensley, S. (1995). *Frances Tustin.* London: Routledge.

Spitz, E. (1996). In pursuit of the lost object: Paintings of René Magritte. Presented at meeting of Division 39 (Psychoanalysis), American Psychological Association, New York City, April.

Steiner, J. (1993). *Psychic Retreats/Pathological Organizations in Psychotic, Neurotic and Borderline Patients.* The New Library of Psychoanalysis, vol. 19. London: Routledge.

Stern, D. (1985). *The Interpersonal World of the Infant.* New York: Basic Books.

Stolorow, R. (1975). The narcissistic function of masochism (and sadism). *International Journal of Psycho-Analysis,* 56:441–448.

——— Brandchaft, B. & Atwood, G. (1987). *Psychoanalytic Treatment: An Intersubjective Approach.* Hillsdale, NJ: The Analytic Press.

Tanazaki, J. (1933), *In Praise of Shadows,* trans. T. Harper & E. Seidensticker. New Haven, CT: Leete's Island Books, 1977.

——— (1931–32). *The Secret History of the Lord of Musashi,* trans. A. Chambers. San Francisco: Northpoint Press, 1982.

——— (1943–48). *The Makioka Sisters,* trans. E. Seidensticker. New York: Knopf, 1993.

—— (1955–56). *Childhood Years: A Memoir,* trans. Paul McCarthy. Tokyo: Kodansha International, 1989.

Tate Gallery (1988). *Late Picasso.* London: Author.

Tausk, V. (1919). On the origin of the "influencing machine" in schizophrenia. *Psychoanalytic Quarterly,* 2:519–556, 1933.

Thalen, E. & Smith, V. (1994). *A Dynamic Systems Approach to the Development of Cognition and Action.* Cambridge, MA: MIT Press.

Tomkins, S. (1962–63). *Affect/Imagery/Consciousness, Vols. 1 & 2.* New York: Springer.

—— (1987). Shame. In *The Many Faces of Shame,* ed. D. Nathanson. New York: Guilford, pp. 133–161.

Tustin, F. (1981a). Psychological birth and psychological catastrophe. In *Dare I Disturb the Universe,* ed. J. Grotstein. London: Maresfield Library, pp. 181–196.

—— (1981b). *Autistic States in Children.* London: Routledge & Kegan Paul.

—— (1986). *Autistic Barriers in Neurotic Patients.* New Haven, CT: Yale University Press.

—— (1990). *The Protective Shell In Children and Adults.* London: Karnac Books.

van der Kolk, B. (1994). The body keeps the score: Memory and the evolving psychobiology of posttraumatic stress. *Harvard Review of Psychiatry,* 1:253–265.

Winnicott, D. W. (1950). Aggression in relation to emotional development. In *Through Paediatrics to Psycho-Analysis.* New York: Basic Books, 1975, pp. 204–218.

Wittgenstein, L. (1953). *Philosophical Investigations.* New York: Macmillan.

Young-Bruehl, E. (1982). *Hannah Arendt: For Love of the World.* New Haven, CT: Yale University Press.

Index